KT-429-751

OCR
RECOGNISING ACHIEVEMENT

HODDER EDUCATION

Official Publisher Partnership

OCR Information & Con Technology GCSE

OCR
RECOGNISING ACHIEVEMENT

HODDER
EDUCATION

Official Publisher Partnership

OCR Information & Communication Technology GCSE

Student's Book

■ **Steve Cushing**
■ **Brian Gillinder**
■ **George Rouse**

HODDER
EDUCATION
AN HACHETTE UK COMPANY

The publishers would like to thank the following for permission to reproduce copyright material:

Photo credits:
p.2 © Adam Hart-Davis/Science Photo Library; **p.3** *t* © Science Museum/Science & Society, *bl* Steve Connolly, *bm* Steve Connolly, *br* Steve Connolly; **p.4** *tl* Steve Connolly, *tm* Steve Connolly, *tr* © Ace Stock Limited/Alamy; **p.5** *all* Steve Connolly, *except bl* Lawrence Berkeley National Laboratory/Science Photo Library; **p.6** *all* Steve Connolly; **p.9** *tl* © ISP Photography/Alamy, *tm* © imagebroker.net/Photolibrary, *bl* Steve Connolly, *bm* Steve Connolly, *br* Steve Connolly; **p.11** *t* © Corbis Super RF/Alamy, *m* Steve Connolly, *b* © Ingram Publishing Limited; **p.12** *all* Steve Connolly, *except b* © bob deering things/Alamy; **p.13** Steve Connolly, © Ingram Publishing Limited, © Leslie Garland Picture Library/Alamy, Steve Connolly, © QED www.QEDonline.co.uk; **p.14** *tr* © Photofusion Picture Library/Alamy, *mr* © WoodyStock/Alamy, *ml* Jakub Semeniuk/iStockphoto.com *bl* Steve Connolly, *br* Steve Connolly; **p.15** *t* Steve Connolly, *m* Steve Connolly, *m* Ronen/iStockphoto.com, F1 Online/Photolibrary; **p.17** *t* Steve Connolly, *b* © Steven May/Alamy; **p.18** Steve Connolly; **p.20** *all* Steve Connolly, *except r* © Eye-Stock/Alamy; **p.22** l Steve Connolly, *m* Steve Connolly, *r* © www.datenrettung.de; **p.33** Steve Connolly; **p.51** Courtesy of Jon Williamson; **p.66** © pina1970/Fotolia; **p.67** *both* Steve Connolly; **p.72** © www.jalopnik.com; **p.85** © Steven May/Alamy; p.99 © Luminis/Fotolia; **p.102** *tl* © QED www.QEDonline.co.uk, *m* © WoodyStock/Alamy, *bl* © Genie+/Unique Perspectives Ltd; **p.119** © Stuart Kelly/Alamy; **p.123** *t* © www.eltekdataloggers.co.uk, *m* © www.contral.co.uk, *b* Courtesy of ScienceScope; **p.124** *t* Martyn F. Chillmaid/Science Photo Library, *m* Courtesy of RV Safety Systems, *m* © Richard Heyes/Alamy, *b* Martin Shields/Science Photo Library; **p.129** © beerkoff/Fotalia; **p.131** *t* © 67photo/Alamy, *b* © PHOTOTAKE Inc./Alamy; **p.133** Courtesy of Wikipedia Commons; **p.141** © Michael Willis/Alamy; **p.145** © JoeFox/Alamy; **p.147** *t* © Shadow Robot Company Ltd, *b* © AFP/Getty Images; **p.188** © Len Kaltman/iStockphoto; **p.196** © webphotographeer/iStockphoto; **p.197** *t* Steve Connolly, *m* Getty Images, *b* Steve Cole/Getty Images; **p.198** *t* Pasieka/Science Photo Library, *b* TopFoto/Keystone; **p.199** *t* © donald_gruener/iStockphoto, *b* © ra-photos/iStockphoto; **p.200** Steve Connolly; **p.201** *both* Steve Connolly; **p.205** © Sean Locke/iStockphoto; **p.207** © Joshua Blake/iStockphoto; **p.211** © Steve Cole/iStockphoto; **p.217** © Gerenme/iStockphoto; **p.219** *l* © Volker Steger/Science Photo Library; **p.220** © Godfried Edelman/iStockphoto.

Acknowledgements:
Brand names mentioned in this book are protected by their respective trademarks and are acknowledged: ArtiCAD software, screenshot from www.articad.cc; Bluetooth; ClamWin, screenshot from www.clamwin.com/content/view/23/55; Gemba Solutions, screenshot from www.oeeimpact.com/images/overview%20graphic.jpg; Gendan Ltd., screenshots from www.enginecheck.co.uk/screens.php; Google, screenshots of search engines and Google Mail; Microsoft, screenshots of Windows Live Messenger; NHS Direct: Self-help expert system tutorial, from www.nhsdirect.nhs.uk (Used under Click-Use PSI Licence C2009002464); Ticketmaster UK, screenshots of online booking.

Every effort has been made to trace all copyright holders, but if any have been inadvertantly overlooked the Publisher will be pleased to make the necessary arrangements at the first opportunity.

t = top, *b* = bottom, *l* = left, *c* = centre

Although every effort has been made to ensure that website addresses are correct at time of going to press, Hodder Education cannot be held responsible for the content of any website mentioned in this book. It is sometimes possible to find a relocated web page by typing in the address of the home page for a website in the URL window of your browser.

Hachette UK's policy is to use papers that are natural, renewable and recyclable products and made from wood grown in sustainable forests. The logging and manufacturing processes are expected to conform to the environmental regulations of the country of origin.

Orders: please contact Bookpoint Ltd, 130 Milton Park, Abingdon, Oxon OX14 4SB. Telephone: (44) 01235 827720. Fax: (44) 01235 400454. Lines are open 9.00–5.00, Monday to Saturday, with a 24-hour message answering service. Visit our website at www.hoddereducation.co.uk

Cover photo © Sebastian Duda/iStockphoto.com
Illustrations by Barking Dog Art
Typeset in Minion Pro 12pt by Fakenham Photosetting Ltd, Fakenham, Norfolk
Printed in Italy

A catalogue record for this title is available from the British Library
ISBN: 978 1444 108644

Contents

Unit 1 ICT in Today's World

Chapter 1 ICT in Today's World   2
Chapter 2 Exchanging Information   28
Chapter 3 Presenting Information   50
Chapter 4 Manipulating Data   64
Chapter 5 Keeping Data Safe and Secure   84
Chapter 6 Legal, Social, Ethical and Environmental Issues when Using ICT   96
Chapter 7 Using ICT Systems   104
Chapter 8 Monitoring, Measurement and Control Technology   123
Chapter 9 ICT and Modern Living   137

Unit 2 Practical Applications in ICT

Chapter 10 Investigating a Need   156
Chapter 11 Practical Use of Software Tools to Produce a Working Solution   165
Chapter 12 Practical Use of File and Data Structure to Produce a Working Solution   171
Chapter 13 Present a Solution   176
Chapter 14 Evaluation   180

Unit 3 ICT in Context

Chapter 15 ICT Innovation in Five Businesses: Introduction   186
Chapter 16 Art Gallery: IndepArt   188
Chapter 17 A Fashion Retailer: Ote KoKotur   196
Chapter 18 A Theatre: Pea Hints on Halfsbery Avenue   207
Chapter 19 A Dentist: Dr Jay Maloden   211
Chapter 20 A Manufacturing Company: Hedsup   217

Unit 4 Creative Use of ICT and Coding a Solution

Chapter 21 Introduction to the Creative Use of ICT and Coding a Solution   222
Chapter 22 Analysis   227
Chapter 23 Design   232
Chapter 24 Development   239
Chapter 25 Testing your Solution   246
Chapter 26 Evaluating your Solution and Working with Others   249

UNIT 1

ICT in Today's World

Chapter 1 ICT in Today's World

Chapter 2 Exchanging Information

Chapter 3 Presenting Information

Chapter 4 Manipulating Data

Chapter 5 Keeping Data Safe and Secure

Chapter 6 Legal, Social, Ethical and Environmental Issues when Using ICT

Chapter 7 Using ICT Systems

Chapter 8 Monitoring, Measurement and Control Technology

Chapter 9 ICT and Modern Living

1 ICT in Today's World

What you will learn in this chapter

● The different types of ICT system and their uses
● The difference between hardware and software
● The hardware components of ICT systems
● The software used in ICT systems

Just for a moment imagine a world without information and communication technology. What would your life be like without ICT? You would have no mobile phone, no MP3 player, no television, no internet for email and web browsing, no computer games – no computers at all! All these you could probably live without, even if you were miserable and bored – but think also about all the ICT in use around us – we rely on ICT to provide us with power for lighting and transport and as a way of managing car engines, and keeping airlines, buses and trains running to time without which our life would, as we know it, be impossible. There are places and people in the world today that manage quite well without all the information and communication technology that we take for granted but they would find it impossible to run many aspects of their lives the way we do. Our modern societies would not be as pleasant and may not survive as we know it without ICT.

ICT is all around us, in our homes, in our schools and businesses and in the infrastructure that allows our society to work and function. In this section you will find the ICT systems in today's world that you need to know about.

ICT systems

What is a computer?

A computer is a programmable machine that follows a set of instructions. Early computers were mechanical with levers and cogs such as Charles Babbage's Difference Engine which was an automated, mechanical calculator, large enough to fill a small room! Babbage's Analytical Engine was designed to be a general purpose computer but was never built, some believe, because the technology of the day was either not good enough or too expensive. Babbage was still working on the design when he died in 1871. A working model was built in 1992 and can be seen in the Science Museum in London.

ACTIVITY 1

Make a list of three items that you own or use regularly – apart from your laptop or PC – that use ICT and that you think you could not do without, and then write down what your life would be like without them.

Charles Babbage's Difference Engine

Charles Babbage's
Analytical Engine

Analogue computers

Analogue computers existed long before digital computers were invented. Guns were targeted using mechanical analogue computers during World War I and the Korean War by the United States Army Air Force.

WEBLINKS

http://oro.open.ac.uk/5795/1/bletchley_paper.pdf#
http://dcoward.best.vwh.net/analog/
These have explanations and documents about analogue computers

WEBLINKS

http://en.wikipedia.org/wiki/Analog_signal
http://en.wikipedia.org/wiki/Digital
These have explanations of analogue and digital signals.

KEY WORDS

Analogue
Analogue signals are continually variable and even small fluctuations in the signal are important. Analogue systems use continuous ranges of values to represent information.

Digital
Digital signals have discrete values such as on/off, 1 or 0. In-between values are not used.

Digital computers

Modern computers are not mechanical but are electronic and, while some analogue computers are used in universities for research, most computers now are digital.

Computers can follow or execute a set of prewritten or recorded instructions, called a program, and respond to commands entered by a user.

All computers used today have the same basic structure, although the way the components are arranged in the structure differs depending on the use to which the computer will be put. The photos show some examples of modern computers:

Desktop PC

Laptop

Netbook

WEBLINK

http://en.wikipedia.
org/wiki/Computer

This describes
digital computers.

PDA

Mobile phone

Mainframe computer

Personal computers

You will be most familiar with the personal computers that you use in schools and at home that you use for tasks such as writing reports or letters in a word-processor, doing calculations or data modelling in spreadsheets, photo and video editing or playing games. These personal computers are often connected together on a network and the internet which also allows them to be used for searching the World Wide Web, sending and receiving email messages, accessing chat rooms or instant messaging, writing blogs and using social networking sites.

Personal computers include netbooks, laptops, notebook computers, palmtops, desktop computers, tablet computers, PDAs and handheld computers. Modern mobile telephones can also carry out many of the tasks normally associated with personal computers with the added advantages of being able to keep in contact with friends by text message or telephone, having an inbuilt camera and playing music or video files or using applications when out and about away from home.

Personal computers are often found in businesses and are used for general tasks such as running database management systems, business spreadsheets and for specialised business purposes such as computer-aided design and computer-aided manufacture such as making cars or televisions. Also, personal computers can be used for capturing and monitoring data received from sensors such as for recording temperatures and pressures of the weather.

ACTIVITY 2

For each of the different types of computer shown, write down some typical tasks that it would be most suitable for.

Desktop computer

Laptop computer

Smart mobile phone

Personal Digital Assistant (PDA)

Other types of computer system

Large organisations such as banks, insurance firms and utility companies (these supply gas, electricity and water) may use mainframe computers. Mainframe computers are computers which work not as a single computer but as if they were many, often dozens or hundreds, of computers each running their own operating systems and carrying out many tasks at once. The term 'mainframe' is now somewhat out of date but it originally referred to the construction of mainframe computers on a set of 'frames' or racks that held the component parts. Mainframe computers are used where large amounts of data needs to be processed in bulk, e.g. the processing of bank statements, utility bills or stock control.

Supercomputers and mainframes

Supercomputers are the fastest computers that exist in terms of the speed of calculation and are used, for instance, in university research departments where fast and complex calculations need to be carried out. This includes the complex calculations needed for simulations or modelling scenarios such as those needed for modelling climate changes. Here large amounts of data collected from many areas will need to be used to try and predict what will happen to the climate.

The distinction between mainframe computer and supercomputer is often not that clear today but supercomputers are usually 'one of a kind', built for a particular purpose, although supercomputers often contain the same components as other computers – just more of them!

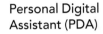
Cray or IBM supercomputer

Embedded computers

At the other end of the scale, embedded computer systems are found in everyday devices and carry out only one or two tasks so they do not need to be as flexible as a personal computer. An embedded computer system controlling traffic lights at a road junction does not need to do anything else. Music players, mobile phones, microwave ovens, washing machines, digital watches and calculators all contain embedded systems. The components and software in these devices only have to carry out their designed function and no other; for instance, in an iPod there is only a need for software to organise and play music and videos. A mobile phone will contain software that controls the connection, address lists and text messages but will not usually have to do much else. Of course, as the device such as an iPhone becomes more complicated and able to carry out more functions, the embedded software has to be added to, but simple devices like a washing machine will probably only ever be required to wash clothes.

Digital watch

Calculator

Music player   Microwave oven   Washing machine

KEY WORDS

Type of computer	
Personal computer	These include netbooks, laptops, notebook computers, palmtops, desktop computers, tablet computers, PDAs and handheld computers. Used for web searching, email, running applications, e.g. word-processing, spreadsheets, databases, and many other software applications in homes and offices
Mainframe computer	Large computers used in banks, insurance firms where very large amounts of data have to be processed quickly
Supercomputer	Very fast computers used in universities and other areas where complex calculations are needed and speed of calculation is important

ACTIVITY 3

Use the internet to find out what is meant by 'microcomputer' and write down the names of two famous makes of microcomputer.

WEBLINKS

http://www.teach-ict.com/gcse/hardware/types/teacher/types_theory.htm

http://computer.howstuffworks.com/10-types-of-computers.htm

http://en.wikipedia.org/wiki/Personal_computer

http://www.webopedia.com/TERM/P/personal_computer.html

http://www.historylearningsite.co.uk/personal_computer.htm

These provide explanations and descriptions of different types of computers.

Hardware and software

The physical components of a computer system are called the 'hardware' and the instructions that make the system work and which the system follows are called 'software'.

Hardware is all of the physical components that can be touched, held and seen.

Software is used to 'program' the computer system which means to create a set of instructions, usually stored or saved for later use, that the computer will follow. Different types of software are used for different tasks, e.g. the software that controls the hardware and allows a user to interact with a computer system is the operating system while software that enables users to carry out tasks is called application software – or simply applications. Other types of software include utility software that does a specific task such as checking a disk drive for errors, and 'drivers' that allow the operating system to communicate with, e.g. a printer. Today, many utilities and drivers are included in the operating system and are already present after the operating system has been installed but if new hardware is added then new drivers may have to be installed.

Hardware

Whatever the type of computer, it will always have the same basic hardware structure. The table on page 8 shows the hardware and what it is for.

There will also be all the components, nuts, bolts, screws, wiring and connectors, etc. to allow all the other components to work together but essentially a computer system consists of INPUTS, OUTPUTS, PROCESSING and STORAGE devices and data flows around the computer system from one to another as shown in the following diagram.

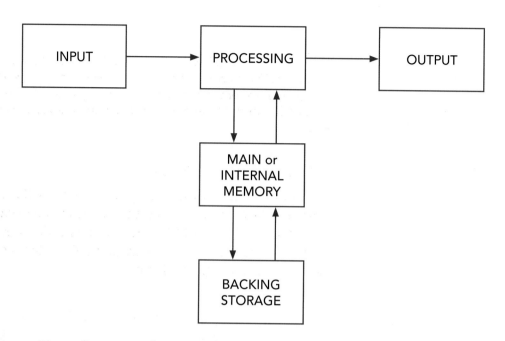

Depending upon the type of computer system in which they are fitted, the hardware components will look different and be larger or smaller in size but will perform the same function.

Hardware	Function
Input devices	Components to allow users to enter data such as instructions
Processor	Component for deciding what the instructions mean and what to do – this is the processing of the instructions or data
Output devices	Components for showing the results of the processing to the user data such as instructions
Internal or main memory	Components to **store** the data and/or instructions that are about to be, are being, or have been, processed
Backing storage	Components to **store** the data and/or instructions when the computer is switched off so the computer system or a user can come back to them later

KEY WORDS

Input
Entering data into a computer system is input.

Processing
Data is converted it from one form to another. This is done by following a set of instructions and commands.

Output
When the results of processing are shown, this is output.

Storage
Data is kept or recorded while waiting to be used or for future use.

Data, such as instructions and commands or information to be used for calculations, is entered using the INPUT devices, worked on (processed), and OUTPUT so the user can see the results. If you are typing a memo, the input would be the keystrokes on a keyboard for the letters, the processing would be where the letters should go and the output would be the memo on a monitor. If you decide to stop and leave the memo for later, the memo could be stored on a flash memory device or hard disk.

ACTIVITY 4

Imagine that you have a list of your friends and want to keep it on your laptop. You carry out three tasks: typing in the list, sorting the list into alphabetical order of name and printing yourself a list to keep at home. Identify which of the three tasks is input, output and processing.

More components

Often, other devices may be present such as the components needed to connect the computer systems to others on a network.

Other devices could be the communication devices such as modems, network interface cards, routers and hubs. Other connection systems may also be present, e.g. USB interfaces.

Network interface card

Router

Hub

USB Flash memory stick

CPU

Modem

ACTIVITY 5

Find out what a 'user interface' is and what it is for.

KEY WORDS

Network

When computers are connected together so that they can share data and devices such as printers, they are said to be in a computer network.

Interface

This is where data is transferred between computer devices or between people and computers.

USB interface

The Universal Serial Bus interface was designed for use on personal computers to connect peripheral devices such as printers, keyboards and flash drives. It is now commonly used to connect other devices such as cameras. USB connections are also now found on many other devices such as PDAs, mobile phones and can also be used to charge batteries.

Peripheral device

Any device that is not actually part of the computer but is attached to a computer is called a peripheral device. Peripheral devices are seen as expanding the system and include scanners and printers.

Communication devices

The function of these devices is shown here:

Device	Function
Modem	This device encodes digital information on to an analogue signal. Often used to send digital data along ordinary telephone lines
Network interface cards	This device is often just called a network card or NIC; these provide the electronic circuitry for computers to communicate on a network
Hub	This device connects different networks sections
Routers and switches	These devices connect different networks and can be used to control where the data is sent. They are often found in homes and used for connecting to the internet
USB interface	This is used to connect a computer with another device such as a flash memory device

Processing data

The processing in computer systems is carried out by the Central Processing Unit or CPU for short. The CPU is a collection of electronic circuits that carry out, or **execute**, the instructions either in a program or which are entered by the user and which make decisions using the instructions. How these

CPU

instructions are executed is not important here but the instructions have to be entered into the computer, stored in the computer's main memory, or in some special memory actually inside the CPU itself, and the results output from the computer for every task that the computer is asked to perform.

If the computer is switched off, then the data that users need to carry on with their work when it is switched back on and all the instructions needed to start and operate the computer have to be kept on a storage device. If this data was not stored safely, the users would have to redo all of their work every time they switched off and restarted the computer; if the instructions to start the computer were not stored, then it wouldn't restart!

The components used for input include not only the familiar devices such as the mouse and keyboard found in personal computer systems but also more specialised input devices such as microphones designed to capture sounds, suck and puff switches used by those people unable to use their hands to manipulate a keyboard or mouse and the input devices used in computer games (such as wireless games controllers) and at supermarket terminals.

Input devices

Some examples of input devices are shown here:

Input device	Typical use
Mouse	Choosing options from an on-screen menu and selecting icons
Keyboard	Entering characters when typing a letter
Joystick/game controller	Moving on-screen objects in a computer game

Input device	Typical use
Scanner	Importing a printed image into a computer system
Barcode reader	Reading the data stored in a barcode
Chip and PIN reader	Reading the data stored in a chip on a bank or ID card
Magnetic stripe reader	Reading the data stored in a magnetic stripe on a bank or ID card
Keypad	Entering numbers at a supermarket checkout

Input device	Typical use
Webcam	Capturing still or moving images
Microphone	Capturing sounds
Sensors	Capturing data about physical conditions such as temperature, light and pressure sensors
Remote control units	Sending the user's decisions to, e.g. a TV
Puff-suck switch	A mouth-operated switch for use by those who are physically impaired

ACTIVITY 6

Persons with physical disabilities often have difficulties using computers in schools to do their work.

Find out about the specialised equipment and software that can help those people to use computers.

Digital camera

Digital video camera

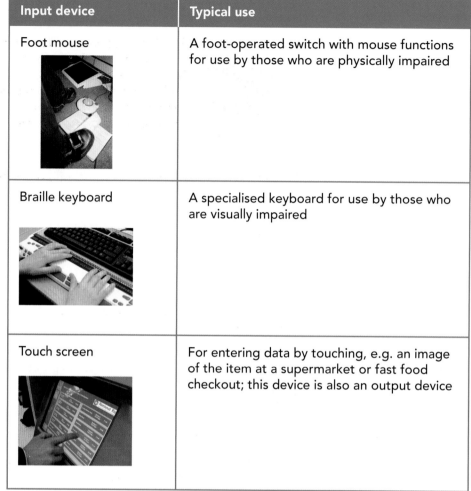

Input device	Typical use
Foot mouse	A foot-operated switch with mouse functions for use by those who are physically impaired
Braille keyboard	A specialised keyboard for use by those who are visually impaired
Touch screen	For entering data by touching, e.g. an image of the item at a supermarket or fast food checkout; this device is also an output device

Other devices that could be considered to be input devices are digital still and video cameras as these can be directly connected to computer systems and the images passed directly to the computer system. Digital cameras usually capture images and store the images on internal storage devices before these are downloaded to the computer system so, strictly speaking, they are not input devices when used on their own and then the images downloaded.

WEBLINK

http://schools.becta.org.uk/index.php?section=tl&catcode=ss_tl_inc_ac_03&rid=9813
This gives a description of the use of ICT for assisting with disabilities.

Output devices

Output devices are needed so that a user can find out the results of processing the input. Some output devices and their uses are shown here:

Output device	Typical use
Monitor	This is the 'screen' or 'display' found on most computer systems and used to see the results of processing. Monitors are now nearly all LCD with flat screens, and the older-style 'vacuum tube' displays are no longer used. They are found in all shapes and sizes but 'widescreen' monitors are best for viewing movies
Printer	Printers produce copies of the results on paper – this is 'hardcopy'
Speakers/ headphones	These produce sounds
Actuators	These produce movement, e.g. motors to move a barrier or door

ACTIVITY 7

During one school week, make a list of each different input device that you use, why you use it and how many times you use it.

Storage devices

The storage of data and instructions is important because the CPU needs to be able to access the data or instructions quickly and easily and a user needs to be able to store their work for future use. A computer system has two types of storage for its data: the main memory (also called internal memory), where the data that is being used, is about to be used or has just been used by the CPU is kept, and a backing storage for longer-term storage of data.

Storage	Function
Main (internal) memory	Holds the data that is currently in use
Backing storage	Holds data for long-term storage

ACTIVITY 8

The size or capacity of storage devices is measured in bytes.
(a) Find out what is meant by a 'byte'.
(b) Find out how many bytes make up a kilobyte (Kb), a megabyte (Mb) and a gigabyte (Gb).

Computer memory

The main, internal memory consists of two types:

Read Only Memory (ROM) which is used to store data or instructions that do not need to be changed such as the instructions needed when the computer is first switched on. When a computer is first switched on, the CPU does not know what to do so there are a few instructions stored in ROM that tell it where and how to find the instructions to get started.

ROM is a type of memory from which data can be read but which cannot usually be changed or erased such as the data that a computer needs when starting up or the instructions in a washing machine. Users must not be able, or have any need, to alter these instructions because if they do then the machines would not work.

Also, ROM does not lose its data when the electrical power is switched off. It is said to be nonvolatile, i.e. keeps its data without the need for electrical power. Special types of ROM can have the data changed, e.g. an EEPROM (Electrically Erasable Programmable Read Only Memory) can be erased and reprogrammed and there are other types that are used for specialised purposes such as storing the configuration details of a router. Sometimes, the initial startup instructions of a computer (called the BIOS) are stored in EEPROMs so that they can be updated in the future.

Random Access Memory (RAM) makes up the bulk of the memory found in computer systems. RAM does not keep any data if its power supply is switched off (it is said to be volatile) but, usually, data in RAM can be accessed much faster than in ROM. More importantly, the data in RAM can be accessed quickly wherever it happens to be stored.

Data stored on tapes and hard disks is accessed much more slowly, although data stored on flash memory, such as memory sticks, can be accessed more quickly.

RAM is used to store the data and instructions such as the operating system that the CPU is currently using, and the data and software applications being used by the user.

A typical laptop computer would have some internal memory (ROM and RAM) and a hard disk. When it is switched on, the instructions stored in its ROM will be used to start it and load the operating system from the hard disk into its RAM. When it is ready for use, a user may start an application like a web browser and this will also be loaded from the hard disk into RAM ready for use.

WEBLINKS

http://www.hardware.windowsreinstall.com/memory.htm

http://www.computersecuritynews.org/computer_memory_explained.htm

This provides an explanation of computer memory.

KEY WORDS

ROM
Read Only Memory is a permanent storage area of memory that does not lose its data when power is turned off – it is said to be nonvolatile. Data can only be read from ROM, not written to it.

RAM
Random Access Memory loses its data when power is turned off – it is said to be volatile – but can be written to as well as read from.

BIOS
The Basic In Out System that is needed to tell the computer what to do on startup.

Hard disk drive

Tape drive

Losing all your work when the power supply is switched off is very annoying, so computer systems have backing storage, such as a hard disk, where users can store – or save – their work. Backing storage is used to keep the instructions that the CPU needs to function – the operating system – and the instructions that a user will need to carry out a task – the software applications – and any data needed or used by a user of the system. Modern applications provide an automatic backup of a user's work so, in the event of a power failure or other disaster such as a program crash, most of the work can be recovered easily.

Hard disks are commonly found in modern computers and, as the name suggests, are made of metal disks, inside a sealed casing, on which data is stored by magnetising the surface of the disk. The correct term for the hard disk device is 'hard disk drive' or 'hard disk device'. The actual data is stored on the metal disks which are the 'medium'.

It is important to use the correct terms in ICT or computing so a device or drive is the physical mechanism that is used to hold the 'medium' (the metal disks in the hard disk example above) on which the data is stored. A tape drive uses magnetic tape as a medium and a USB memory stick uses flash memory as the medium and the now rather outdated floppy disk drive is the device and the floppy disk is the medium.

Some backing storage devices, e.g. DVD drives, have a removable medium, e.g. a DVD-R, so that when one is fully used another disk can be substituted or the disk can be taken to another computer which can read the data using its DVD drive.

Flash memory

USB memory stick

Flash memory is becoming more commonly used as the technology becomes easier and cheaper to manufacture. Flash memory is similar to ROM in that it retains its data when the power to the computer is switched off (it is nonvolatile) but it is like RAM in that it can be erased and used over and over again.

Flash memory is a very specialised type of EEPROM that can be erased and rewritten to many times over and is used in memory cards (such as those used in mobile phones and digital cameras) and USB flash drives. Because flash memory needs no power to keep its data intact, allows fast access times to its data and is not easily damaged, many people store important data on their 'USB key sticks' instead of on their hard drive.

Some computer manufacturers are now using flash memory instead of hard disks in their smaller computer systems. Flash memory is used in systems such as mobile phones, music players, PDAs, game consoles and digital cameras. Digital video cameras now use flash memory to store images as flash memory is more reliable and can hold more data than the conventional video tapes that were used previously. One disadvantage of flash memory is that the devices that use it, e.g. USB key sticks, are small and easily lost! However, they do appear to be resistant to damage, surviving being dropped or put through washing machines cycles when left in pockets!

Removable storage media

Some storage devices can have the medium removed so that the data can be transported to another computer or stored safely and securely away from the computer system. Flash memory (in USB sticks) is removable, and DVD and CD are commonly used for storing video and music. Modern computers no longer use floppy disks and do not usually have a floppy disk drive but there are still a few uses for the floppy disk. Invented in the mid-1970s by IBM, the floppy disk was once the most common form of backing storage. Billions of floppy disks were made before they were super-seded by flash memory in USB drives, or CDs and DVDs. Most people no longer use floppy disks, although there are older industrial computer systems for automatic control of drilling and manufacturing equipment (oddly, some of these are used to make the printed circuit boards that are found in modern computers!) that still have them. But even here flash memory devices are being made to replace the floppy disks, giving the equipment a new lease of life.

DVD and CD are optical storage systems. Both disk formats can hold large amounts of data but the technology is always advancing so more and more data can be stored. Blu-ray technology, using a disk the same size as DVD, allows a disk the size of a DVD to store over ten times the amount of data compared to a DVD. Blu-ray, DVD and CD drives read and/or write the data to a disk.

Optical storage systems use lasers to read and write data to the removable medium in specially sealed devices or drives.

The correct spelling of the media used by computers is disk but often the spelling 'disc' is used in names.

The storage capacity of storage media is measured in megabytes (mb), gigabytes (gb) and terabytes (tb).

Storage Device	Medium	Full name	Typical use
CD	CD-ROM CD-R CD-RW mini-CD	Compact Disk	This disk was the original digital disk used for storing music and replaced vinyl LP discs. Later, CD-drives for computers that could read and write data to the disks were made available. CDs can store about 700 mb of data which is about 80 mins of music. Computer games are often sold on CD-ROM as these cannot be erased. Most people refer to the CD-ROMs that carry music simply as CDs
DVD	DVD-ROM DVD-R DVD-RW DVD+R DVD+RW DVD-DL mini-DVD (There are two types of DVD available for use – the plus or minus varieties are two competing standards but do much the same thing)	Digital Versatile Disk	This is used mainly for videos and movies. It has a large capacity which depends on the type of DVD disk used but single-sided DVDs can store 4.7 gb and double-sided around 9 gb. DVD-ROM is used to store computer software for sale. Most people refer to the DVD-ROMs that carry movies simply as DVDs

Storage Device	Medium	Full name	Typical use
Blu-ray	BD-R BD-RE mini-BD disk (BD-RE is the reusable version)	The name comes from the type of laser used – it has a short wavelength in the blue-violet part of the spectrum	This is used to store very large amounts of data and is used for high-definition audio and video
Multilayer disks	BD	These have been made with up to eight layers for storage.	These are enhancements and developments of the Blu-ray disks and may have 100 to 200 gb capacity. The disks will need new types of drives to use them but the capacity should allow ten hours or more of high definition video to be stored on one disk

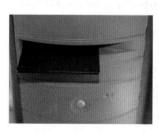

Floppy disk drive   CD/DVD drive   A flash memory card   Blu-ray player

In all the optical disk formats shown above, the medium can be disks that are used once only (shown by an R) and those that can be reused (RW) – the RW disks are often much more expensive than the cheap use-once only disks! As with all technology, the advances in storage devices and media mean that the list above will be added to as time goes by. The increased capacity of the latest Blu-ray disks will mean that the amount of user data that can be stored on a single disk will be huge, making them ideal for backups. These disks will also allow many hours of high-definition video and multichannel sound to be easily stored.

Each of the backing storage devices and media used by computer systems has its use and its advantages and disadvantages. For example, flash memory is easy to carry around but can be easily lost or stolen, DVDs can be used to store vast amounts of computer data but can be damaged by scratches. Some advantages and disadvantages of the different storage media are shown here:

Storage medium	Advantage	Disadvantage
CD	● Write once, i.e. CD-R are cheap to buy – so cheap that most people use CD-R instead of CD-RW and ● CD-RWs can be written to more than once ● all modern computers can use them	● CD-ROM cannot be written to after manufacture ● small capacity compared to DVD, Blu-ray, flash memory ● easily damaged by, e.g. scratches
DVD	● Write once are cheap to buy ● all modern computers can use them ● large storage capacity	● rewritable DVD-RWs are expensive ● double-layer DVDs are expensive ● some devices cannot use both the plus and minus type of DVD ● cannot be used on the CD drives of older computers ● easily damaged by, e.g. scratches
Blu-ray	● very large storage capacity	● devices and media are expensive but prices will fall as more people buy them ● not usable by DVD or CD drives so a new optical drive is needed ● easily damaged by, e.g. scratches
Floppy disk	● easily transported ● all older computers can use them ● not as easily damaged as hard disks	● not commonly used in modern computers ● very small storage capacity ● easily lost or stolen ● can be damaged by magnetic fields, or mishandling
Hard disk	● very large storage capacity ● relatively cheap for large storage capacities compared to removable devices/media	● easily damaged by knocks, heat, magnetic fields ● not as suitable for removable devices as flash memory as hard disk should not be moved especially when in use
Flash memory	● all modern computers can use flash memory via USB ● large storage capacity ● not easily damaged	● very expensive for the very large storage capacities needed to replace hard disks ● slower access to data than hard disks ● they can only be reliably used about 10,000 or so times ● easily lost or stolen when used as removable USB sticks

WEBLINKS

http://www.
computerhope.com/
jargon/s/stordevi.
htm

http://en.wikipedia.
org/wiki/Data_
storage_device

http://www.
howstuffworks.com/
flash-memory.htm

http://www.
manifest-tech.com/
media_dvd/dvd_hd_
multi_layer.htm

These provide
descriptions and
explanations of
storage devices.

It is possible to attach any or all of the storage devices to a computer system via USB so a large hard disk can become a removable device. Often, hard disks attached in this way are used for storing private files or backups as they can be locked away from the computers.

CD disk   Floppy disk   Multi-layer disks

Connecting computers together and networking

Many ICT systems are connected together so that data can be shared between them. The hardware needed to do this is not essential to the working of the system but many ICT systems have the components already built in by the manufacturer. Laptops, PDAs and mobile phones have the components already fitted to allow them to connect to other devices via wireless networks and often by more conventional wired networks. These allow the users to communicate with each other and to share data easily.

If the ICT system is to be able to communicate with other systems, it has to have a network interface card which can use wires or radio waves (wireless connections) to communicate with other devices on a network or networks. Often these are already installed in the ICT system, e.g. all laptops have these built in and a mobile telephone would be useless without one!

In the network itself there are the physical connectors, i.e. the wires or radio (wireless) connections, and additional hardware to connect the system together. Such hardware components are routers, hubs and repeaters.

A router is used to connect two networks together or to connect to the internet. Often in the home, a router is called the 'modem' as it is used to connect home computers or networks to the internet but it really is just a router. This device consists of hardware and software that directs data from one network to another – one of the networks could be the internet – which is one very large network! Routers have a number of connections called ports and can be programmed to direct data to whichever port the user wishes. Users can also program the router not to send data to particular ports and this can be used to make networks secure. Often a router will have a wireless port and this can be used to share a single internet connection between multiple computers. The wireless connection is separately programmable as wireless connections are less secure than wired connections.

Hubs and repeaters are similar to routers but they are much simpler than routers as they cannot be programmed and just forward all the data

WEBLINK

http://www.
didcotgirls.oxon.sch.
uk/depts/it/gcse/
notes/hardware/
index.htm

This provides
explanations of
hardware.

they receive. Most hubs have multiple connection ports and all the data from one port will be sent to all the other ports. They are used to share one network wire between a number of computers.

Software

Software is the set of instructions that the computer follows. The software that controls the whole system is called the operating system and this has a number of specific functions such as:

- manages the CPU usage by hardware and software
- managing the hardware including peripherals such as printers using, e.g. device drivers
- provides an environment for software applications to run
- provides a suitable user interface
- manages software on the computer system
- provide a multitasking environment that allows a user to carry more than one task at once
- manages inputs and outputs
- manages memory resources.

Operating systems and utility software

Operating systems on most computers today use windows, icons, menus and pointing devices for the user to access the facilities but other operating systems exist, the most common being a command line interface.

A window is an area of the screen used to interact with a software application. An icon is a small image used to represent an element of the interface or application. A menu is a list of items to choose from and a pointer is the on-screen icon or image that is used for selection.

A Graphical User Interface (GUI) has advantages over a command line interface in that the user does not need to be highly skilled in ICT or even know how to use the software in any detail to get started. There is help available from menus if the user needs it. Using a GUI means that the user does not need to access all the features of the operating system or software to carry out tasks. A command line interface requires the user to know the exact commands needed to use it and to have some experience of using computers. A command line interface usually allows full access to all aspects of an operating system or software application but can be quite difficult for inexperienced users.

Operating systems often have utility software included but occasionally these are extras and have functions such as:

- managing the hard disk to keep it working at its best, e.g. defragmenting the files
- compressing files so that they become smaller
- encrypting files for security
- scanning for viruses.

Utility software is used by users to fine tune their computer system and to keep it running efficiently. Utility software usually is designed to perform only a single task.

Applications software

Users of ICT systems often do not seem to notice the operating system at all – especially if it is really easy to use and performs well – but are more familiar with the applications that allow them to carry out tasks such as writing a letter or creating a video. This software is called application software.

Application software includes:

- applications for creating and managing data and information:
  - word-processors
  - desktop publishing software
  - spreadsheet
  - database management software
  - multimedia software
  - slideshow software
  - web authoring software
- applications for creating and managing still, moving and video images:
  - photo-editing software
  - animation software
  - video-editing software
  - graphics manipulation software
- applications for communicating with others:
  - web browsing software
  - communications software, e.g. social networking software, e.g. chat, instant messaging, web browsers, file transfer and email clients
  - gaming software

and more.

Programming

The instructions that are found in all software have to be written by programmers who use specialised software to create and check their work. Programmers will create the instructions in a language that computers can follow. This special software includes the programming software such as:

- editors which programmers use to type and create the instructions which are known as source code; while the programmers can understand the source code computers systems usually cannot!
- compilers which are special applications that convert the source code into a language that the computer can understand – this is called the object code; the code produced depends on the type and make of the computer it is designed for
- debuggers used to find errors in code
- linkers to link or join parts of the programmers code together with other code.

WEBLINKS

http://www. didcotgirls.oxon.sch. uk/depts/it/gcse/ notes/software/ index.htm

http://en.wikipedia. org/wiki/Computer_ software

These provide explanations of software.

Some software is designed to be used on different types or makes of computer and this often involves the use of 'interpreters' so that the same code may be understood on different computers in much the same way as interpreters are used to make different human languages understood. Code written in interpreted languages is often slower but has the advantage of working on many different computers. This is especially important when many applications have to work on different computers over the internet. An example of an interpreted language is Java which is used by some websites and has to work in many different web browsers on all sorts of different computers.

User interfaces

All software used to control or create requires a user interface. This is where the user tells the computer what to do or enters data that the computer will use. The operating system of modern computers is responsible for providing the user interface to the computer system and to the software being used and programmers creating applications have to make sure that their software sticks to the rules!

Data is raw numbers, letters or other characters. Information is the data put into context so that it means something.

ACTIVITY 9

Find out what is meant by:
(a) a command line interface
(b) a graphical user interface (GUI)

and write down the main features of each.

A good user interface:

- will be logical to use, e.g. all the menus and options will be in the same place as those in other applications
- will have options and tools in logical and sensible order; they will follow the normal reading directions of the user, e.g. left to right
- will have similar colours and sizes of windows, text and images and they will be easy to find
- will have suitable colours, e.g. not too bright or contrasting or too pale for the user to see and take into account, e.g. colour vision problems
- will have only a sensible amount of information on the screen at any one time
- will have any tools, e.g. buttons needed to move to a different page or screen, in a logical place and similar for all applications.

File types

One of the advantages of using ICT systems is that your data can be saved on a storage device and retrieved for later use. To save data for later use, it has to be recorded on the, e.g. USB memory stick's flash memory in a file. The data is encoded in a file format. The data saved by e.g. word-processors or video-editing software is recorded in files in a format that can be opened later. So that the operating system knows which application made the file and what to do with the file when the user tries to open it, extra data is also stored in the file or as an extension to the name that tells the operating system that the file contains data about, e.g. an image or a document that should be shown in a web browser. For instance the first two lines of a web page would look something like this:

```
<!DOCTYPE html>
<html>
```

which tell the operating system that this is a web page and to send it to a web browser.

Some operating systems use extensions to the names used when saving the files, e.g. Microsoft's Windows operating systems have many file extensions, some of which are:

- jpg, gif, tiff used for different types of image files
- wav, mp3, aac used for audio files
- mpeg2 and mpeg4 used for video files
- doc, xls, ppt, rtf for document files.

The different 'file types' are used to show that the files contain a particular arrangement of data and to help choose which application should be used to open and view the file. Using the incorrect file type when saving a file is not usually possible but sometimes a user will change the file extension when renaming a file and when the file is accessed an error will be shown because the operating system either doesn't know what to do with it or sends it to the wrong application.

ACTIVITY 10

Open a software package that you would use to manipulate images and find out what image file types it can export. Find out why there is more than one file type for saving images.

EXAM TYPE QUESTIONS

1 Explain what is meant by hardware.

2 For each of these tasks, state the most suitable input device that you would use:
   (a) for typing text into a document
   (b) for reading the data on a chip in a credit card
   (c) for reading the data in a barcode
   (d) for recording a spoken commentary
   (e) for importing a printed photograph

3 For each of the tasks listed below, write down the most suitable software application you would use to carry out the task:
   (a) view web pages
   (b) compress a file
   (c) manage memory resources
   (d) convert source code into object code
   (e) edit an image

4 Imagine that you have to continue with some school work at home and you wanted to transport a very large number of files of work from your computer at school to your computer at home. You are not allowed to send them home by email. Explain how you would take them home.

5 You are going to be given a new computer as a present. You are asked if you want a laptop or a desktop computer and you decide that you would like a laptop. Write down the difference between the two and explain why you would prefer to be given a laptop computer.

6 What are the main functions of these types of software?
   (a) an operating system
   (b) utility software
   (c) antivirus software

2 Exchanging Information

What you will learn in this chapter

- How ICT systems are used to exchange information
- How ICT systems are used to communicate information
- How to keep data and information safe when ICT systems are used to exchange and communicate information
- Web browsing and searching the World Wide Web for information
- The use of email for sending messages and attachments
- Instant messaging, chat rooms, blogs and video-conferencing
- File sharing
- Online banking and the selling and buying of goods and services

KEY WORD

Online

A peripheral such as a printer is said to be online when it is connected and ready for use.

A computer system or user is said to be online when they are connected to a network or to the internet.

How we use ICT systems to communicate

Using text messages, talking on the phone, sending emails, instant messaging and chat rooms to keep in contact with our friends, families and others are all services that use ICT, often but not always over the internet. We can also share files and look at web pages using the internet.

The use of ICT to communicate provides a cheap and reliable set of services that spans the entire world but it does mean that we have to be more organised and careful when using it than we would normally be when, e.g. writing and posting a letter on paper.

Using instant messaging is quite simple: the user will log into a service and be shown any friends or contacts who are also logged in and can be invited into a conversation. Instant messaging is different from email in that both persons have to be online and in contact – rather like a normal phone call – and is a typed conversation. Sometimes, a video image is also arranged at the same time but usually if there is video there is also sound and the conversation is then a video call and the participants don't need to type anything! The main advantage of instant messaging is that a real conversation can be held but disadvantages include that both users have to be using a computer and, usually, logged into a service, and the conversation is only between two people at one time.

Chat rooms are similar to instant messaging but more than two people can be involved. Often, video images can be shared using webcams. The

Instant messaging system

main purpose of chat rooms is to share information between a group of people. The advantages of chat rooms is that more than two people can join in at once and this can be used for multiplayer online games featuring virtual worlds which users may be able to create themselves. The main disadvantage is the problem of not really knowing who the other people really are as users can easily pretend to be someone they are not. For this reason, young persons are discouraged from using chat rooms.

Features of instant messaging

Participants can get an immediate reply and conversations are held in real time and can be saved for later reference. Additional features include the possible use of a webcam to view the participants, or a microphone to talk directly.

Features of chat rooms

Chat rooms allow instant messaging between two or more people who have a text-based conversation. Conversations and participants can be moderated which means that the contributions are checked before being posted.

Chat rooms can be used for sharing text-based information or playing online games with a graphical user interface.

ACTIVITY 1

You have to explain to a group of younger persons in your school why they should not use instant messaging or chat rooms unless they are very careful about whom they chat to. Write down what you would say to them.

WEBLINKS

http://en.wikipedia.org/wiki/Instant_messaging

http://en.wikipedia.org/wiki/Comparison_of_instant_messaging_clients

http://www.teach-ict.com/gcse/theory/communication/miniweb/pg15.htm

These provide explanations of instant messaging.

Email

Email is a popular method of communicating and is used by businesses and individuals. Simple use of email involving quickly typed and short messages is the most common way it is used but, more and more, people and businesses are using email to send important documents and long letters. One advantage of email is that there is no need for the person sending the email to wait for the person receiving the email to be online; the message is sent and the recipient can pick it up at a later time. Conversely, a disadvantage is that there is often no way that the sender knows if the message has arrived or has been read.

WEBLINK

http://www. teach-ict.com/ gcse/theory/ communication/ miniweb/pg8.htm

This provides explanations of email.

Email addresses

If you have an email address, it will be unique to you and no-one else will have the same address.

ACTIVITY 2

Write down why every email address should be unique.

ACTIVITY 3

A typical email address looks like this and has two main parts:

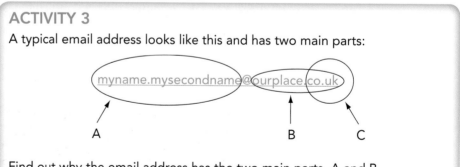

myname.mysecondname@ourplace.co.uk

A   B   C

Find out why the email address has the two main parts, A and B.
Part C is often different and it could be .co.uk, .com, .org.uk. Why is this?

Organising emails

The use of text messages and emails means that we generate many files and have many more names and addresses (most people call these 'contacts') than previously. It is sensible to organise our files and contacts logically so that we can find them. This is quite easy to do on mobile phones and computers and users are advised to set up their systems carefully. Many people do not do this properly and files and contacts are often lost. With email, messages can be filtered (using rules applied as the message

ACTIVITY 4

Open an email client and find out how to send an email using these features:
cc
bcc
return receipt
and write down why you would use these features.

arrives) into folders for each of our contacts or documents. Lists of contact addresses can be made up of single or many contacts so we can easily find the addresses of contacts and send messages to individuals or groups at once. Messages that we don't want to read can be filtered into folders or automatically deleted.

A disadvantage of email is that many messages are unwanted – so-called 'spam'. People who abuse the email system by sending unsolicited bulk messages indiscriminately are called spammers and are responsible for over 95% of all email messages. This large amount of email messages causes problems for users who find many unwanted messages filling up their system and it slows down the email system itself with needless messages getting in the way of productive messages, but it is difficult to stop.

WEBLINKS

http://www.teach-ict.com/gcse/theory/communication/miniweb/pg9.htm
http://www.teach-ict.com/gcse/theory/communication/miniweb/pg10.htm
These list the advantages and disadvantages of email.

Spam emails

Spamming is useful to advertisers who have no costs beyond the management of their mailing lists which they can purchase from less reputable companies, and it is difficult to discover who is actually sending the mass mailings.

A forum

KEY WORD

Posting

A posting is a contribution to a conversation placed on a website, or into a conversation by a participant.

ACTIVITY 5

You are at home and want to discuss some ideas about an English project with a group of friends before you write your project. You have a choice of using instant messaging, a chat room, a blog or email to do this. Write down as many advantages and disadvantages of using each form of communication with your friends.

KEY WORD

Protocol

A protocol is a set of rules that must be followed for the communication to work.

Email service providers and individual users can set up spam filters to try and stop unwanted messages but these are not perfect and they sometimes filter out messages that the user would like to read.

Online communities use ICT to communicate with others who have similar interests and who use email and instant messaging but they are also often web-based, which means that people use websites to share photos, video, news and other information with each other. Blogs are a type of website which is frequently updated on a regular basis with news and information, rather like a diary. Other people can add their comments and this makes blogs interactive. Podcasting is similar but uses audio messages.

An example of a blog is Twitter, where the messages are short (usually around a 100 characters) and when updated are sent to those who want to keep up to date. The messages can be sent via the website or by text message; most choose the website as using text messages may be costly. Twitter users can restrict who sees their postings or allow everyone access.

The first and most common use of the internet is the sharing of files either as web pages or directly between users.

The World Wide Web comprises a vast amount of documents written in a language suitable for viewing in a web browser. The documents are written in hypertext and are linked together. The documents are usually called web pages and pages can contain text, images, videos and other multimedia and users navigate between different pages using hyperlinks.

Files can be easily transferred to others across the internet. Many people attach the files to emails and send them but there are limitations on how many files can be sent and how large they can be.

Special file transfer services, such as FTP (File Transfer Protocol), exist for the specific purpose of moving files and these are often used for uploading new websites or pages. Mobile phones can allow file sharing over Bluetooth and/or WiFi connections to send files to other phones.

Unfortunately, file transfers between individuals are also commonly used for the illegal sharing, i.e. copying and distribution, of videos and music files as well as the legal downloading of, e.g. MP3 music or MPEG4 video files from commercial websites such as iTunes or the BBC and much of the publicity about file sharing has focused on this.

ACTIVITY 6

Why are the publishers and broadcasters of music and movies so worried about illegal file sharing? Find out how they are trying to prevent computer users from sharing music and movies that have not been paid for.

Facsimile or fax

This is a system that normally uses telephone lines to send images of documents to others. Originally designed to send copies (facsimiles) of documents quickly to others using cheap telecommunication lines, fax has

Fax machine

WEBLINK

http://www.
teach-ict.com/
gcse/theory/
communication/
miniweb/pg5.htm

This explains about fax.

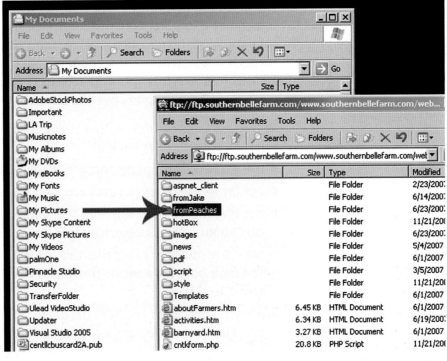

FTP transfer of file

been largely replaced by the sending of email attachments. Fax is still used where security and legal issues are important.

Using ICT in a safe and secure way

When we use any method of communication, we have to be careful to make sure that our data, particularly personal details, are kept safe from those we would not wish to see them. This is why letters are posted in envelopes! When using ICT to communicate, it is important to be careful because electronic data is so much easier to copy, steal, read or otherwise interfere with compared with information on paper.

With paper files, documents can be locked in rooms or cabinets for security, take time to copy and if stolen are quickly missed by the owners. With electronic files, access can be gained over a network or even via the internet; copying can be done very quickly and there is no need to steal the file if it is easily copied so usually no-one notices. Furthermore, because electronic files are so small compared with paper documents, many files can be taken at once and carried away on a flash memory device such as a USB memory stick. Someone would notice you if you stole a filing cabinet full of paper documents but a USB memory stick would be easy to hide.

Using ICT to exchange information requires you to be sensible and to make use of the services appropriately and responsibly. You will learn more about these in later chapters but you should:

- keep backups of files so that if you lose or damage the original, you have a copy to refer back to
- use passwords properly and not share them with others
- not try to use other person's accounts, details or passwords
- not give out your, or anyone's, personal details to anyone you are not sure about – this is especially important
- not share music or other files that are not yours to share – just because you have paid for a music download does not give you permission to give it to others
- not send private or confidential details or information to others unless you know who they are and can be sure that the information is kept secure – email and other internet services are not very secure!
- not abuse others by sending offensive materials or messages to anyone
- not view websites that could be seen as inappropriate and if you do come across these by accident, move off them quickly – these sites may be illegal, offensive, abusive or carry viruses.

Using the internet to exchange information

Before networks became commonplace and the internet was easily and cheaply available, information was exchanged within organisations or between people or by copying the files onto portable storage devices and physically moving them from one computer to another; many still prefer to use, e.g. CDs for transferring files as these offer a higher level of security than simply emailing files over the internet.

Web browsing

The World Web Web is an extremely large collection of pages of information that can be viewed using a web browser.

A web browser is a software application that displays the content of web pages; viewers use browsers to see text, images and other features of the web pages.

The owner or publisher of the web pages can choose to include text, images, videos, sounds, animations as well as other features such as email links, hyperlinks, file downloads and feedback forms. A website can also include navigational aids so that viewers can find their way about easily.

Web browser

KEY WORDS

World Wide Web
A collection of pages of information stored on servers and accessed via the internet.

Website
A collection of pages about related topics or information and accessed from the same or related servers.

Web page
A text document which usually contains instructions to tell the browser how to display the page. The document is usually written in HTML.

HTML (Hypertext Markup Language)
A set of instructions used to tell a web browser how to display a web page.

Web server
A computer that holds web pages or other files and allows access to these by others over a network or the internet.

Web browser
A software application that allows users to view text, images and other features on web pages and to navigate between websites and pages.

On a good website, it should be easy to navigate between pages and to find the information that you want.

Navigational aids in a web browser

All web browsers have built-in navigational features to help users find their way around websites and from one site to another. These features include:

Navigational feature of browser		Purpose when clicked
Home button		This takes the user to their home page, not the website's home/main page
Back button		This will take the user back to the previous page
Forward button		This will take the user forward to the next page

Navigational feature of browser	Purpose when clicked
Reload button	This will reload the page to refresh it
Stop button	This stops a page from loading
Bookmark or Favourite button Bookmarks	This will show a list of pages that the user has made. A user can click on an item in the list and go to that page
History History	This shows a list of all the pages visited so that they can be found again

The amount and methods of storing history and bookmarks or Favourites vary between different web browsers but all of them store these to make it easy for users to find pages again.

ACTIVITY 7

There are several good web browsers available from different companies. Open two different web browsers and make sure you can find these features and know how to use them in each browser:
- home page button and how to set the home page to your choice
- back and forward buttons
- history list
- bookmarks (Favorites) list
- how to clear the history list so that no-one know what the browser has been viewing

Finding information on the internet

There is so much information on so many pages that finding the exact piece of information that you want can be quite difficult and can take a long time.

Search engines were invented to help people find the information that they want. There are many search engines and the one you use is your choice.

Using a search engine

Using a search engine needs some thought and care if you are not be faced with thousands of results, many of which may not be quite what you wanted. If you are trying to find information about a new smart mobile telephone that you may want to buy, typing 'smart phone' into the search engine will probably give you hundreds of thousands of pages to look through and you may not find anything of use.

Careful use of a search engine can narrow down the results considerably. Here are several ways to do this.

Google offers an advanced search page where you can be more specific about what you want to find.

Putting specific words into the boxes will give you fewer but more useful results.

Another way to narrow your search is to use search techniques that use the logical terms AND, OR, NOT. Using these can force the search engine to find what you want.

- Typing 'smart AND phone' will search for pages that have both of the words 'smart' and 'phone' together.
- Typing 'smart OR phone' will search for pages that have either of the words.

Use the form below and your advanced search will appear here

Find web pages that have...

all these words:

this exact wording or phrase: tip

one or more of these words: OR   OR   tip

But don't show pages that have...

any of these unwanted words: tip

Need more tools?

Results per page: 10 results

Language: any language

File type: any format

Search within a site or domain:

(e.g. youtube.com, .edu)

⊞ Date, usage rights, numeric range, and more

Advanced Search

An advanced search screen

- Typing 'smart NOT phone' will search for pages that have the word 'smart' but not the word 'phone'.

ACTIVITY 8

You are looking for a new mobile phone and want one that will take photos and play MP3 files, but is not pink in colour.

Use the advanced features of the Google search engine to make your search. Try the same search using another search engine, e.g. Yahoo.

How successful were you with each?

Search engine limitations

Unfortunately, not all search engines will follow your instructions exactly and some will tell you that you do not need to type the words AND, OR, NOT because they will do it automatically.

Search engines have very complex ways of finding pages of information and a search engine may display results that the owners of websites or advertisers want to be shown rather than the precise results that you want.

Types of search engine

Crawler-based search engines trawl around the World Wide Web looking for pages and when you carry out a search will only search those pages that they have already found before displaying the results to you. This is much quicker than carrying out a completely new search of the whole World Wide Web every time but may miss the actual page that has the information you need.

Directory-based search engines rely on humans to send into them information about their pages or websites and, when someone does a search, will send out lists of those pages or sites.

Hybrid search engines can use both methods but whatever method is used, the results are displayed for you to see.

The order of the list can be changed by the owner of the search engine. Some website publishers will pay the search engine owners to show their website higher in the lists than others, or will pay for advertising on the search engine so that the site always appears.

As long as you are aware of the limitations of using search engines, you can find what you want quite easily.

ACTIVITY 9

Ask your teacher how, for what reasons and who decides what websites are filtered before they are allowed to be seen in school.

Advantages and disadvantages of using the internet to find information

Advantages	Disadvantages
A vast amount of information is available	Can be too much information to look through
Information can be found quickly compared with manually searching a library of books	Some results of searches may not be useful or the links provided may be out of date
Information is provided by anyone	Can be difficult to decide which information is useful or accurate or out of date. Some information may be false
You can find information on almost any topic	Some information may be inappropriate for reading or viewing
Information is already in electronic format and can be stored and used again	Having information in electronic format sometimes means that it has not been read properly or that it has been re-used without checking or following copyright restrictions

Email

Email is a way of exchanging messages electronically.

To use email, you must have an email account and access to the internet using a computer or other device such as a mobile phone.

Messages are written, stored and sent to the recipient which means that the sender and recipient do not have to be online at the same time.

The stages in sending an email are as follows.

- Open the email application (this is often called an email client) and choose the option to write or compose an email.

- Write the text of the email and check it for accuracy and for spelling mistakes. Many people do not bother to check emails for spelling mistakes and often use shorthand or 'textspeak' but this shows a lack of care and can cause misunderstandings when the message is read.

- Put in the email address. This can be typed or chosen from an address book. More than one address can be entered so that the message can be sent to more than one person without the need to retype it.

- Choose the 'send' option to transmit the email.

KEY WORDS

Email
An electronic message is made up of a 'header', which includes the address of the person who sent them email and the recipient's address, and the 'content', which is the actual message. Emails were originally designed for text-only messages but can carry attachments with other forms of information.

Email client
A software application used for sending, receiving and storing emails.

Email address
This is made up of two parts: the user name of the person followed by a name of the domain which provides the email services. A typical email address is:
myname@emaildomain.co.uk

Domain
Domains are names given to the addresses of computers on a network or on the internet. All the addresses are numbers which are difficult to remember so they are given names to make it easier for humans to use.

The email message will be stored in the senders 'outbox' ready to be sent. It is either sent immediately or when the sender next connects to the internet. From the outbox, the message goes to the sender's internet service provider's computers (servers) where it may be stored for a short time or sent straightaway over the internet to the recipient's ISP servers.

The recipient's ISP will store the email until the person logs in and then will send it to their 'inbox' where it will wait until the recipient reads it.

How an email travels

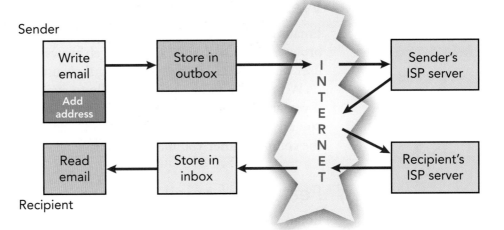

How an email travels

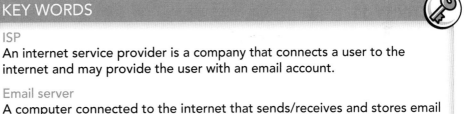

KEY WORDS

ISP
An internet service provider is a company that connects a user to the internet and may provide the user with an email account.

Email server
A computer connected to the internet that sends/receives and stores email messages.

Email outbox
A folder on a computer used to store outgoing emails.

Email inbox
A folder on a computer used to store incoming emails.

Emails are mainly used for short text messages but can be used to send documents and other files. Files such as video, sound or documents that are sent along with emails are called 'attachments' and can be very large.

Some ISPs restrict the size of emails that can be sent or received so that users often have to compress the files to make them smaller.

ACTIVITY 10

Imagine you are sending an email to your best friend who uses a different ISP than you. Copy this list and fill in the outline details of the main places where your email would travel when leaving your outbox and ending up in your friend's inbox.
- my outbox is in............................(name of my email client)
- my ISP server is..........................(name of my ISP)
- my friend's ISP server is................(name of my friend's ISP)
- my friend's inbox is in..................(name of my friend's email client)

Webmail

Emails can also be sent from mobile phones, smart phones and from web browsers. Webmail, as email from web browsers is called, is useful when the user cannot access their email using their usual email client.

Webmail should be used carefully to avoid being overlooked by others if you are in a public place and by making sure that you log out properly. If you are using a public computer in a library or café then anyone who uses the computer after you may see your details if you do not log out properly.

Features of email software

Email clients should provide a number of features to make using email easier for the user. The features found in most email clients are shown on the next page.

ACTIVITY 11

Find out how to add a signature automatically to your emails.

Find out what is meant by a digital signature.

KEY WORDS

Chat room
Users log in and exchange text-based messages with one or more people

Instant messaging
Real-time text-based messages are sent between people.

Video-conferencing
Using video cameras, microphones, speakers and monitors to hold business conversations over the internet between two or more people.

Chat rooms

Chat rooms are mainly used to share text-based information with others over the internet in real time. So-called 'rooms' are set up and users log in and can 'chat' to one or more people at the same time.

Chat rooms have become less popular for conversations but are very popular for online gaming where whole virtual worlds can be constructed to involve hundreds of players.

Feature	What it is used for
Address book	The names and email addresses of contacts are stored here. This may sometimes be called a contacts list
Cc	This is used to send the same email to other contacts at the same time. All the recipients can see who it has been sent to. _cc_ stands for 'carbon copy' which comes from the use of carbon paper when typing letters on a typewriter to make more than one copy at a time
bcc	This is used to send the same email to other contacts at the same time. The recipients cannot see who it has been sent to. _bcc_ stands for 'blind carbon copy' meaning that others do not see who other copies have gone to
Return receipt	The sender can set this to be automatically told if the recipient has received and read the message. This is not reliable as the recipient can refuse to send the receipt
Security options	This can let the user decide how sensitive or confidential the information is and may be used to encrypt the message
High/low importance	This indicates how urgent the message is and may put the message at the top of a list or flag it for immediate attention
Signatures	This may be a short message added to all outgoing emails to give some details of the sender
Special folders to organise mail	Outboxes, inboxes, sent boxes and other folders are used to store and organise email messages. Users can create new folders to store emails from individuals so that these are grouped together
Message rules or filters to redirect emails and to organise emails into folders	Users can set up rules or filters to send any incoming email messages to the correct folder so that, for instance, all the messages for a sender are stored automatically in the folder of that person
Spam filters	These are rules or filters set up to stop spam emails or send them to a separate folder
Archive	Email clients can archive older emails for long-time storage and free up space for new ones
Attachments	Files such as documents, video, sound and so on can be attached to emails. It is possible to attach more than one file at a time and this is called using multiple attachments
Distribution lists	These are lists or groups of contacts collected together under a single name so that an email can easily be sent out to everyone in the group by sending it to the group name
Spellcheck	Most modern email clients include a spellchecker to check the spellings of the words

Instant messaging

Instant messaging allows users to type short messages to another person and the message is instantly delivered. The difference between instant messaging and 'chat' compared to email is that it appears that the 'chatters' are having a proper conversation while email doesn't. However, as modern instant messaging systems do allow users to leave messages for others to pick up and email can be very quick to send and deliver, the differences may not be so noticeable. Instant messaging is now more popular than the use of chat rooms.

Online conversations happen in real time between people from anywhere in the world where they can connect to the internet. To use instant messaging, users have an account with a provider and use instant messaging software. It is possible to save a conversation to read later.

It is possible to add video using webcams to see the other person while typing and to use microphones so that people can talk instead of having to type, but to be able to talk and see several persons at once requires the use of video-conferencing.

Many people also use text messaging from their mobile phone to hold text-based conversations with others.

Video-conferencing

Video-conferencing is used to connect two or more persons over a network or the internet so that they can see and hear each other. To use video-conferencing, the users must have a video input such as a webcam or digital video camera, a microphone to capture the sound of people speaking, a video display such as a monitor, and an audio output such as speakers or headphones. They must also have suitable software to allow video and audio from a number of people to be shared with all the others.

There are a number of advantages and disadvantages of video-conferencing:

Advantages

- meetings can be called at short notice as there is no need to arrange for people to travel to the meeting or for people to completely re-arrange their work
- the cost of travel is saved
- the cost of hiring a conference venue is saved
- the time spent travelling is saved for other work
- it can be used to keep in easy contact with employees who work from home.

Disadvantages

- the initial cost of the software and hardware can be high
- there must be a reliable connection via the internet or network; if this fails then the conference is disrupted
- some people do not like be 'on-camera' and become self-conscious
- there is a lack of personal contact between participants
- the different timezones around the world mean that, for some people, the conference may be out of working hours or even in the middle of the night – some people do not function well out of normal working hours
- there is difficulty when handing out documents to others as they will have to be sent and then printed in advance.

Social networking

People who share the same hobbies, interests or backgrounds like to communicate with each other. People who go to the same school may like to keep in contact with their friends and teachers after they leave school, for instance, and to do this they may use email, set up a website or use a social networking service.

While it is also possible to use email or instant messaging, most social networks are web-based using a website specially designed for people to share videos, photographs and post text-based information.

Weblogs

Some people like to write down their activities on a website for others to read giving a commentary on what they have been doing. Weblogs or 'blogs' can have pictures or video but most are text-based and written by individuals so that their friends can follow their lives. A common type of blog will follow a person's travels so that others can see where they are or where they have been.

Clubs and societies use blogs for showing their activities and commercial companies often use blogs for internal communications and for marketing their products. These are 'corporate blogs'.

Blogs are useful because they can be viewed and updated from any device that can connect to internet so you could use a mobile phone to update your blog as you travel – there is no need to sit at a computer.

'Twitter' was created in 2006 and is a free social networking service where you can read short messages called 'tweets' from others; 'tweets' are very short and text-based so that they can be sent and read from most devices with internet access, although if you use a mobile phone you will have to pay.

Twitter is very popular but users should be aware that a great deal of the time can be spent using it and that, without care, very personal details can be revealed to others.

SMS

Short message services (SMS) are used to send short text messages between mobile phones. This is the most used messaging service in the world with billions of messages being sent. SMS text messages are limited in the number of characters that can be sent at once so a shorthand language has developed to keep the messages short. Textspeak uses initial letters such as B4 for 'before', ALOL for 'actually laughing out loud'. Most of the shorthand is quite recent but some like AWOL (for 'absent without leave' or 'missing') has been used for generations.

There is a maximum number of characters that you can send in one text message. Why is this and what is the maximum number of characters?

Dangers of social networking

Users of social networking should be aware that, while it can be quite fun and a good way to keep in contact with others, there are dangers.

Personal details should not be revealed to others, especially by posting them on websites or in instant messages.

Care should be taken when 'chatting' to others if you do not know them personally as it is very difficult to be sure exactly who they are, and even if they are who they say they are. It is easy for anyone to sign up with false details in order to contact young people for inappropriate reasons.

Users should never arrange to meet anyone they have met online, nor should they tell others where they live or what they are going to be doing. Who knows who the person really is, and if you give out your address and say you are going on holiday next week, then others know the house will be empty.

File sharing

Sharing information with others has been made far easier than in previous times. The internet allows any electronic document to be shared with others.

The document can be placed on a web page for all to see. It can be emailed to others as an attachment, can be made available for download from websites or by file transfer via FTP.

File Transfer Protocol (FTP) is a useful way of moving files via the internet. A software application, called an FTP client, is used to connect to a server directly and files can be uploaded and downloaded. Most importantly, there is no limit on the size of file that can be transferred, although very large files can take a long time to transfer. For this reason, FTP is used for sharing software, CD or DVDs and for uploading web pages to servers ready for displaying in a website.

File can be shared in other, more complex ways, for sharing music or video files from TV stations or online music sellers.

Document sharing

Whole documents can be shared online so that many users are able to check, edit and update them simultaneously.

This can be done by posting the document online and allowing others to have access to it so that they all can alter and update the document.

Google wave is an online tool that allows real-time conversations and document collaboration and numbers of people can work together using email, text, images, videos and sounds.

E-commerce

The internet allows individuals and companies to buy and sell items, goods and services online. The amount of trading online is now immense and many companies sell more goods online than they do in their stores and some companies only sell goods online.

The greatest difficulty with online buying and selling is payment. Credit cards and debit cards can be used for most transactions but there are problems with buying or selling goods than cost very little (these are called micro-transactions) so alternative methods are used.

Bartering, i.e. swapping some goods for others, has been used, but is not that easy to arrange. There are now companies that specialise in micro-transactions but the problem of making sure that the buyer actually pays for the goods still remains.

Individuals selling goods over the internet can lose their goods if the person buying them does not send the money, and buyers can lose their money if the seller does not send the goods. Websites that specialise in buying and selling by individuals try to make sure that the transaction goes well and may offer compensation if it does not, but there is always a small risk to both buyer and seller.

KEY WORDS

Microprocessor
An integrated circuit that carries all the functions of a CPU.

RFID
Radio frequency identification used to tag goods or pets.

GPS
Global positioning systems use satellites to allow GPS devices to work out where they are.

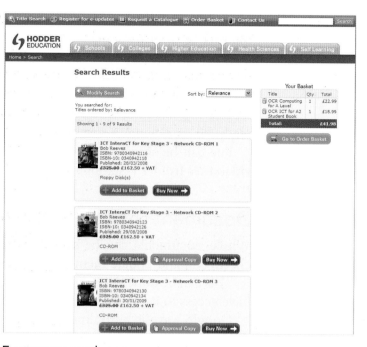

E-commerce web page

Using ICT for control, monitoring and tracking

Many people's lives have been made easier or more enjoyable through the use of ICT to control devices in our homes.

Entertainment systems, including televisions, satellite and TV set-top boxes, DVD players, Blu-ray players and games consoles, are all computers using microprocessors.

Washing machines and microwave ovens have microprocessors that can be programmed to control their functions. Users of a washing machine can program the machine for temperature, time and other settings when washing clothes.

Microwave ovens can be programmed for different times of cooking, temperatures and types of food to be cooked.

ICT can also be used to track people or items. Radio frequency identification (RFID) is commonly used to track pets or goods. A tag is inserted into the pet (it is harmless and painless) and can be read remotely by a RFID reader.

The tag can be read from several metres away and can be used to hold information that can identify the goods or animal.

RFID tags are used in pets. A tag will hold a code that can be used by vets to identify the owner of a pet. This is useful if a lost animal is taken to the vet as it allows the owner to be contacted or an owner can prove that a particular dog or cat is really theirs.

RFID tags are being put into airline baggage so that the baggage can be tracked more easily to help avoid its loss in transit.

Cars and people are often electronically tagged. Cars are tagged with a device that sends details of their location to be monitored.

Criminals can be electronically tagged so that their whereabouts can be monitored. This can be used to make sure that the criminal does not go out when they shouldn't or does not go where they are told not to.

Electronic tagging of cars and people uses the mobile phone network to send details of their location back to a control centre. The location is determined by a GPS receiver in the device.

EXAM TYPE QUESTIONS

1 What is meant by the following terms?
  (a) online
  (b) offline

2 State three differences between email and instant messaging.

3 Explain why the sender of an email would use 'bcc' rather than 'cc' to communicate with others.

4 Explain how a typical email address is constructed.

5 You are researching a science project on global warming and are looking on the internet for information to put in your project. Discuss the issues that you should consider when using the information that you find.

6 Give two reasons why an email carrying a large attachment may not arrive at its destination.

7 Give two reasons someone might prefer to use webmail rather than a 'normal' email client.

8 A global company has started to use video-conferencing to communicate with its managerial staff around the world rather than gather them together in a conference room at its headquarters in a big city.
  (a) Explain why they might prefer to hold conferences in this way.
  (b) What are the disadvantages they might have to overcome?

3 Presenting Information

What you will learn in this chapter

- How ICT tools are used to present information
- The features and facilities of software applications and how these can be used to present information
- How information can be shared between software applications and why this is useful

An audience will understand any data and information if it is presented properly. Using software to present information properly and sensibly is quite easy to do once the features and facilities offered by the different applications is known. It is important to try and use the most suitable application for the presentation you require. For example, normally a letter is written in a word-processor and not a spreadsheet. The word-processor will offer all the facilities needed to present the text of the letter so that it is easily read by the recipient – who, in this case, is the audience. If a newsletter was being written with multiple columns and pictures, a desktop publishing application might be more suitable. Animations and video require facilities not usually found in word-processing or desktop publishing software, and while it is possible to create web pages and whole websites in word-processing or desktop publishing software, specialised web authoring software is a better choice.

KEY WORD

Audience
An audience is the person, or group of people, at which the work is aimed. Different age groups or people with different interests or backgrounds should be considered when producing a piece of work such as a report or presentation.

Word-processing and desktop publishing applications

If you want to write a report or a letter, the most appropriate software to use is a word-processing or a desktop publishing application. These are designed to allow text and images to be combined easily and for you to be able to see how the final product will appear when printed on to paper. Today, many documents are never printed but sent to others by, e.g. email but we still need to set out the document so that it is easy to read.

Word-processing (WP) software and desktop publishing (DTP) software have many features in common. Both allow text to be entered from the keyboard and displayed on screen in various ways ready for printing or saving for later use.

Text can appear in different styles or typefaces which is a set of characters such as letters, numerals and punctuation marks. A particular typeface can be made up of a number of fonts with different characteristics such as italic, bold and weight, all of which are used to make text appear differently on screen or paper.

Fonts and typefaces

This is italic text which is sloped and can be slightly rounded as well in some typefaces.

This is bold text

This is heavy bold text

This is narrow text

This sentence `is printed in` various type faces.

This sentence is printed in various sizes of font.

The size of a font is measured in units that originate from eighteenth-century French printers when all printing was done using hot metal and a printing press. The unit of font size is a 'point' or 'pt' and originally

A well-designed poster

depended upon the length of a foot (a real foot was once used!) and was 0.2 to 0.4mm. This is not accurate enough for use today or when using computers and is now set at 0.353mm – this is not an easy size to remember so we refer to font by their size in 'points'. The most common point sizes used in documents are 11 and 12 as these appear to be 'just right' to the eye but remember that what looks good on screen does not always look good when printed on paper, e.g. a large point size may be easy to read on screen but when printed will take up most of the page and look dreadful!

Also, as you can see from the examples, using too many different typefaces and fonts in one sentence makes the sentence quite difficult to read so it is advisable not to use more than one or two fonts in your work. You should always think about the audience, i.e. who is going to read your work, and make sure they are not distracted or put off reading your work by using too many features.

However, the careful use of typefaces and their fonts can make a document look appealing and will catch the attention of a reader.

When choosing a font to use, you should consider:
its proportions – fonts can have their width fixed or be monospaced like this:

Monospaced

where each letter takes up the same width. Proportional text looks like this

Proportional

where each letter's width is different.

Fixed-width text is easier to align properly and is best for, e.g. tables of letters or figures as all the letters will line up neatly in columns. It is often used in, e.g. spreadsheets and for computer programming so that all the code can be easily studied on screen or paper.

Manuscripts for new books are sent to publishers printed in fixed width text as it is easier to edit and count the words.

Proportioned text is becoming more accepted for documents and most modern reports, letters and books use this type of font as it is easier to read large amounts of text in a proportional font.

ACTIVITY 1

Use a word-processing or desktop publishing package and type your name. Enlarge the font to a size that fills the whole line.

Now choose at least four different font types and look at the differences in how your name is displayed. Make sure you look at serif and san serif fonts.

Why are some fonts not suitable for documents when they are printed out?

Bullets and tables

When displaying lists, indentation and bullets are used, sometimes with numbers. Text can be indented so that it is placed away from the edge of the page.

This is an example of indented text using various bullet styles:

- this is a bulleted indent
  - with a further indent here.

and this is a bulleted indent using numbers to pick out the items:

a font can have a different shape depending on its:

1 size
2 weight
3 proportion

Sensible use of bullets and numbering can make lists very easy to read – and to learn.

There are other ways of displaying text on screen and on a page. Word-processing and desktop publishing offer the use of tabs. These should be used to avoid repeated use of spaces to place text across a page a set distances and are useful, quickly indenting the start of a new paragraph for lining up lists, e.g.

This is a list of features that can be used to display text in different ways:

font	can be different shaped letters
bullets	can be spots or numbers
italic	the letters are sloped
indent	spacing the word over the page

Here each of the columns has been 'tabbed' across the page so that it lines up neatly.

A better way of making lists with multiple columns is by using tables. Putting lists in tables and using lines with no colour for the tables means that, when printed, the table doesn't show on paper.

This is a table with no lines showing. The words are in neat columns:

City	Country	Places to see
London	United Kingdom	The Tower of London
Paris	France	La Tour Eiffel
Madrid	Spain	Royal Palace of Madrid
Brussels	Belgium	Cathédrale de St-Michel

Being able to change the colour of table lines is very useful as different parts of tables can be made to stand out or be used as headings. The cells in the table can be changed as well. This is the same table as previously but lines and colour have been added:

City	Country	Places to see
London	United Kingdom	The Tower of London
Paris	France	La Tour Eiffel
Madrid	Spain	Royal Palace of Madrid
Brussels	Belgium	Cathédrale de St-Michel

Tables can be a useful way of displaying information but care must be taken to make them look pleasing so beware of using too much colour. A better way to display this table is:

City	Country	Places to see
London	United Kingdom	The Tower of London
Paris	France	La Tour Eiffel
Madrid	Spain	Royal Palace of Madrid
Brussels	Belgium	Cathédrale de St-Michel

Text can be made to stand out or be highlighted by using the different borders supplied by the software:

EXAMPLE   EXAMPLE

and borders can be placed around whole pages too.

Text can be placed on the left or right of a page so that the left edges of the words are aligned:

This is an example of LEFT justification

This is called left alignment or left justification and is the usual way of placing text and is most easy to read. It is the default setting and often there is no need to change it.

If the text is lined up by the right edge it is said to be right aligned or right justified.

This is an example of RIGHT justification
This is often used on posters or advertisements for artistic effect but large
amounts of text aligned in this way are not so easy to read.

It is possible to place the text in the exact centre.

this is an example of CENTRE justification
Text can be centred in between the edges of a page or column
and this is useful for headings or items in advertisements
that need to stand out.

Again, using too many changes of alignment in a document can be very
distracting but careful use can make text stand out and be eye-catching.

Text can also be displayed in different colours and can be underlined to
make it stand out. This is useful for headings and subheadings but again
should not be overused.

Both word-processing and desktop publishing packages, along with
many software applications, offer the facility to check your spelling and
grammar but these are not perfect and should be used as aids rather than
a cure and with some caution – there's no real substitute for knowing the
correct spelling and grammar so you can choose the correct ones from the
options offered.

Word-processor with spell-check window

ACTIVITY 2

Open up your word-processing software and find out what these tools are.
For each, write down what you would use them for.

Word count
Spelling and grammar
Track changes
Mail merge
Autocorrect
Customise

ACTIVITY 3

Open word-processing and find out how to make a page with three columns of text such as that found in a newspaper. Do the same with a desktop publishing package.

While you can put pictures into your documents with modern WP, the facilities for adding and displaying images are really quite limited. Although you can do all this in word-processing, the latter is better suited for documents that do not contain many pages, have only a few images and do not use multiple columns such as letters, memos, business cards and simple posters.

For more complicated documents such as brochures, newsletters, reports, magazines and booklets, DTP is used because it can reliably provide multiple columns and pages, and images and text can be combined more easily. Further, DTP offers more accurate placement of images and can output the document in formats that printers can use. Complex reports which include images, graphs and text with tables and columns are usually produced in DTP software.

Today, the differences between the features of WP and DTP are not so obvious to most users as they once were but a careful choice of software application means that the end product is properly produced without difficulty.

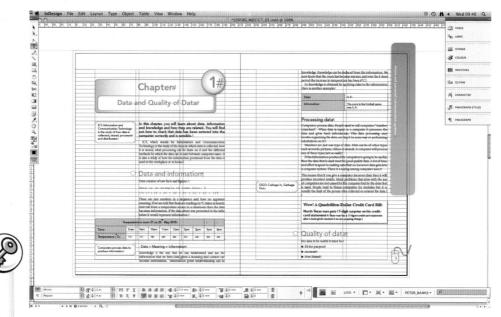

DTP package

Slideshow software

Presentations to audiences can be made more interesting if the presenter can show animations and have sound effects. Slideshow software allows a user to put text, images, video and animations along with sounds together and display the information as a series of slides, usually on a large screen.

Features of slideshow software include:

- inserting text
- inserting images

KEY WORDS

Slide
This refers to a single page of information in a slideshow.

Slide transition
The way one slide changes to another can be changed so that the slide may change abruptly, dissolve into the next or use some other method of showing the next slide.

ACTIVITY 4
Open a slideshow package and make a presentation with at least four slides on how to send an email. Make sure that you include some text and images, and at least two different slide transitions.

- choosing an animation style for the text or images
- adding sound effects
- linking or adding video
- grouping text or images together
- layering the text and images.

Multimedia software

This is used to combine text, images, video, animations and sounds into a presentation that usually allows the user or viewer to interact with it by, for instance, choosing which route to go through it, answer questions, receive feedback or even interact with the presenter.

Web authoring software

You can make a web page in any text editor because web pages are written in markup language and you can just write the code needed to make a page. This code will make a simple web page:

```
<html>
<head>
<meta content='text/html; charset=ISO—8859—1'
http-equiv='content-type'>
<title></title>
</head>
<body>
This is my page on the World Wide Web
</body>
</html>
```

and can easily be typed but it doesn't make a very interesting page:

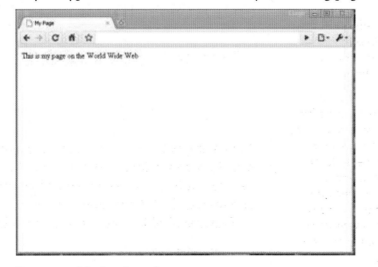

Browser with simple web page

To create interesting pages and whole websites, web-authoring software is used. This has many features, much like a word-processor and will generate all the codes for you.

ACTIVITY 6

Look up the 'rules' for good web design and write them down.

Explain how website owners have to make sure that people with disabilities can access their web pages.

ACTIVITY 5

Start up a web-authoring application and look on the toolbars to see what features it includes. Look for these features and find out how to use them by creating some new pages:

- text formatting
- creating tables
- inserting images
- linking to other pages.

Web-authoring software should include features that make creating web pages and websites easy but the user has to make sure that all the pages are accessible to everyone. Different users will use different web browsers so your websites with all their pages have to work in all of them – even when the user is viewing the pages on the small screen of a smart phone. Also, some people have disabilities so cannot see or hear very well, so good web pages and sites must allow these people access. Good web design will include the ability to make the text on the pages larger, have text in different colours, have images replaced by descriptions or have the text read out to them by their computer.

ACTIVITY 7

Look at four different websites and write down who the information is aimed at and what it shows. For instance, a school website shows information for parents about term dates and parents' evenings.

Web pages and sites are used in many ways to give information to people; schools use websites to provide information for students and parents; businesses use websites to display and offer their goods for sale; and the government uses websites to provide information on, for instance, laws and taxes.

Graphics manipulation and photo-editing software

Graphics manipulation software is used to create and manipulate images. Photo-editing software is used to edit digital photographs.

The features of these graphics packages include being able to:

- select part of an image to work on
- create and use layers which are rather like making parts of the image on different transparent sheets and putting them on top of each other in layers
- change the size of the image making them smaller or larger; this is scaling
- crop an image by removing rectangular sections from the top, bottom or sides

Pixel
Digital images are made of dots or squares called pixels arranged in a grid. Each pixel has information giving its intensity and colour.

Colour balance
The overall intensity of the different colours in an image or video.

Resolution
The number of pixels across the image and down the image is used to measure the resolution of an image.

- cut parts of an image; this is different from crop as the piece can be any shape and from anywhere in the image; unwanted parts of an image can be cut and replaced so that it looks as if they were never there; this can often be done automatically in modern graphics software
- paste a part or whole of an image into another image
- zoom into parts of image to see them or work on them easily; this is not the same as resizing
- change the image orientation so that it is tilted, upside down, sideways or otherwise re-orientated; this can be done by rotating the image
- mirror the image so that it looks like a reflection in a mirror
- correct or changing the perspective of an image
- make selective colour changes to a parts of an image
- sharpen or soften images; this can correct poor photographs or be used for artistic effect
- reduce red-eye: this is used to remove the red spots in the eyes of people in pictures taken by flash photography.

ACTIVITY 8

Choose a package and produce an example of the use of each of these features:

- crop
- copy and paste part of an image into a new image
- cut part of an image
- use a layer to add a new object to the image.

Input your examples into a presentation and add some notes to explain how you made your examples.

Because modern graphics packages can change the content of a digital image, it is sometimes difficult to tell what is original and what is enhanced or changed.

Celebrities often look much better in a digital photograph than in real life; people or objects can be added to or removed from photographs, parts of images can be put together to create photographs that mislead people or make people believe things that are not true.

Video-editing software

Many people now own a digital video camera or can create video sequences on a mobile phone and want to edit them.

Video-editing software can be used on most modern PCs. The video is imported or transferred from the camera to the computer and opened in the software which allows the user to:

- alter the amount of video by cutting, joining, cropping and pasting sections of video
- add or alter the soundtracks
- insert still images if needed
- change the colour balance
- add some special effects to the video or sound
- export the video and sound to, e.g. DVD or back to the camera.

Gaming software

Playing games on a computer system can be great fun. Computer games are made in many different ways but most include objects, sounds, backgrounds, rooms or levels. Objects can be characters or objects that the player interacts with such as wall, weapons, vehicles or tools and these are created by the game-maker and combined to make a playable game.

Communications software

Often social networking software, such as chat and instant messaging software, web browsers, file transfer and email clients, can be used to arrange information in different ways for others to view.

Spreadsheets and database management software

The main features of these are described in another chapter but one of the most important uses of spreadsheets and databases is to manipulate and display data in different ways so that users and viewers can get as much information from it as possible, or to convey the information that is there in ways that can be understood.

The mass of numbers shown is not displayed clearly. It is not easy to understand and use the numbers to compare the rainfall of 1998 and 2008 in Cambridge, UK.

| Month | Rainfall in mm | |
	1998	2008
January	48	58
February	5	13
March	45	69
April	120	51
May	6	63
June	102	35
July	26	52
August	16	65
September	104	60
October	77	56
November	55	69
December	60	21

The information about whether or not the summer months of 2008 had more rainfall than those of 1998 can be seen but it takes some time to work it out.

The comparison can be made easier if the data is manipulated and displayed differently as in this chart:

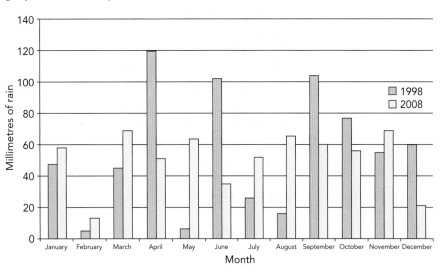

Monthly rainfall chart

ACTIVITY 9

Look up the rainfall for 2009 and produce a chart to show whether or not it had a wetter or drier summer than 2008.

WEBLINK

http://www.
metoffice.gov.
uk/climate/uk/
stationdata/
cambridgedata.txt

This gives rainfall
data from the UK
Meteorological
Office.

It is easy to see from the chart that in Cambridge, UK there was a lot more rainfall in some months but a lot less in others in 1998 compared to 2008, April, June and September being much wetter but May, July and August were drier.

Moving data between software applications

Sometimes data has to be moved from one software application to another. This may be because it can be manipulated or displayed better or because it is needed to add to, say, a report or presentation.

Copy and paste

Nearly all software applications allow users to select and copy all or part of a document, image or data ready for moving to another application. The data is stored temporarily in an area of the computer's memory set aside for this purpose. This area is often called a 'clipboard' but is just a temporary storage area.

The user can then go to the other application and paste the data into the place in the document where it should go.

Cut and paste removes the original data while copy and paste leaves it in the original document.

Sometimes the data can be saved to a new file and then imported into another document. Most applications that can use images, text, video and animations allow users to import data from files that they have already stored.

Object Linking and Embedding (OLE)

This is a very useful way of exporting and re-importing data. Software that supports OLE will allow a user working on a document with text and images to click on, for instance, an image and export it to a graphics package, do some editing to change the image and then re-import back into the original document. The user does not have to choose a graphics package or select from options as the software takes care of all the details automatically.

EXAM TYPE QUESTIONS

1 Explain why the creator of a presentation should consider the requirements of the audience.

2 For each of the tasks shown choose the most suitable software package, and give a reason for your choice.
(a) creating a text-only letter
(b) creating an advertising poster with images and text
(c) creating a web page
(d) creating a presentation with many slides

3 Explain why a book publisher may prefer to have the text of a book sent to it in monospaced typeface.

4 Explain the difference between 'copy and paste' and 'cut and paste'.

5 An original shape is shown on the left. The original image is then manipulated in a graphics package to produce the image on the right.

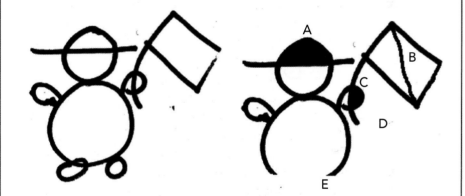

(a) For each of the areas A, B, C, D and E, state which graphics tool would have been used to make the change.
(b) Further changes have been made to this new version of the image. Explain how the changes may have been made.

Manipulating Data

Data types

Computers can only deal with numbers and so the data we see and use has to be in the form of numbers when a computer system is using it. To make processing, e.g. calculations, sorting, etc., run faster and be less complicated for the processor to carry out, we assign store forms of data in different ways – we call these data types.

There are a number of different data types commonly used by computer systems, each type being used for a particular form of data:

Text: this is the most commonly used and text data can be any character such as letters, numbers, punctuation, space and other characters such as &, £, % and so on. Examples of text data are First Name, Family name, such as Brian Gillinder. If data is stored as text, we cannot carry calculations on the data. This data type can be known as alphanumeric.

Numeric: this data can only be numbers; either whole numbers or numbers with decimal places. Whole numbers are called integers while numbers with decimal places are often called real numbers. Numbers can be displayed or formatted in different ways, e.g. 234.89 is an example of a number with decimal places (a 'real' number) and can be displayed or formatted as £234.89 which is currency. Numbers with decimal places are also called floating point numbers and such numbers are more complicated for the computer to store and process than whole numbers, which is why there are the two data types for numbers.

Boolean or Logical: this data can have only two values, TRUE or FALSE.

Sometimes the choice is not shown as TRUE or FALSE but by two other choices, e.g. MALE or FEMALE, YES or NO, or just M or F, Y or N.

Date/time: the data for this type must be a time or have only days, months and years. 11:25 is a time, 09/04/2010 is a date. Times and dates can be formatted and displayed in different ways, e.g. 9th April 2010 is the same data as shown before but in a different format.

Image

Some databases use this to store graphics and photographs.

It is important to choose the most suitable data type for the data that you want to store.

Data type	Example	Sample data	Examples of use
Text, also called alphanumeric string	This type of data can be any character, punctuation mark, letter or number	nkasjfca.,?ad,a.1,6,5,a	Used to store telephone numbers, names
Date	This type of data indicates a date or time	22/10/1950	Used to store dates of birth, dates of events
Integer	This type of data is a whole number	22	Used to store quantities of stock
Real	This type of data is a number with a decimal point and some decimal places after the point	22.15	Used to store prices
Boolean, also called logical	This type of data is value that can only be true or false. True or false can be represented in other ways, e.g. on or off, male of female, open or closed but there are only two choices	Y or N M or F 1 or 0	Used to store gender, Yes or No answers in questionnaires
Image	This can be hold a graphical image		Used to store photos

ACTIVITY 1

Write a list of the name, address, postcode and telephone number of your school. For each entry in the list, choose a suitable data type and give a reason for your choice.

WEBLINKS

http://en.wikipedia.org/wiki/Data_type
http://dev.mysql.com/doc/refman/5.0/en/data-types.html
http://www.teach-ict.com/gcse/software/db/miniweb/pg7.htm
These provide explanations of data types.

Capturing data

Music keyboard using a midi interface

Data capture is the process of collecting data for use in a computer system. Data can be captured in many ways but, however it is done, the data must be in a form that the computer can understand and use, otherwise it is useless. Data capture is collecting data ready to be typed into a computer, making measurements that can be typed in and asking people for information that can be entered into a computer system.

Data capture should not be confused with data entry. **Data capture** is the collection of data while **data entry** is the process of inputting the data into the computer. Although they may occur at almost the same time and may appear to be happening all in one go but they are quite separate processes, e.g. a barcode scanner will collect the data from a printed barcode (data capture) and send it to the computer terminal, e.g. at a supermarket checkout (data entry) to be processed. The result of the processing is shown on the checkout terminal or printed on the customer receipt.

The method of capturing data depends on what the data is going to be used for and where it is being collected.

Sounds can be captured with the use of a microphone, or input directly from, e.g. a music keyboard using a midi interface, and new still and video images can be captured with digital cameras. Scanners can be used to capture or input documents or printed images such as photographs and graphic tablets can be used to draw new images on a computer.

Some data is captured automatically without much involvement by humans once the system is set up and working.

- Barcodes and magnetic stripes hold data that is captured by a reader or scanner.
- Optical character recognition reads data from documents and converts it into text on a computer ready for use.
- Optical mark readers gather data from pre-printed forms which have been marked up.
- Radio frequency identification (RFID) is used to track or identify objects which have had a chip implanted, e.g. a pet or a product and, increasingly, baggage carried on aircraft.
- Voice recognition is used to turn speech into computer data so that a voice or speaker can be identified or the spoken words entered into a word-processor for editing.
- Sensors can gather data for use by computers.

When we want to use data that we have collected ourselves, we should collect the data in a way that makes it easy for us to enter it into our computer system so data capture needs careful thought before it starts.

A common method of capturing data is to use a data capture form. This can be a simple tally sheet that is used to count, e.g. the number of vehicles passing a road junction or a long, complex questionnaire that collects data on people's background and educational history when applying for a job.

Scanner

Graphic tablet

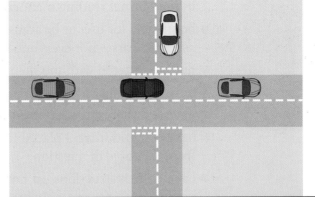

Time	No. Cars (east to west)	No. Cars (north to south)
12.43 am	–	9
12.44 am	–	7
12.45 am	3	–

Data capture form

A commonly used data capture form is a questionnaire and these are useful when we wish to collect a lot of data from many people and do not have the time to talk to everyone in person. Also, questionnaires allow people to fill them in privately and in their own time.

A good data capture form should be designed so that it:

- is simple and easy to use, i.e.:
  - only asks for the data that needs to be captured and not ask for any unnecessary information
  - has a minimum of printed text or instructions
  - is not too long
  - is not boring to read!
- provides clear instructions on:
  - what to do and how to fill in the form
  - where to send or hand in the form
- has the spaces to be filled in as close to the questions as possible
- is logically laid out so that questions follow on from each other
- collects the data in a way that be quickly and easily entered into the computer system
- has the reason for the data capture clearly shown so people know what the data is to be used for.

The same sort of care should be taken over the design of all the forms, printouts and screens that are used by computer systems.

WEBLINK

http://www.
teach-ict.com/
gcse/software/
datacapture/
miniweb/index.htm

This provides
explanations of data
capture

Any form that appears on screen should:

- be logically laid out so that the reader moves from one item to another in the normal reading manner, i.e. from left to right
- be suitable for use, or be adjustable so that it can be used, on different size monitors – not everyone has a large, high-resolution display!
- not be cluttered with too many items of information
- only have items that are relevant to the topic
- have text that is in a suitable typeface and font, e.g. size
- have text and images placed in suitable positions so as not to distract from the topic in question
- have clear instructions on how to use the screen or have access to a help screen
- not use colours that are difficult to see or tell apart – persons with colour vision problems may not be able to read red text on a green background, or bright yellow on red background may be dreadful to look at by some people
- have a simple and consistent method of moving between screens.

Similarly, forms and documents printed on paper should be carefully designed so that the reader finds them easy to view and use. With paper documents, room should be made for any headers or footers, and for the possibility that the pages may be stapled together, e.g. leave a gap on the side of the page so when several are stapled together the text is not hidden. When printing booklets or books, gaps must left on alternate left and right edges so that the pages can be bound together without hiding the words. When making a flip-over calendar, the gaps have to be at the top and bottom of alternate pages – so we need to think about the final product before we start.

ACTIVITY 2

Open a desktop publishing package and find out how to alter the left and right margins to allow for gutters when printing.

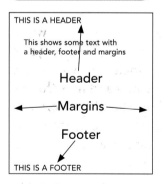

THIS IS A HEADER

This shows some text with a header, footer and margins

Header

Margins

Footer

THIS IS A FOOTER

KEY WORDS

Margin
A margin is a part of the page that is not used for printing.

Gutter
The part of the pages in a book that cannot be used for printing because of the binding. In a comic, a gutter is the space between panels of the comic strip.

January 2010						
Sunday	Monday	Tuesday	Wednesday	Thursday	Friday	Saturday
					1	2
3	4	5	6	7	8	9
10	11	12	13	14	15	16
17	18	19	20	21	22	23
24	25	26	27	28	29	30
31						

February 2010						
Sunday	Monday	Tuesday	Wednesday	Thursday	Friday	Saturday
	1	2	3	4	5	6
7	8	9	10	11	12	13
14	15	16	17	18	19	20
21	22	23	24	25	26	27
28						

Flip-over calendar

KEY WORDS

Random access
Random access is when an item such as a record can be accessed directly without having to search through all the others.

Serial access
With serial access all the items or records have to be searched one by one until the one needed is found.

Designing files for storing data

Most users of ICT systems never have to worry about how, or even where, their data is stored because the software application or the operating system will do it for them. If you are designed a database, then you will need to consider the layout of the fields and the number of tables and how they are linked but rarely do we bother with considering how the file is stored on, e.g. a hard disk. But this is important even though most are unaware that the designers of the software will have taken great care to ensure that data is stored securely and safely and can be easily retrieved.

Example

In a library, to find a book with a title beginning with P using serial access you would start at the first book with a tile starting with A and look at all the titles until you came to those starting with P and continue until you found the one you wanted. It could take a long time. With random access you would go straight to the book you wanted. Random access is also called direct access.

Designers of software that stores data need to consider:

- the type of storage medium to use, e.g. a hard disk or a removable optical medium or flash memory; a database needs fast rewriting or data would run very slowly using a small USB flash memory stick so most designers assume that the user has a hard disk for their data
- how the data is to be accessed, e.g. is it by random access or by serial access?
- how the data is to be grouped, e.g. related data should be grouped together and data that is not to be used often can be stored away from that in constant use; a TV set-top box for digital TV recordings has to have software that constantly monitors this so that any video files are properly stored to ensure smooth playback of movies, DVDs for movies have to have their files carefully arranged for the same reason
- how the data is linked together so that users can search for or extract data quickly and easily
- the number of accesses to files should be kept to a minimum by careful arrangement of the data files on disk so that the hard disk is not constantly searching for data all over the disk
- it should be possible to add or delete data.

Checking data

It is important that any data that is used is the data that we want to be used.

When capturing data it is our responsibility to make sure that we put the right questions on the data capture form so that we get the sort of answers that we can use.

We should always make sure that the data we collect is accurate and correct – computers cannot do that for us. If we collect data on the data capture form that is wrong, e.g. if we ask a person's age and write down 45 years instead of 54 years or we record a temperature of 21 degrees Celsius instead of 12 degrees Celsius there is no way that the computer will know that the data is wrong. This is one reason why measurements are made by sensors instead of recording them manually but some data cannot be recorded by sensors.

Once the data has been collected and we have checked that it is correct, e.g. we have the age of the person correctly recorded, the data can be entered. Often it is typed in by the user at a keyboard. This can introduce errors and mistakes as typing is slow and laborious and needs a great deal of concentration.

The first check that should be made on any data that is being entered is to make sure that the data being entered is the data that we want to be entered, e.g. we are typing what to appear in our document, spreadsheet or database. There are many ways that errors can occur when entering data from a data capture sheet including:

- the data may not be read properly from the data capture sheet
- a typing error may occur, e.g.:
  - a spelling mistake
  - data may be omitted, e.g. 2 instead of 12
  - the same data may be entered twice, e.g. 11 instead of 12
  - characters may be switched around, e.g. 21 for 12 or 'fats' instead of 'fast'
  - an extra character may be added, e.g. 20 instead of 2
  - typing the wrong character, e.g. when typing fast T might be entered instead of Y because the wrong character on the keyboard was hit
- rarely, there may be a faulty input device sending the wrong data to the computer.

This means that a check on the data typed into the document compared to the data on the data capture sheet has to be made. This is verification.

Verification

WEBLINK

http://www.
teach-ict.com/
gcse/software/db/
miniweb/pg11.htm
This provides an
explanation of
verification.

Verification is the process of making sure that the data that appears in a document or database is the same as the original source data on the data capture sheet.

When entering a small amount of data, it is sufficient to check the data by reading the source document and comparing it with the data in the computer system – this is a *visual check*. Visual checks only pick up transcription errors and do not detect inaccuracies in the original data.

When there is a large amount of data to be entered from many source documents, such as those used in, e.g. creating payrolls for paying wages, visual checks cannot made as the data has to be entered very quickly and there isn't time. In this case, it is much faster to have two data entry clerks typing in the same data and the computer will compare the two sets of entries. Any differences in the entries are reported to the clerks for correction. This is known as *double entry*.

Visual checking should not be confused with proof reading even though it would seem to be similar.

Proof reading

ACTIVITY 3
Write down three reasons why you should get someone else to proof read your work.

Proof reading is the reading through of documents to check for factual and other errors. Proof reading should be done by someone other than the original author and is used to spot inaccuracies in the facts and layout as well as any spelling or grammatical errors that may have gone unnoticed. A proof reader will mark up a document and send it back to the author for corrections to be made. Proof reading does not check the data against the original source data that was collected.

When proof reading an electronic document on a computer, these symbols cannot be used. Find out what facilities a word processor will provide for a proof reader to mark up a document.

Validation

Validation is the process of checking that the data being entered, usually into a database or spreadsheet, is acceptable and reasonable. Validation is carried out by the computer according to rules set by the designer of the database who decides on what sort of data is wanted in the database or spreadsheet.

Again, validation does not check that the data is correct or accurate but checks that it is sensible and meets any rules that have been set up. For instance, if the age of a person is to be entered, then the database can check that the age is sensible by setting rules such as 'the age must be over 0 years' so a minus value cannot be entered, or the age must be over 18 years so that an age of 18 or under 18 years will be rejected.

Validation can be a powerful way of ensuring that only reasonable or sensible data is entered into a database.

There are a number of useful validation checks that can be set up and these include the following.

Range check

This checks that a value is in a given range. Range checks can be simple, e.g. a number is between 18 and 65, or a date is between, e.g. 4th April and 1st September, or can be quite complicated checking, for instance, that the date entered in February is not over 28 or 29 depending whether or not it is a leap year.

Format check

This is sometimes called a picture check and makes sure that the individual characters in the data are valid, e.g. no numbers in a name, no letters in numerical data or that there is the proper mixture of the two in, e.g. a vehicle identity number (VIN).

Since 1981, VINs have always had 17 characters not containing I, O or Q (so that these are not confused by readers with numbers) arranged in a

Vehicle VIN plate

format that records details of the manufacturer, model and serial number of the vehicle in a complicated sequence of letters and numbers. A format check will ensure that only valid letters and numbers are entered in the correct positions in the sequence.

In the UK, a National Insurance number must be in the format XX 99 99 99 X and the first two and the last characters must always be letters. All the other six characters are numbers with the total length always nine characters. If any other format is entered the computer system will reject it with an error message.

Length check

This checks that the correct number of characters have been input, e.g. a date must always have six characters such as 01/01/01 or must have eight characters such as 01/01/2001. It can also can determine maximum length of the data, e.g. those of phone numbers.

Presence check

Sometimes a rule can be set to ensure that a piece of data is always entered. This is a presence check but as it is not really checking the data but checking to see if it is there, some people do not regard this as a true validation check. However, it is useful to make sure that all the required data is entered and is often seen on web pages where specific details, e.g. a contact telephone number, must be entered and must not be left blank.

WEBLINK

http://www.
teach-ict.com/
gcse/software/db/
miniweb/pg10.htm
This provides an
explanation of
validation.

KEY WORDS

Spreadsheet
A spreadsheet is a
software package
used for displaying
and manipulating
numbers.

Database
management
software
This is used to
store data in fields,
records and files.

Check digit

Some data is very complicated, such as the VIN mentioned above, so it has to be checked extremely carefully. Check digits are extra digits added to the end of codes such as product codes, bar codes, bank account numbers which must be entered correctly every time. The value of check digits is determined by the values and positions of other digits and characters in the code and are calculated when the data is entered and compared to a stored value. If the checks match then the data is accepted, if not an error is generated.

Validation checks must be created before any data is entered into a database or spreadsheet.

Often, a field in a database can be set only to accept data of a certain type, e.g. only numbers can be entered, and this is often used as a simple validation check. It is not a flexible method of validating data but can be useful.

Spreadsheets

A spreadsheet is used to edit, format and carry out calculations on numbers. Spreadsheets are grids of cells and each cell is identified according to its position on the grid, usually with a reference to the column and row, like this:

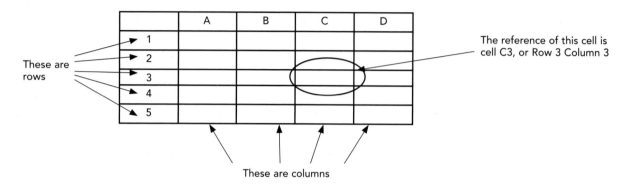

Spreadsheet with labels

Features of spreadsheet software

Spreadsheet software provides many features for displaying and manipulating numbers, and for presenting the results of any calculations.

Spreadsheets also provide the usual formatting features such as bold, italic, underlining, left, right and centre formatting of characters in the cells.

Cells can also be highlighted in colours, have borders, merged with others, or even hidden from view.

Functions

For manipulating numbers, spreadsheets provide many built-in functions along with the usual adding, subtracting, dividing and multiplying of numbers. You can carry out calculations and comparisons of numbers using any of the built-in functions and you can create formulas of your own.

Some built-in functions include:

Function	Used for ...
=SUM()	Add up all the values in the cells in the range
=AVERAGE()	Work out the average of all the values in the cells in the range
=MAX()	Show the maximum value in the range
=MIN()	Show the minimum value in the range

KEY WORDS

Cell
The basic unit of a spreadsheet, used to hold data or mathematical functions.

Range
A collection of related cells.

Replication
This is the copying of the contents of one cell into other cells.

Relative cell references
When a cell's contents are copied or moved the references are automatically updated to refer to other cells.

Absolute cell references
The references to other cells do not change when the cell contents are moved or copied elsewhere in the spreadsheet.

Formula
This is a means of carrying out a calculation using references to the contents of other cells.

Formulas

Formulas are a powerful facility in spreadsheets. For instance, if you want to find out how much you are spending over a period of time, you can use a spreadsheet to do it.

	A	B	C	D
1	Item bought	Week 1	Week 2	
2	Music downloads	4.99	2.99	
3	Drink	3.95	2.95	
4	Bus fare	2.50	2.50	
5	Lunch	4.80	4.35	
6	New clothes	12.60	25.99	
7				
8				
9				
10				

Formulas could be used in these cells to work out the total spent each week

Formulas could be used in these cells to work out the total spent each week.

A suitable formula to add up the amounts shown in the range B2 to B6 would be:

=SUM(B2:B6)

There is no need to type a formula into cell C8 as most spreadsheet software provides a simple way to do this. The formula can be copied from cell B8 and pasted into cell C8 or it can be replicated by dragging the contents from one cell to the next. In both cases, the formula will be automatically updated to add up the new range of cells, in other words,

=SUM(B2:B6)

when copied into cell C8 will be automatically updated to become:

=SUM(C2:C6)

This is because the cell references are said to be relative. If you don't want this automatic updating to happen when the formula is put into other cells, then the references have to be made absolute. If the references are made absolute then when the formulas are copied or replicated, they do not change.

To make the formulas absolute, a dollar $ sign is placed before the cell references like this:

=SUM($B$2:$B$6)

Sometimes only part of the reference has to made absolute, like this:

=SUM($B2:$B6)

In this case, when the formula is copied the column reference will stay the same but the row reference may change.

Absolute referencing is useful if the formula refers to a value that doesn't change. In this spreadsheet, the value for savings is the same every week:

	A	B	C	D
1	Item bought		Week 1	Week 2
2	Music downloads		£4.99	£2.99
3	Drink		£3.95	£2.95
4	Bus fare		£2.50	£2.50
5	Lunch		£4.80	£4.35
6	New clothes		£12.60	£25.99
7				
8	Savings	£10.00		
9				
10			£38.84	£48.78

so when the formula in cell C10

=SUM(C2:C6)+$B$8

was copied into cell D10, it became:

=SUM(D2:D6)=$B$8

and still referred to cell B8 because the cell reference $B$8 is absolute.

WEBLINK

http://www.teach-ict.com/gcse/software/spread/student/shome_spreadsheet.htm

This provides explanations about spreadsheets.

Uses of spreadsheets

Spreadsheets are used in many different ways but most involve calculations.

Teachers can use spreadsheets to keep records of the marks given to students work and to keep records of class attendance. Engineers have to carry out calculations when designing new structures such as bridges, cars and aeroplanes. They must carry out calculations to see if their designs are strong enough or that the aerodynamics of a new aircraft will allow it to fly safely.

ACTIVITY 5

Copy the spreadsheet shown into a spreadsheet package and write a formula, using the information in the spreadsheet above to calculate:

(a) the total spent in the two weeks
(b) the average amount spent on drinks over the two weeks

Use the features of the spreadsheet software to underline and embolden the totals.

Print out the spreadsheet to show your new formulas.

Databases

Database software is used to store, sort and retrieve data and is properly called database management software (DBMS). It also allows users to import data and set up security to stop unauthorized users from accessing the data.

Databases store data in a structured way inside a file.

A database file contains a group of related records, often arranged in a table. A record is collection of fields, each of which holds an item of data.

If you are keeping a database of your friends' details, you would put their first name in one field, their family name in another and other details in more fields.

KEY WORDS

Database
A database file is stored on a storage medium and contains records.

Record
A record contains a number of related fields.

Field
Field contains a single item of data.

Database search
A database search is the interrogation of a database to find some data.

Database sort
A sort of a database puts the data into a specific order. Descending order puts the data into an order with the highest or largest first, e.g. Z to A, 1 December before 1 January.
Ascending order puts the data into an order with the smallest or lowest first, e.g. A to Z, 1 December after 1 January.

No.	First Name	Family Name	Telephone Number	Date of Birth
1	Dave	Jones	0113 496 0995	1 Jan 1996
2	Iqbal	Patel	0115 496 0994	10 October 1995
3	Jasmine	Carr	0117 496 0556	3 March 1996
4	Wenxi	Wong	0191 498 235	4 June 1996

Reasons for using a database

People use databases instead of paper files or other software because databases are designed to manage large amounts of data efficiently.

You can store vast quantities of data in a much smaller space in a database that you can if it were on paper, and you can add new data and delete or edit the data much easier. If you had 10,000 names and addresses in a list on paper and had to delete a few of them, the list would soon become messy and untidy and need retyping. If you had to add a few in the middle then you would have to retype them all to keep the list in order. Databases make this unnecessary.

Finding data can be quicker than looking through long lists of records or searching through many paper files, and the data can easily be exported from the database into other software applications such as presentation software, desktop publishing software or spreadsheets.

More than one person can look at or use a database at one time which is difficult with a single paper copy.

Data in paper files may be less secure than that kept in databases in that a backup of a database can easily be made, encryption can be used to keep the data from being understood if someone manages to steal it and passwords can be used to stop people accessing it.

However, some electronic files can be less secure than paper ones as it is easy to copy an electronic file without the owner being aware that it has been copied.

Features of databases

Database software provides a number of features that make viewing and retrieving stored data much easier for users.

Entering and editing data

You can easily enter new data and edit the data that you have. This is not so easily done with paper files and you may have to retype large amounts of data.

Sorting

When data is entered into a database it may not be in any sensible order. Databases allow you to sort the data easily into order.

Sorting in ascending order puts the data into an order in which the lowest piece of data appears first. Sorting the friends database into ascending order of Family Name gives this:

No.	First Name	Family Name	Telephone number	Date of Birth
3	Jasmine	Carr	0117 496 0556	3 March 1996
1	Dave	Jones	0113 496 0995	1 Jan 1996
2	Iqbal	Patel	0115 496 0994	10 October 1995
4	Wenxi	Wong	0191 498 235	4 June 1996

Descending order puts the highest value first. Sorting it into descending order of Date of Birth gives this:

No.	First Name	Family Name	Telephone number	Date of Birth
4	Wenxi	Wong	0191 498 235	4 June 1996

3	Jasmine	Carr	0117 496 0556	3 March 1996
1	Dave	Jones	0113 496 0995	1 Jan 1996
2	Iqbal	Patel	0115 496 0994	10 October 1995

The advantage of using a database to sort data is that the whole record with all its fields is sorted at the same time.

Searching

The data in a database is only useful if you can find what you are looking for. Searching the database to find what you are looking for can take a long time if you just look through it one record at a time so database management software provides a way of searching for data.

Queries

A database query is a question that you ask a database so that it can find and retrieve the data that you want. Queries are usually written in a special language designed to find the data but most database software will provide an easy way for a user to make queries and use them. Queries can be saved for later use so that the information can easily be found again.

When making a query, the user gives the database a set of criteria to use to find the data and the query will find the data that matches the criteria.

For example to find all of the friends who were born before 31 December 1995, a suitable query would be:

Date of Birth, 31 Dec 1995

or to find all the friends called Dave:

First Name = 'Dave'

Queries can use several criteria at once, which is a powerful feature of databases.

Date of Birth > 1 Jan 1996 AND Date of Birth, 4 March 1996

will find all the friends born after 1 January 1996 and before 4 March 1996. In this case there are two.

Relational databases

Databases can store a large quantity of different data items and can become very complicated to design, create and use. Relational databases keep data in tables which are related to each other.

KEY WORDS

Query
A query is a question asked of a database to find some data.

Criterion
A criterion describes the data that you are looking for.

Boolean or logical operators
These are used to compare the criteria you set:
< is used to select all those less than
> is used to select all those more than
= is used to select all those exactly equal to
NOT is used to select all those that are not equal to
OR is used to select alternative criteria at the same time
AND is used to select more than one criterion at the same time

Tables contain records which are made up of fields, each of which holds a single item of data and each field must have a unique name.

Tables can be related to one another in several different ways depending on how the data is organised.

Primary key

A primary key is the field in a record that holds unique data and allows that record to be identified amongst all the other records. Every value in a key field must be different from all the values in the same field in the other records.

In this extract from a database of a class, there are many first names that are the same, and more than one student of the same gender:

Student No.	First Name	Gender
10021	Anne	F
10022	Jamil	M
10023	Jamil	M
10024	Anne	F
10025	Kathryn	F
10026	Karen	F

The only field with different values in every record is the Student No. so this is the only field that is suitable for use as a key field.

There are other keys that can be applied to fields. Secondary keys are used for sorting and foreign keys are used to link tables.

A relational database holding details of MP3 music files might have two tables, one with the ID of the file, names of the track and the record label. Another table may hold the name and contact details of the record label.

Uses of databases

Databases are used by individuals to store data about relatives, friends,

> **KEY WORD**
>
> Primary key
> This is a field that contains data that is unique. All the records that have this field have different data stored in this field.

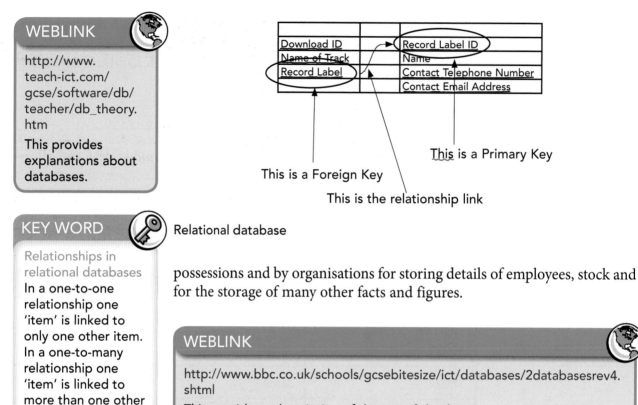

This is a Primary Key

This is a Foreign Key

This is the relationship link

Relational database

possessions and by organisations for storing details of employees, stock and for the storage of many other facts and figures.

Presenting data

Data stored in tables can be difficult to read and understand so data management software such as spreadsheets and databases provide facilities for presenting the data in ways that make it easier to follow.

EXAM TYPE QUESTIONS

1 (a) (i) What is meant by verification?
    (ii) Describe two ways that data is verified.
 (b) What is meant by validation?
 (c) Why are both verification and validation necessary when entering the details of workers' hours and pay into a computer system that works out their wages?

2 This is part of a database:

No.	Item	Description	Number in stock	Selling price
1	Inkjet Printer	Colour	12	£34.89
2	Keyboard	USB type	23	£12.99
3	Monitor	22in LCD	42	£140.76
4	USB key stick	4GB	56	£21.90
5	Mouse	Blue	121	£4.99
6	Keypad	USB	4	£9.99
7	Scanner	Flatbed A4	13	£45.87
8	USB hub	4 port	2	£19.99

 (a) Suggest a suitable field or data type for each of the fields and give a reason for your choice.
 (b) Which field should be chosen, if required, to be the key field and why?
 (c) Suggest a suitable validation check for the 'Number in stock' field, and give a reason for your choice.
 (d) If the data shown was sorted into a list by ascending order of price, which item would be at the top of the list.

3 Describe the features of a spreadsheet package that make it suitable for storing and using financial data.

4 Why would a company that stores records of its employees use a database to this?

5 Keeping Data Safe and Secure

What you will learn in this chapter
- Backups
- Archives
- How to use ICT safely
- Why it is important to use ICT responsibly
- How to keep your data safe and secure

In businesses, it is vital that all documents and records are kept so that they can be referred back to as and when required. Some documents are private and confidential and must be kept secure from those people who are not authorised to view them.

While paper documents can be lost or destroyed through carelessness or accident or even deliberate actions, it is much easier to delete or alter electronic files and lose the data forever. At home or in school, the documents can usually be retyped or created all over again, but in business the loss of important documents or files may be disastrous. Also, the loss of a whole term's coursework would not be easy to redo. For this reason, it is sensible for everyone to be organised and careful with their files.

There are some simple ways to make sure that your work is not lost or does not have to be redone because of accidental alteration or deletion:

- Never work on the only copy of a document, always use a copy.
- Save your work every few minutes, don't leave it until the end of a lesson to save the document – who knows if there will be a power cut or fault, or if you will forget!
- Save your work with different filenames, e.g. as mydoc_version1 and then mydoc_version2 so if you make a mistake or alter something you didn't mean to do, you can go back to the earlier version and retrieve it.
- Use a password on you work if you are worried that someone else might read it – but remember than passwords can cause you problems if they are forgotten!
- Keep a copy of your work in several different locations so that if you lose one, then you still have the other copies; these are *backups*.

Backups are copies of files that are kept so that if anything happens to one copy, then the others are available to use and the data is not lost. Sensible computer users make backups of all their files or whole hard disks to ensure that, in the event of a computer failure, their work and data are not lost.

Rules for using backups

There a few rules that you should follow when creating and storing backups:

- Make a backup regularly. Businesses will make backups at least once a day and often more frequently if their data is vital to their organisation.
- Make more than one backup and don't create a new backup 'over' the first in case it doesn't save properly.
- Use sensible names, maybe with the date included, for each backup so you can find it again.
- Keep each backup separate from the others and keep them away from the original file – copy them onto a removable medium, e.g. a flash memory stick, or removable hard disk, or on a CD or DVD.
- Store the backups carefully and safely – don't store them on the same desk as the computer – if the computer is stolen or damaged then so will the backups be!

Backups in businesses

Large organisations or business will have a set time for backups to be created – often after the day's work has been done or at some convenient time in the day – and use specialised data storage systems for their backups. These still include specialised tape drives with magnetic tape used for the data because this can hold vast amounts for a reasonable price and the media (the tape in cartridges) are removable. These backups are part of their disaster recovery plan. If a complete loss of data happens, i.e. a disaster, the data can be recovered and restored from the tapes. The company will use the tapes in rotation so that there are several copies available and a common system is the grandfather, father, son scheme which will work for any backup scheme The idea is to decide on three sets of backups such as daily, weekly and monthly. The daily, or son, backups are used in rotation on a daily basis with one being upgraded to father status at the end of each week. The weekly or father backups are used on a weekly basis with one becoming grandfather status each month. Often one or more of the grandfather backups is removed from the site for safekeeping and in case of a total loss when it is used for disaster recovery.

Tape drives used for backups

Frequency of backups

Sometimes, the use of scheduled backups is not enough, e.g. in banking or financial organisations where data is being changed all the time. In such cases, continuous data protection is needed and in this case a copy of the changes to any data is saved automatically every time the data is altered. A user or administrator can restore lost data at any time.

It is not necessary to have such a complex system at home but a school with all its data stored on its ICT systems would require a disaster recovery plan.

Backups should be kept away from the buildings in use, i.e. offsite and where they can be retrieved if required.

Archives

At intervals, a copy of data is taken and stored away for permanent safekeeping. These are *archives* and should be stored on removable media and keep in a safe place. Archives are used for reference purposes, e.g. for tax inspection, for research at a later date or for producing reports at the end of a financial year.

Archives differ from backups in a number of ways:

ACTIVITY 2

Make a new folder and call it 'archive'. Look through all your files and folders and move any files and folders that you are no longer using but want to keep into this archive folder. Make a backup of the archive folder and store it safely. Make a backup of the other files as well.

Backup	Archive
Consist of data in use, i.e. live data	Consist of data no longer in use
Made at frequent intervals	Made at set intervals, often some time apart
Can be used for disaster recovery	Have little use on disaster recovery
Not useful for reference/research	Can be used for reference purposes

Security of files

When documents are kept on paper, they can be locked away and it is quite difficult and time-consuming to read them or to steal them if you are not supposed to view them. Paper documents are bulky and office workers would, or should, notice someone reading their files in the office, and it takes time to photocopy them but electronic files are much smaller, easily and quickly copied and, more importantly, no-one would normally notice if the files have been copied.

WEBLINK

http://www.teach-ict.com/gcse/theory/protectingdata/teacher/protectdata_theory.htm
This provides explanations of how to protect data.

KEY WORDS

Personal data
Personal data is data that can be used to identify you or to provide information about you or your activities, such as your name and telephone number.

Unauthorised user
This is anyone who does not have permission to access, see or use the data or information.

The need for security of data and personal information when using ICT

Any person who is allowed to use, read or have access to computer files is an authorised user. In many cases, it is not important if someone else reads your letters, documents or reports but most people would like to keep their work and details private and to have some control over who can see them.

Personal data and information can be misused in many ways and measures have to be taken to ensure that unauthorised users are prevented from seeing, and possibly using, data that is not meant for them.

Businesses have to keep their company data private for commercial reasons and any information could be used by competitors. Also, the personal information of the employees and customers has to be kept safe and secure so that it is not misused.

Employees have to be trusted to use any information they need in their work in an appropriate manner and while there are laws to try and ensure that they do, the company must take steps to protect the information.

Misuse of data

Data can be misused in many ways from simply gossiping with others about customers to selling contact details to advertising companies.

One of the greatest dangers associated with the misuse of data is the use of other people's personal data to obtain money or goods. This is fraud and is illegal but it is very difficult to stop or to catch those responsible. Typically, a criminal will use the personal details of another person to apply for and obtain a bank card – usually a credit card – and then use the card to buy items or services, often online where there are fewer checks. Sometimes, goods and services can be purchased online by simply using the details for another person's credit card without them knowing and by the time the real owner discovers the fraud, it is too late to stop it. The use of 'chip and pin' systems has helped reduce the amount of card fraud in Europe itself but many countries do not use chip and pin and often the fraud will take place in countries far away. This is one of the disadvantages of having ICT systems that span the globe and connect banks.

Identity theft is not very common but is becoming more so. This involves a person using the details of another to pretend to be them. This can allow them to buy goods and services, and to, e.g. travel as that person, while the real person gets the bills! The person whose identity has been stolen usually only finds out when they receive large bills that they do not recognise or are prevented from, e.g. travelling because someone else has used their identity.

Young people should be especially wary of giving out, or letting others, have their personal details. While most people are honest and safe to converse with, there are many who would use the details to track down and harm young people and obtain details from young people by pretending

KEY WORDS

Hacking and hacker
Hacking can be legal as it means accessing, or trying to access, an ICT system without the proper user names or passwords. Legal hacking would be trying to recover a password when it has been forgotten and the owner has asked the 'hacker' to do it. Illegal hacking is trying to access data or information without permission and is properly known as unauthorised access.

to be friends. Unfortunately, it is often very difficult to tell the difference between those who mean no harm and those who do, especially when online and using, e.g. email or social networks. So young persons are always advised not to give out details of their mobile phone numbers, home addresses, email addresses or indeed, even where they go to school, nor to arrange to meet anyone.

Protecting data

There are a variety of ways to try and prevent unauthorised users from seeing your data when using ICT systems:

- Don't allow others to look over your shoulders or see the screen when typing your work. This may seem obvious but having a computer screen facing a window will allow outsiders to just look at what you are typing! Many companies have their windows screened or have the screens facing away from the window to prevent just this – and banks will have their computer screens placed so that customers cannot see them.
- Keep the computers in rooms or areas that only authorised people can enter.
- Have some physical security to prevent unauthorised use of the computers.
- Do not keep data on laptops when they are being transported or taken away from the office/home.
- Keep removable media safe and secure – and try not to lose, e.g. the USB flash memory sticks which stored your data.
- Have a unique user identity for each person for logging into the computer systems.
- Use passwords properly.
- Use passwords or access codes on files and folders on the computer system so that other users cannot access your files.
- Encrypt your files so that if they are stolen they cannot be understood.

Physical security

A simple act of putting, e.g. locks on the doors can help prevent others from seeing your work. Companies will use this and will employ security guards and put bars on windows; if they have them, they will have their computer rooms on floors other than the ground floor; they will have their computers fixed to desks so that they cannot be stolen; and they will use security cables to tether laptops to fixed objects so they are not easily stolen.

Many laptop users also have small safes in their cars in which their laptops are locked when travelling and most sensible laptop users carry their laptops in ordinary bags so that other people don't even know they have a laptop with them and don't attract attention. Using a laptop in a public place advertises the fact that you have a laptop ready to be stolen from you!

Using a laptop in a public place

If you are typing or reading private information or entering passwords make sure that no-one can see what you are typing or looking at. Some criminals can train themselves to observe and remember the keys that you press when entering passwords or codes and then use them to access your work, accounts or even bank details.

User IDs and passwords

A user ID is essential so that when you log into a computer or network system, it can identify you and assign to you all the folders, files and access rights that you should have. User IDs are used by the system only to identify you and not really for security so you should set a password or change the one given to you.

A password should be:

- something that only you know
- not written down
- not shared with anyone, i.e. don't tell it to a friend or let them use it
- not be easy to guess, e.g. your pet or best friend's name, or even a word at all
- can be remembered easily but be complicated enough not to be

worked out; it is recommended that a password be a mixture of letters in upper and lower case and include digits, preferably at random

- changed regularly and often

- not be used for every account! i.e. use a different password for different accounts because if someone else discovers it then they can only access one account.

PINs

Personal identification numbers (PINs) can be used instead of passwords. At a bank machine (ATM or automatic teller machine) or a supermarket checkout, the PIN number is used to check that the user of the bank card is the correct user. Sometimes not all of the numbers in the PIN are requested by the system and the numbers may not be in the same order as they are in the PIN so as to reduce the chances of fraudulent use. This is common when accessing a bank account online.

Example of PIN use

If a PIN is 8967, a website may ask for the 2nd, 4th and 1st numbers of the PIN so the user will have to enter: 978. The next time the person uses the website, it may ask for the 1st, 3rd and 4th numbers so the PIN this time is: 867. This adds more security to the system.

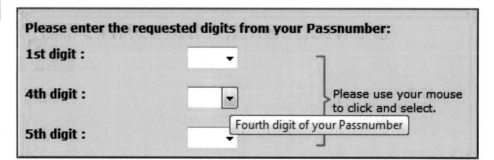

Example of PIN use

ACTIVITY 5

This is a PIN: 4356
How many three number sequences (the numbers can be used more than once in a sequence) can be made from these numbers?
    Find out from bank websites what additional security measures are taken to make sure that only the account owner is accessing an account.

Encryption

Sometimes it is vital that data is not understood by anyone other than those authorised to read it. For instance, banks must keep their customer information private and military or government organisations do not want their secret data read. Encryption changes information from, e.g. plain text that anyone can understand into encrypted information that cannot be understood. The process is called encryption and is carried out by encryption software with the aid of an encryption key. An encryption key, usually the same key as used to encrypt the data, is required for the reverse process, decryption, to make the information understandable again. Without the key, the data is meaningless to a reader so the key must be kept secret and security using encryption relies on the key not being known by unauthorised persons.

Public key encryption doesn't use the same key for encryption and decryption and is easily used. A person will have a public key and a private key for using encryption to secure their data. The public key will encrypt the data and the private key will decrypt it so all the person has to do is allow everyone to know the public key so that they can use it to send encrypted data to them. No matter who has the data or who sees it while it is being sent, once the public key has been used the data is unintelligible. The public key will not decrypt the data. Only the one person who knows the private key can make the data understandable again – so they keep the private key to themselves!

Hacking

Most people associate the term hacking with illegal activities but a hacker is anyone that can, or attempts to, access a computer system by gaining access to security details. This is not necessarily illegal as, if a password is forgotten, a hacker may be employed to discover or reset the password. Many companies will employ hackers legally to try and break their security to test it.

However, most people will think of a hacker as someone who illegally accesses, or tries to access, data that they have no right to access. An unauthorised user who attempts to discover user IDs and passwords and use these to access the data and is often called a hacker.

Key logging

Discovering user IDs and passwords is not as easy as it is made out to be if the owner is sensible and protects them properly. Key logging software records the keys that are used when a person types at a keyboard. The software then either immediately sends the information to another person or records it for sending later. Another person receiving the information could use it to discover passwords. This software goes unnoticed by the user and can reveal anything that is typed on a keyboard.

Security measures by banks

Banks will try and prevent user passwords being recorded by key logging software by asking customers to use drop down lists of letters and numbers to enter their passwords or PINs.

Unauthorised users can try to access networks from outside using the internet if they cannot physically reach and use a computer on the network. Whenever a network is connected to the internet it becomes vulnerable to outsiders who may try and access the data stored on the network by connecting to it from the internet.

With more and more networks being set up in businesses and in homes, it is important for everyone to try and prevent unauthorised access to a network from the internet. User IDs and passwords should always be used but to stop unauthorised access from outside the network, the network must be connected to the internet via a firewall.

Firewall

A firewall can be programmed by its owner to allow only authorised computers and users to access the internet and to stop any unauthorised access from outside the network. A properly configured firewall will be very effective. Most routers and cable 'modems' include a programmable firewall and these should be configured very carefully. If a wireless router or access point is used, this too should be carefully configured using authentication, i.e. requiring users to identify themselves before being allowed access and using encryption for sending data over the wireless connection.

Careful use of firewalls and data encryption can prevent your data from being viewed or stolen and prevent others from using your internet connection without you knowing!

Malware

Some people are exceptional computer programmers and provide us with software applications that allow us to carry out all sorts of tasks. Unfortunately, some programmers use their talents to cause problems for other users. Malware is the term used to describe any computer program that enters a computer system without the owner or user's consent and does them or their computer system harm.

Malware includes:

- viruses
- worms
- Trojan horses
- spyware
- adware that does not tell the truth about a product.

Computer virus

A computer virus is software, i.e. a computer program, that can enter a computer system without the knowledge or permission of the user, copy itself, and possibly pass itself along to other computers without the knowledge or permission of the users. Viruses are usually attached to other software, e.g. files or applications.

ClamWin Scan Status

```
----------------------------
Scan started: Wed Nov  2 23:16:18 2005

-- summary --
Known viruses: 40929
Engine version: 0.87
Scanned directories: 97
Scanned files: 599
Infected files: 0

Data scanned: 6.52 MB
Time: 62.842 sec (1 m 2 s)
----------------------------
Completed
----------------------------
```

Save Report   Close

Example of anti-virus software

KEY WORDS

Spyware
Software that sends details of the data and activities of a computer system to others without the knowledge of the owner of the system.

Worm
Worms are software that copies itself and uses networks to spread around without any user helping them.

Trojan horse
Software that pretends to be a useful application but carries out other tasks.

Some computer viruses are harmless but most will alter, delete or otherwise damage the data in files stored on a computer system. It is not usually possible for viruses to damage actual hardware but a virus can corrupt the embedded software that enables the hardware to function, rendering it unusable, e.g. corrupting the BIOS of a computer to prevent it from starting, or corrupting the software that manages a hard disk which will stop it from working properly. A virus that copies itself many times over will slow ICT systems so much that they may not work; other viruses will change the way software applications work so that the user cannot carry out a task, e.g. when using a web browser the required web page does not display properly or at all, and others will delete files or change the data stored within them.

Antivirus software should be kept up to date and used regularly to scan a computer system to remove any viruses. It should also be used to scan for viruses any files that are leaving or entering your computer to try and prevent the spread of viruses.

Using antivirus software properly is vital but there are a number of other ways to try and prevent viruses from affecting your computer system:

- Avoid looking at websites that show inappropriate materials as these often carry viruses or other malware.
- Do not open email attachments unless you are sure that they come from a safe source – or scan them first with antivirus software.
- Do not use other people's removable storage media on your computer without scanning it for viruses first.
- Do not download software, e.g. files or programs, from websites that are not genuine, e.g. do not download illegal music, video files or other software.

Worms

Worms are computer programs that copy themselves and use networks to spread around without any user helping them. Worms, unlike viruses, are not attached to other files and can cause great harm even if all they do is consume network resources and slow the network down. Many worms carry extra code that is designed to damage, delete or alter files or to provide access to the host computer for others to exploit.

Trojan horse

A Trojan horse is a software application that seems to the user to perform a useful task or job but may allow unauthorised access to the user's computer system. Trojan horses, unlike viruses and worms, do not copy themselves.

WEBLINK

http://www.
teach-ict.com/
gcse/theory/virus/
miniweb/index.htm

This provides
explanations about
computer viruses.

ACTIVITY 7

Make sure that your
computer systems
have antivirus
software that is
up-to-date. Run an
antivirus scan on all
of your computers at
home.

Trojans require interaction with another user to fulfil their purpose which is usually an attempt to access networks or computer systems.

Spyware

Spyware collects information about users without their knowledge or consent, rather like spying on people. Spyware software is usually installed without the users knowledge onto their personal computer or laptop and collects data which is then sent over the internet to others. This data can be used for commercial reasons but honest companies will ask first before they collect and use data so mostly spyware is used by disreputable people who are searching for personal details such as names, passwords and bank account details.

A keylogger application that records the keystrokes is also a type of spyware and some spyware will interfere with, e.g. web browsers so that the user is redirected to a page where advertising or even viruses can be encountered.

Installing and running antispyware software is now as important as using antivirus software because personal details must be kept secure.

Adware

Software that is automatically downloaded and installed on a computer system and advertises or directs the user to advertising material is called adware. Usually it is no more than a nuisance but, again, it invades the user's privacy and interferes with their work or tasks so is unwelcome.

EXAM TYPE QUESTIONS

1 What is meant by the term 'computer virus'?

2 Describe how you can protect your computer system from computer viruses.

3 What is the purpose of:
   (a) a user name
   (b) a password

4 What are the precautions you should take when setting and using passwords?

5 Explain what is meant, in ICT, by:
   (a) a worm
   (b) spyware
   (c) adware
   (d) key logging

6 Explain how the data stored on a computer network can be made secure from viewing by unauthorised users.

Legal, Social, Ethical and Environmental Issues when Using ICT

What you will learn in this chapter

- The main principles of the legislation relating to the use of ICT/computer systems
- Health and safety when using ICT
- Physical safety
- How good design can minimise health problems of ICT
- How ICT can enhance the lives of people

Computer use and the law

With so many people using computers today, and with many of the computers connected to the internet, many users worry that others will misuse their computers and, e.g. steal their data to commit fraud. Over the years, a number of laws have been passed to make misusing computers to do harm to others, steal their ideas or their data or to reveal information about others illegal. While the laws will not stop people misusing computers, they do act as a deterrent to try and prevent computer misuse and to offer the victims some way of recovering their losses.

Computer Misuse Act(s)

This Act of Parliament relates to:

- the unauthorised accessing of materials stored on computers, which means that any access to materials that you do not have permission to view is against this law, as is using a computer to access data or programs stored on other computer; this is often what people refer to as 'hacking' but hacking is only illegal if you do not have permission to access the data or use the computer to access the data

- any access to computer material with the intention of using the information to commit further offences is against this law; this means that if you access information, even if you have permission to do so, with the intention of using it to commit, e.g. fraud, you are breaking this law

WEBLINK

http://www.teach-ict.com/gcse/theory/computer_misuse_act/miniweb/index.htm

This provides an explanation of the Computer Misuse Act.

- any unauthorised alterations you make to computer materials is against this law; this means that if you change some materials stored on computer when you do not have permission, then this is breaking this law; for instance, if you access someone else's computer files and change the contents, then you are breaking this law; also, unauthorised altering of files to make the computer malfunction, alter its workings or damage other data breaks this law – so sending a virus is against this law.

Penalties for breaking this law can be a prison term of several years, or fines, or both.

Data Protection Act

The Data Protection Act aims to protect the rights of the owners of the data. It does not actually protect the data. The Act sets out rules on how the data should be stored and used and provides a means for the owners of the data to complain and sometimes to claim compensation if their data is misused.

Data on ICT systems

Storing data on computers makes it easier for that data to be accessed and retrieved by the user, but it can also make it more available to those who would misuse it.

The Data Protection Act tries to protect individuals by giving them rights to access any data stored by others and to try and make sure that the data is processed appropriately. Further, many people would prefer that their personal data is kept private and not known by everyone.

Everyone has the right to know what data is stored about them on computer systems and the right to view it. If someone feels that they are not being allowed to view the personal data stored about them, or that the data is not being processed properly according to the Act, they can contact the Government Information Commissioner's Office and ask for help. The Information Commissioner's Office will investigate the matter and if necessary can enforce any actions to deal with the complaint.

The Data Protection Act lays down eight principles about how personal data should be handled by anyone storing the data.

These principles are that:

- Personal data must be fairly and lawfully processed.
  This means that personal data must not be collected by deceiving or misleading the person into providing it and the personal data can only be used lawfully.
- Personal data must be processed for limited purposes.
  This means that personal data must only be used for the purpose for which it was obtained. For instance, a person's email address

ACTIVITY 1

Find out and make a list of the types of data that your school keeps about you. Do not list the actual data but write down items such as:

- name
- date of birth

– collected so that a company can reply to enquiries – must not be used, without the person's permission, for any other purpose.

● Personal data must be adequate, relevant and not excessive.
This means that personal data that is stored should be just enough for the task to be carried out, only relevant to the task and should not include other data. A bank would only need to hold a customer's name address, for instance, and not any details of their medical records, while a hospital would hold the patient's name and address and medical details but not their back account details.

● Personal data must be accurate and up to date.
This means the person storing the data has a duty to ensure that any data they hold is accurate and free from errors. This is the principle that most people worry about because inaccurate data stored by, e.g. banks and credit companies can cause many difficulties. Most people who ask to see what data is being held about them are concerned that companies hold data that is not accurate and want to get it corrected.

● Personal data must not be kept for longer than is necessary.
Data should be discarded when it is no longer needed. However, the data should be discarded in a way that others cannot read or access it.

● Personal data must be processed in line with your rights.
This principle ensures that the person's data is processed so that a person's rights are respected.

● Personal data must be kept secure.
Any stored data must be kept secure. The Data Protection Act ensures that people who hold data take all technical and organisational precautions against its loss, unauthorised access and damage. The Act does not dictate what measures must be taken but it means that a company must use proper security to protect the data. Companies will set passwords, levels of access and use physical methods of protecting their data to comply with part of the Act.

● Personal data must not be transferred to other countries outside of the European Economic Area that do not have adequate data protection.

Other countries around the world may not have the same level of data protection as the UK, so the Act states that personal date must not be sent to countries with levels of Data Protection lower than in force in the UK.

WEBLINKS

http://www.
teach-ict.com/
gcse/theory/dpa/
miniweb/index.htm

This provides an explanation of the Data Protection Act.

Copyright, Design and Patents Act(s)

Computers make copying of many publications so much easier! Multiple copies of, e.g. video, music, images and documents are easily made with the aid of computers so authors are concerned that their works be protected and that they earn the royalties that they deserve.

In the UK, unlike some other countries, there is no copyright registration. An author of, e.g. a book automatically owns the copyright to that

ACTIVITY 2

Find out how long an author has copyright over a new book. Is this the same as for music or films?

WEBLINK

http://www.teach-ict.com/gcse/theory/copyright_patents_act/miniweb/index.htm

This provides an explanation of the Copyright Acts.

book when the book is created. Copyright applies to any work of art, music, book, dramatic work, e.g. a play, and is subject to international treaties so that other countries recognise the copyright as well.

Copyright lasts for many years after the initial publication of the work but only gives limited protection to creative work. Owning copyright to a piece of work will not stop others from copying it but only allow the author to bring action in the courts, and often the person copying the work cannot be traced. This is particularly a problem with computer software, images and other digital data, e.g. audio and video files where copies are so easily made and shared.

Any copying or sharing of digital files that you have not created yourself is a breach of copyright; copying and sharing MP3 files made from music CDs, copying movies from DVDs and using other people's images are all breaches of copyright.

Health and Safety at Work Act(s)

Almost everyone, not just all employees and employers, have a duty under the Health and Safety at Work Acts to work and behave safely; also the Act makes it illegal to act recklessly or intentionally act in such a way as to endanger yourself or others. Employees must take reasonable care for their own and others safety and cooperate with their employers in doing so.

The Act applies to those using computers for their work but not necessarily to those using them at home – unless the person is working at home.

It would, however, be very silly not to take care when using computers at home as prolonged use of computers may damage your health. There are a number of conditions that may be caused by long periods of use of computers.

Health

Repetitive Strain Injury (RSI) may be caused by the repetitive clicking of the buttons of a mouse or a keyboard and shows itself as pain in the arms; the pain gets worse with any activity and the area affected may be weak. RSI is a term that is often used to cover other conditions such as Carpel Tunnel Syndrome (CTS) where there is muscle paralysis or numbness in the hands caused by damage to the nerves in the wrist and arms. It is not certain that RSI or CTS is actually caused by repetitive actions when using computers but these actions do seem to make the conditions worse.

Headaches are often caused by problems with vision and having a computer monitor too far way, too dim or too bright, or having the text on the screen at the wrong size, may cause headaches.

Neck or back pain may be associated with incorrect postures. Sitting at the wrong height, distance or for long periods at computer desks may cause back or neck pains. Using a proper 'computer chair' such as one that

Computer chair with back support for RSI

WEBLINK

http://www.teach-ict.com/gcse/theory/healthsafety/miniweb/index.htm

This provides explanations about health and safety.

provides proper back support and is adjustable will lower the risk of back pain or damage. Also, having computer monitors at the wrong distance or angle may cause neck or back pains.

Eyestrain or sore eyes may be caused by using computers for long periods. Staring at a computer screen for long periods without blinking will cause the eye to dry out, having the wrong size text on screen will strain the eyes when trying to read it, having too bright or dim colours will cause eyestrain and not setting the resolution of the monitor appropriately will strain the eyes. Another consideration is the light level and reflections for monitors as these can affect how easily the work on the screen is seen. Using computers will not damage your eyes but might make them sore or cause headaches.

ACTIVITY 3

Copy out and fill in this table with all the hazards you can find:

Health problem	Description of how the problem might happen	How to try and prevent it

Physical safety

Using computers can also cause physical damage to you if you are not sensible. You should:

- use a proper office chair with proper back support and adjustable height; the chair should have a single, central leg that allows the chair to swing around and that leg should have at least five supporting points, possibly each with a wheel so that the chair can move easily
- not drink or eat when using a computer due to the possible electrical hazards, and the possible spillage of food and drink into the computer itself!
- not tamper with any cables or computer parts
- place the computer equipment safely so it cannot fall or be knocked over
- not behave in a manner to cause possible damage to the computer equipment or place others in danger, e.g. don't run around or push people or place bags in throughways.

ACTIVITY 4

Obtain a copy or make a copy of the rules about using the computers and computer rooms at school.

Next to each rule write down why the rule is imposed.

ACTIVITY 5

Copy out and fill in this table from the information on the previous page:

Safety hazard in the room	What might happen	Prevention
Equipment not placed properly	A monitor might fall on someone and hurt them	Place all equipment properly
Food and drink in the room		

ACTIVITY 6

Draw a sketch of your computer room at school and mark on it the exit routes and where the fire extinguishers are. Are the extinguishers the correct type? Find out what each type of extinguisher is used for.

Design of computer rooms

When computers and computer rooms are designed, the designers take into account the safety of the users. Computers and peripherals are all made to a high level of electrical safety, have no sharp edges and will withstand some misuse without becoming dangerous.

Computer rooms must have safe electrical installations, have proper and adequate surfaces for computers, be secure from unauthorised access, have easy and safe exit routes in case of, e.g. fire and provide adequate working space for each individual.

How ICT can enhance the lives of people

ICT has made many everyday tasks easier or safer and many persons with disabilities or impairments have found that the use of ICT has made their life easier and allowed them to take part in employment or other aspects of life that would normally be denied to them.

Computer software often has facilities which many people do not normally use but which can make using it far easier:

- Voice recognition will take spoken words or sounds and turn them into commands or words on a screen. This can be used by persons physically unable to type to create documents, make the computer carry out tasks or to initiate or answer telephone calls when driving. In most circumstances, using a mobile telephone while driving is illegal but answering by voice command is still allowed.
- Voice synthesis will turn words on a screen into vocal sounds so it can be used to tell a visually impaired user what is on the screen. Drivers can have incoming text messages on their mobile phones read to them while driving. This makes driving safer.

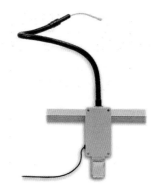

Puff-suck switch

- Zooming into parts of a screen can make the images or text easier to read.
- Predictive text can save time when typing a text message on a mobile phone.

Persons with limited physical abilities can control computers by using specialised input devices.

A puff-suck switch (also called a sip and suck switch) is used by simply sucking or puffing down a tube and the action is input into a computer via an interface box.

A mouse can be adapted for use by a foot rather by a hand. These switches are pressure-sensitive and can be made to respond to one touch or several so as to emulate mouse clicks or movements.

Head pointers work by tracking the movements of your head so that up-down, left-right, etc. inputs can be made into the computer.

Braille keyboards are designed for the visually impaired and allow entry of characters just like a normal keyboard. This is a typical Braille keyboard:

Braille keyboard

Wheelchair ICT mobility device

Some Braille keyboards have specially designed connections to the keys to allow easy editing of characters, e.g. the key is pressed on one edge and the character can be removed.

In severe cases of physical disability, ICT can be built into mobility devices such as this chair.

By fitting appropriate inputs and outputs, the person can have a degree of freedom and independence that would not normally be possible for them.

EXAM TYPE QUESTIONS

1 A bank stores details of its customers in a database. Describe the obligations that the bank has to the customers when storing and using this data.

2 What is meant by hacking?

3 A student is producing a poster for the school play. She downloads a picture of the writer of the play that she found on the internet and uses it in her poster. Explain the issues relating to this use of the picture.

7 Using ICT Systems

What you will learn in this chapter

- How ICT systems are started, accessed and shut down
- How ICT systems settings are adjusted
- How to manage files and folders
- Networks
- How ICT facilitates modern living
- Troubleshooting

Starting an ICT system

When an ICT system such as a desktop computer is first switched on, it takes a short amount of time before it is ready to be used. It has to check its hardware, load and run the operating system and any utilities or other software needed and then check and make any connections to networks or other systems before you can use it.

The initial startup is carried out by built-in instructions, called the BIOS, and is meant to check hardware such as memory chips and then load and run the operating system. The BIOS is usually stored in ROM so that it is readily available when the computer starts up. The BIOS will check to see what secondary storage devices are attached and will look for a suitable device to start from and then load the operating system. If the BIOS cannot find a suitable boot device, it will stop the startup and display an error message on the screen like this one:

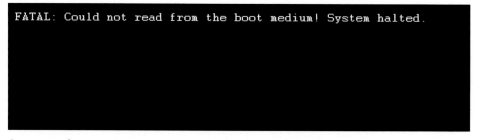

```
FATAL: Could not read from the boot medium! System halted.
```

Screen with error massage when BIOS can't find a boot device

Storage of the operating system

Most personal computers store the operating system (OS) on a hard disk or flash memory. Hard disks are the most common because they have a huge storage capacity and very fast access times so that all the software can be loaded quickly. Flash memory is used in small computer systems like netbooks or smart phones because it requires less power, takes up less physical space and is less likely to be physically damaged by movement. However, although prices are coming down, flash memory can be very expensive when large capacities are needed.

The device that the PC starts from can be altered by changing the setting in the BIOS so that the PC can start from devices such as an optical drive or another hard disk. This is useful for installing or updating operating systems.

Once the operating system has fully loaded and carried out its checks and made any necessary connections, it is ready for use. It is best to allow the OS to do all this before starting to use the PC as interrupting it can prevent it working properly or loading all its required software components.

KEY WORDS

Login
The process of identifying yourself to a computer system using a user name and password.

Logout
The process of exiting a computer system.

ACTIVITY 1

Find out how to access the BIOS on your computer home. Be careful to ask your parents or the owner if you can do this and remember not to change anything if you do not know what you are doing in case you cause the computer to stop working.

Look at the settings for several things like boot device, storage devices and so on.

Explain why it is not a good idea to set a password on the BIOS.

Accessing a PC

A computer at home will often ask for the user to log in and enter a password but it can be set up so that is not necessary. Not using a user ID or password makes the PC less secure as anyone can use it but in the home, people don't worry about this, preferring to have the PC up and running as soon as possible. This lack of care about security can have dire consequences if others can see and use the data stored on the computer, and inexperienced users can alter the settings so that the PC becomes difficult to use.

Login

In schools and businesses, however, security is very important so users have to log in and identify themselves to the ICT system whenever they wish to use the computers. A user name has to be entered and the system uses this to identify who the user is and then asks for the password linked to that user. Only when the correct password is entered will the system allow the user to log in to the account. When login happens the system provides the user with access to the software, files and data that have been assigned to that user. Using the login identity and password of another person means that you have access to their files and data, and to areas of a network, for instance, that you normally may not have and is considered a serious breach of the rules and regulations. It may also be breaking the laws on computer misuse if the person using another user name and password accesses data that they are not authorised to use or see.

User names and passwords

User names should be unique so that all users can be identified easily by the system and passwords should be robust and difficult to guess but not too difficult to remember.

Shutdown

it is not advisable to just switch off a computer system at the power supply as doing this does not allow it to close any files, exit applications and save any settings for later use.

A user should shut down any system properly to make sure that it is not damaged, is left so that others can use it later and is safe while unattended.

When you have finished using a computer, you should:

- save any work or files that you have been using
- close any software applications that you were using
- log out properly.

Logging out/off

Logging out (or logging off) properly is important because it makes sure that all your files and data are safe for the next user. This is particularly important in schools, businesses and when using a computer in a public place like a library or internet café. Not logging out of a computer and getting up and leaving it unattended means that anyone can sit down and use your files and data. They may also use your account for unauthorised or illegal activities and you could be blamed.

After you have logged out, you can turn off the computer. Check that the monitor and any other peripherals such as printers are also turned off and are safe. This is important at home as it saves electricity and reduces the fire risk. In schools and businesses, printers and other peripherals are usually left on but monitors may be turned off. Ask your teacher!

Adjusting the settings

Most users want to set up their desktop computer, netbook or mobile phone to suit themselves. Adjusting the settings of school computers is usually actively discouraged as it makes the job of the technicians more difficult if everyone changes the settings each time they use a computer, but at home there are some settings that can easily be changed to make the computer easier to use:

- The screen size can be altered on monitors to suit the task and the vision of the user.
- The time and date can be adjusted.
- The type and size of the fonts used on screen for messages and instructions can be changed.
- The size and shape of the mouse pointer can be adjusted and its speed of movement can be adjusted.
- The mouse can be altered for left- or right-handed use.
- The image used, the size and position of icons can be changed.
- The user name and password can be changed.

Managing files and folders

All files and folders must have sensible and meaningful names if they are to be found, recognised and used again.

Managing how and where the folders and files are put on a storage medium is the job of the operating system but the user is responsible for choosing filenames and putting the files into the correct folder.

There is usually a home folder, although it is sometimes called by different names such as 'My Documents', assigned to a user into which all the files should be put. On a networked computer, this folder may be on the server or other remote computer and may be called by the user's name.

A user can create any number of subfolders with different names to store all related files:

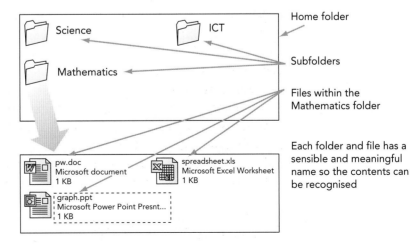

Files and folders

Once a folder has been created, a user can use the facilities provided by the operating system to manage the folder.

A user can carry out these tasks on folders.

Task	Action
Create a new folder	This creates a new folder within the home folder or subfolder
Rename	This changes the name of the folder
Move the folder	This removes the folder from its current location to a new one
Copy the folder	This makes a new copy of the folder
Delete the folder	This removes the folder and its contents

Care should be taken when carrying out these actions; some can be irreversible.

A user can carry out these tasks on files:

Task	Action
Create a new file	This is usually the responsibility of the software application when the data is saved to a new file
Rename	This changes the name of the file
Move	This removes the file from its current location to a new one
Copy	This makes a new copy of the file
Delete	This removes the file from the folder

Most files are made by a software application that labels the file so that it can be reloaded into the application. There are several ways to do this, the more common being:

- add an extension to the file that is specific to the application or contents of the file, e.g. jpg indicates that the file is a graphic file
- insert a code into the file that identifies its contents, e.g. all html files should have <html> in the first few lines of data to identify it as a web page.

A user should not normally change the file extension or else the file may become unusable.

ACTIVITY 2

Find out what these file extensions refer to:

.bmp
.txt
.zip

Networks

Networks are a convenient way of connecting computers together so that they can communicate with other computers.

To be able to connect to a network, extra hardware components and software are needed.

Network Interface Card (NIC)

This hardware component provides the physical connection to the network and uses cables or wireless. Many laptops, netbooks and PDAs, as well as mobile phones have these cards built into them but it is usual to have to add this to a desktop computer.

Cables are used to connect the NIC to the rest of the network and these have to be installed correctly to be secure and safe from interference or physical damage. Cables can be expensive to install and maintain but are very reliable in use. Some buildings are not suitable for cable use because of the materials in the structure or it may not be possible due to planning rules.

Wireless networking

Wireless networking is a convenient way to connect computers especially mobile computers, laptops, netbooks and smart phones. Wireless networks use radio waves to connect the computers and are common in homes.

Wireless networking is also useful in buildings where cables are not allowed or possible or where connections may not be permanent. Hotels and cafes offer WiFi connections to their customers and many areas have free WiFi connections.

WiFi allows people to connect their laptops, smart phones or PDAs when they are away from home but users need to be careful to make sure that their data is protected from others.

Wireless networking is not as secure as cabled networks because the data is transmitted by radio waves which could be intercepted by others. For this reason, users of wireless networks must ensure that their connection is secure by using passwords and by encrypting the data that is sent over the connection.

The encryption of data over wireless networks is carried out automatically when the user sets a connection password or key. When a computer connects to the wireless network it is asked for the password or key and when it responds with the correct key the connection is allowed. If the correct key or password is not given, the connection is refused.

Unsecured wireless networks allow any users to connect and use the network so all home users are advised to make sure that their wireless networks are set up with passwords and encryption of data.

ACTIVITY 3

Car manufacturers use a network called a CAN.

Find out what this is and what it is used for.

Network topologies

Networks can be arranged in different ways.

A simple network uses cables to connect the computers one after another.

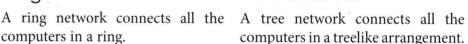

Computer

Terminator which stops the signal being sent

Cable

Ring network

A ring network connects all the computers in a ring.

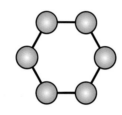

Tree network

A tree network connects all the computers in a treelike arrangement.

Star network

In a star network, all the computers and peripherals are connected to a central device so that each has its own cable connection:

Computer cable

This central device could be a hub router, switch or central server

Each of these could be a printer, server or network storage device

The central device is used to make sure that the data from each computer can reach all those computers that it is meant to. Sometimes it is set up to make sure that the data only goes to the computer or device intended. This means that the data on each cable is kept to a minimum.

Mesh network

A mesh network connects all the computers to the others:

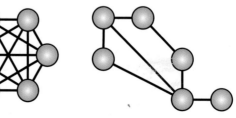

Networks can have peripheral devices such as printers attached so that all the computers can share them for printing, file servers so that all computers can store and access files stored on them or a device to connect the network to the internet so that all the computers on the network can access the internet.

Advantages and disadvantages of different network types

Network type	Advantages	Disadvantages
Bus	<ul><li>Uses less cable so can be quite cheap to set up</li><li>Can easily add more computers to the network</li></ul>	<ul><li>Usually quite slow compared to the other types</li><li>If one cable or connection fails, the whole network will stop working</li></ul>
Ring	<ul><li>Can work faster than star networks when there are many users</li><li>Does not require a hub or centrals server</li></ul>	<ul><li>If one cable or connection fails, the whole network will stop working or only computers next to each other can communicate</li><li>Adding more computers can cause problems for the whole network</li></ul>
Tree	<ul><li>Easy to set up</li></ul>	<ul><li>If the computer 'above' the one in use fails, then there is no network access</li></ul>
Star	<ul><li>Can work faster than other types because the data only goes to those computers that need it</li><li>Easy to add new computers or devices to the network</li><li>There is a central hub or server that controls where the data goes so there can be more control over the data</li></ul>	<ul><li>If the central hub or server fails then the whole network will stop</li></ul>
Mesh	<ul><li>All computers are connected to all others so if one fails then data can still reach its destination as there is always at least two routes for the data to take</li></ul>	<ul><li>Complex to set up and maintain</li><li>Can be expensive to set up</li></ul>
Wireless	<ul><li>Easy to set up</li><li>Mobile computer systems can use it while being carried or moved from place to place</li></ul>	<ul><li>Security can be complicated to set up Can be insecure if not set up properly and data can be viewed by unauthorised users</li><li>Unauthorised users can use the network if it is not securely set up</li></ul>

Advantages and disadvantages of using networks

The advantages and disadvantages of networks are shown here.

Advantages	Disadvantages
Data and files can be shared	● There is less security for the data and files than on a stand alone computer because unauthorised users may try to use the network to access data and files remotely. Networks can make data vulnerable to hackers ● Expensive and complicated security measures are necessary to protect the data and files from unauthorised users
Some software can be shared ● so reducing costs ● making set up and maintenance easier	● Some software is difficult to use over network and network versions may cost more to purchase
One internet connection can be used by many computers on a network	● The connection to the internet must be secure to prevent unauthorised users from accessing data on the network for outside via the internet. Firewalls and passwords must be used ● Viruses can spread more easily over networks to other computers
Peripherals such as printers can be shared	● Can be complicated to maintain and solve problems ● May be necessary to employ a technician to look after large networks
Users can communicate with each other using email or instant messaging	
Often computers for use on a network can be cheaper than standalone computers	It can be expensive to install ● cables, routers, and hubs ● servers and other networking components can be expensive and complicated to install and maintain

Internet

The internet is a collection of computers and servers that are connected together in a global network that is used by millions of people all over the world. It is a network made up of networks used by businesses, universities and government organisations all linked together by optical, copper cables, satellite and microwave links carrying a vast amount of information, resources and services.

All computers using the internet use the same network protocol to access information and services on the internet.

KEY WORDS

Internet
A global network of computer systems using the same or similar protocols to communicate. It allows services such as the World Wide Web, file transfer with FTP, secure and insecure data transfer, VoIP telephone communications, instant messaging, email and many other services. There is no central control over the internet but access to some websites and information can be restricted.

World Wide Web (WWW)
Sir Tim Berners-Lee wrote a plan in March 1989 for what would eventually become the World Wide Web. The World Wide Web is a collection of linked pages and documents written in hypertext that hold information. A web browser is used to view the pages that can hold text, images, video, and sounds, and to navigate from page to page.

HTML
A language that allows documents to be arranged and structured so that web browsers can display them.

Protocol
In ICT, a protocol is a set of rules used by computers for communication with each other. To use the internet, computers use Internet Protocol (IP) and Transmission Control Protocol Internet Protocol (TCIP).

WEBLINK

http://www.teach-ict.com/gcse/theory/internet/miniweb/index.htm
This provides information about the internet.

Uses of the internet

The internet is used to provide information and services for users. Some of the services are listed below.

World Wide Web (WWW)

There is a vast amount of information available on the World Wide Web (WWW) and this is accessed by using a web browser to display and view pages containing text, images and multimedia components.

FTP

The file transfer protocol is used to share and exchange files over the internet between a computer and a server. It is commonly used to upload web pages to a web server.

File sharing

Files can be shared or distributed over the internet using the World Wide Web, by FTP or by peer-to-peer sharing.

File sharing itself is not illegal but many computer users share files that do not belong to them and that is illegal.

Downloading music files from reputable sites after paying for them is legal and is now a very popular way of buying music. The sales of CDs has dropped because more people are downloading music from music stores. Buyers do not need to buy the whole CD but can pick individual music tracks to purchase.

Email

Electronic mail is a way of sending messages over the internet. The message is written and addressed and sent to a server that forwards the message to the recipient.

Telephone

The internet can be used to provide voice communications just like 'normal' telephones. The use of Voice-over-Internet-protocol, or VoIP, uses the internet to connect people in a similar way to ordinary telephones.

Online chat and instant messaging

Users can carry on a conversation using the internet. Most online chatting or instant messaging is text-based with users typing their conversations and sending the messages to each other.

This is different from email in that the people are conversing in real time just like in a real face-to-face conversation.

Remote access

The internet can be used to access computers that are far away in a different location. This is used by technicians for maintaining computer systems in other businesses or by businessmen to access files when away from the office.

Remote access requires a secure connection to be made between the computers so that data is kept safe from unauthorised users.

There are complex systems available for setting up and accessing remote systems.

Video and audio streaming

Video and sound can be viewed and heard over the internet. Video and sound are made available from servers by television companies and users can watch 'live' TV or listen to 'radio' over the internet. Many television providers have made their programmes available in this way and people can watch TV or listen to radio shows as they happen or after they have been broadcast.

Video-conferencing

Business people can hold conferences using video and sound over a network. Video-conferencing allows conferences to be held at short notice, allows participants from all over the world without them having to pay for travel, hotel expenses or having to pay to hire a conference room. The internet allows video-conferences to be held between people who are geographically far apart.

Online banking

People can access their bank account details using their home computers by using the internet. A secure connection is set up to the bank using a user name, password and additional measure such as PINs and secret phrases.

The advantages of online banking are that the bank account can be viewed and maintained at any time of the day or night, there is no need for the account holder to pay for travel to a branch of the bank and access can be from any computer that has access to the internet. Often, online banking can be cheaper than having a 'normal' bank account because the bank does not have to have so many cashiers, does not need so many branches, and has fewer administration costs so the bank saves money and passes the savings on to the account holders.

Teleworking

Many people now work from home by using the internet to communicate with their employers or clients. ICT has enabled more people to produce their work, exchange files with other workers and to maintain contact with other workers or employers without having to actually go to a work place.

The workers can save money because they do not have to pay travelling costs, can work at times that they choose and can work for more than one company at the same time.

Drawbacks for workers include not having any set time of work, being interrupted by family or friends when they should be working and not having regular contact with other employees or managers.

Employers who allow their workers to work at home can save the costs of offices or work places, paying travelling expenses or providing other facilities Disadvantages to employers of allowing workers to work at home include not being able to supervise the employee and not knowing how the work is progressing. Also, the employer may have to pay to provide the ICT equipment and software and the internet connection to allow the employee to work from home.

E-commerce

Online buying and selling of goods and services over the internet allows people to buy and sell at any time of the day and night, when shops and businesses are closed, to save the cost of travel to the shop to buy goods, search for the goods on line, to choose the lowest price or the best supplier and to buy goods from anywhere in the world.

Sellers of goods online can sell their goods at any time of the day, do not have to have actual shops so can save the costs of employing shop assistants and can attract more customers from all over the world.

Individual sellers can offer their goods for sale on auction websites and this can allow them to show their goods to many more possible buyers.

There are many advantages of e-commerce but there are some disadvantages as well. Sellers and buyers have to be sure that each is honest, that the data sent over the internet is kept secure from unauthorised people.

WEBLINK

http://www.teach-ict.com/gcse/theory/ecommerce/miniweb/index.htm

This provides information about e-commerce.

Cloud computing and networking

It is possible for organisations to use the internet to connect many computers instead of having their own large dedicated network. The organisation can make their files and information available to all their employees and workers all over the world without having to build their own private network.

A business using cloud computing:

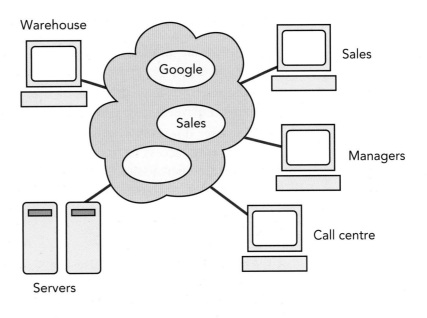

Cloud computing

The organisation can keep its data and files stored on it servers and make its services and business software available using a web browser.

Troubleshooting

Although major problems with computers should be left to trained and experienced people, all users of computers should be able to solve the simple problems that face any user when trying to carry out a task or produce some work on a computer.

ICT systems do not always work as expected but many problems can be resolved by the user.

A failure to print

If a document is sent to the printer and no printout comes out of the printer it could be for any of the following reasons:

- The printer is switched off or offline so it should be switched on and put online.
- There is no paper in the printer so more paper should be added.
- There is no ink or toner on the print cartridge. A new ink cartridge or toner cartridge will have to be installed.
- The user has selected the incorrect printer. Sometimes when several printers are available, it is easy to chose the wrong one. The user should select the correct one and send the print job again.
- The wrong printer driver is in use. The user should check that the correct driver for the printer is in use and change it if need be.
- The user does not have access or permission to use that printer. On a network, access to printers can be controlled and some users may be refused permission to print to that printer. The user should ask for permission or choose another printer.

Unable to open a file

A file may not be opened because:

- it has been moved to another folder so the application cannot find it
- it has been renamed so the application is not looking for the right name
- the file has been corrupted for some reason
- the file extension has been changed so the application does not recognise it
- the file is password protected and the wrong password has been used.

Page not found

This is often shown as Error 404 in a web browser and means that the page is not longer available because it has been removed, moved or its name has been changed. Sometimes the server is not available and this can produce a page not found error.

A link to the page may be incorrect and this can cause this error.

There is little that a user can do other than check that they have typed the name of the page correctly or that the link is correct.

How ICT helps with modern living

Modern life would not be so easy for us without ICT but it is worth remembering that not all the people in the world have access to ICT. Some countries do not have the ICT facilities that we take for granted in our country because the country or the people cannot afford it, there are limited resources or the technical knowledge is not available and some countries actively discourage and prevent their citizens for using the internet. In some countries, access to internet sites outside their own country is restricted or prevented altogether.

In our country, ICT is part of our lives and affects our lives in many ways.

WEBLINK

http://www.teach-ict.com/gcse/theory/social/miniweb/index.htm

This provides information about ICT and society.

ICT and transport

The movement of cars and other vehicles on the roads can be monitored and controlled using ICT. Traffic lights at road junctions are linked to sensors and each other by computer systems so that traffic flow can be managed and make the roads safer. Pedestrian crossings use sensors and control systems to enable people to cross the roads safely.

Railway trains are controlled by computer systems that not only control the actual trains so that driving them is easier but control the passage of the trains on the rail network. Sophisticated signalling uses sensors and tracking systems to make sure that trains can travel at high speeds between rail stations.

Airlines use ICT at all stages of their business. Customers can book their tickets online and check-in online which means that the customers do not have to travel to the airline offices or to a travel agency to choose flights and book their seats. The airline's website will show the destination, flight departure and arrival times and the options that the passenger has. When the booking is complete, the airline will email an 'e-ticket' to the passenger with a reference number. The passenger can then use the e-ticket and the details shown in it when checking in before the flight and so does not have to queue at a check-in desk at the airport.

Airline baggage is now tagged with RFID chips so that it can be tracked from check-in at the airport to the destination. This chip is read by receivers in the airport baggage handling facility so that the bags can be automatically routed from baggage check-in to the aircraft, and back again on arrival.

Aircraft have sophisticated tracking and control systems to control their flights and to help the pilots and flight engineers during the flight. Sensors on the inside and outside of the aircraft send signals to the on-board

Airline baggage tagged with RFID chips

computers so that the systems can monitor the state of the aircraft during the flights to make sure that the environment for the passengers is safe and comfortable.

The position of the aircraft is monitored by on-board computers using the preset flight data about the flight path and the system will make alterations to ensure that the aircraft is flying where it should be. Any changes will be made automatically or the pilot informed that they are necessary.

ICT and the home

Many household appliances now have microprocessors inside to control their actions and to allow users to program them. Washing machines, microwave ovens, central heating systems, air-conditioning systems, game consoles, video recorders, television sets and set-top boxes and other appliances are all controlled by microprocessors.

The advantages to users of having the appliances controlled by microprocessors is that the user can set up the appliance and then go off to do other things. Household chores no longer take so much time so there is more time for work or leisure. Appliances are safer as the microprocessor will not allow unsafe use such as trying to use a microwave oven with an open door, trying to open a washing machine door before it has finished emptying the water, attempting to open the tray of a DVD recorder while it is still recording and the laser is still working.

Microprocessors in cable or satellite television set top boxes can be programmed to change channels, record programs and set up favourite channels quite easily. The set top boxes can also be programmed to prevent young children from watching unsuitable television programs or to require a PIN to allow the program to watched.

The recording of television programs can be controlled so that users cannot copy or keep them for longer than the broadcaster wishes. Digital Rights Management can be sued to restrict viewing, recording or copying by inserting codes into the digital video or audio that signals to the recorder that it cannot record or copy the program.

ICT and commerce

E-commerce and online banking have changed the way people buy and sell things and manage their bank accounts. People can now buy and sell goods and services at any time of the day and can check their bank accounts and make financial transactions without having to pay the cost of travelling to the shops or banks.

Companies can advertise and sell their goods worldwide via the internet and many companies have attracted customers from all over the world.

Individuals can advertise and sell their goods on auction sites and many people have now started small trading businesses using these sites.

WEBLINK

http://www.teach-ict.com/gcse/theory/medicine/miniweb/index.htm

This provides information on medicine and ICT.

ICT in medicine

Expert systems are used in medical diagnosis to assist doctors in making decisions and to provide advice in the prescription of medicines.

ICT systems are used in hospitals and to assist nurses in caring for sick people and monitoring the welfare of patients.

ICT and surveillance

Convicted criminals can be electronically tagged so that their location and activities can be monitored by the police or other agencies.

Vulnerable people can also be monitored with electronic tagging which has been used to track people who are suffering from loss of memory or to track children to make sure that they are safe. This use of electronic tagging has been subject to debate over whether or not it invades the privacy or infringes the rights of the individuals.

Electronic tagging is also used to track property or cars so that a monitoring agency knows the location of the property or vehicle at all times. This is useful if the car is stolen. If the car is reported stolen the agency can find out where it is and notify the police. Many cars have had the tracking devices installed and some new cars have them installed when manufactured.

WEBLINK

http://www.teach-ict.com/gcse/theory/police/miniweb/index.htm

This provides information about the police and ICT.

ICT and communications

The development of the internet and the increasing power of ICT systems has changed the way people can communicate. Communications now cost less as they can be routed via the internet. The internet is paid for by governments, businesses, universities and other organisations but is available to anyone who has a connection so communications can be cheaper than conventional methods like telephone calls or postal services.

Using the internet can also be faster as emails can arrive with the recipient sooner than a letter sent by a postal service.

Instant messaging, email, chat rooms and the use of the internet for voice and video communication means that people can keep in contact with their friends and family wherever they are in the world.

Business can use email, teleconferencing and teleworking to carry out their business and keep in contact with employees, customers and suppliers.

EXAM TYPE QUESTIONS

1 A school has all its computers connected on a network which is connected to the internet.
   (a) Describe the problems it may face when students use the network.
   (b) What are the advantages of connecting the computers on a network?

2 A school is to install a new network using a bus network. You want to write a letter to the head teacher giving reasons why the school should install a star network instead.
   Make a list of the reasons that you would include in your letter.

3 The school stores the students' personal data in a database on a computer connected to its network so that all the teachers can have access to it when in school and at home.
   Discuss the issues that the school must consider when doing this.

8 Monitoring, Measurement and Control Technology

What you will learn in this chapter

- Sensors
- Data logging
- Writing instructions to control screen image/turtle
- Using ICT to monitor and control
- How ICT is used to monitor and control everyday devices/people

Sensors

Sensors are used to capture data about physical conditions and change the data into electrical signals. Sensors can be used to measure physical quantities such as these:

Sensor	Photo	Measures	Example use
Light sensor		Light levels	Amount of sunlight when recording weather data, light levels in a science or Design & Technology experiment
Infrared sensor		Infrared levels	Can be used to detect the heat given off as infrared from a person
Sound sensor		Sound levels	Amount of sound when recording weather data, sound levels in a science or Design & Technology experiment

Sensor	Photo	Measures	Example use
Temperature sensor		Temperature levels	Temperature when recording weather data, temperature in a science or Design & Technology experiment
Pressure sensor		Pressure	Can be used to detect when a person stands on a pad, or to measure the air pressure in a car tyre
'Motion/ movement' sensor		This 'sensor' usually measures light or sound changes to detect the movement of an object so is really a combination of other sensors	Used in security systems
Water sensor		Water, humidity, moisture	Can be used to measure rainfall or water/moisture in soil

ACTIVITY 1

Look around your school and make a note of any sensors that you see. Write down what they are measuring. Do the same at home.

KEY WORDS

Monitoring
The process of being aware of what is happening around you.

Data logging
This is the capture and storage of data from sensors.

Control
ICT can be used to control other ICT systems or external devices by using data from sensors or instructions or commands written by the user.

Sensor
A sensor is a hardware device that is used to measures a physical quantity. Sensors convert the physical quantity into a signal which can be read, when converted, by a computer or by a person.

ADC
An analogue to digital converter changes analogue signals into digital signals.

DAC
A digital to analogue converter changes analogue signals into digital signals.

> ### KEY WORDS
>
> **Actuator**
> A hardware device that moves or controls a mechanism. A motor is an actuator.
>
> **Data acquisition**
> The collection of data from real life situations and conversion into a form that can be used by a computer.
>
> **Data logger**
> A hardware device that collects or acquires data and stores it ready for sending to a computer system.

Data logging

Data loggers are used to collect and store the data from sensors before it is sent to a computer for analysis. They are useful if it is not practical or safe to use a computer system while collecting the data such as when out on a field trip.

Data loggers can have one or more sensors attached and will store the collected data in their internal memory or on a storage device for later use. The data can be transferred to a computer whenever it is convenient to do so.

Analogue to digital conversion

The signals that are sent from the sensors have to be converted into digital signals because sensors produce analogue data but computers can only use digital data. An analogue to digital converter (ADC) is used to do this.

Some actuators can only deal with analogue data so if they are controlled by a computer, a digital to analogue converter (DAC) is used.

Using computers for monitoring and measurement

Connecting sensors directly to computers often does not work because computers cannot read the signals from the sensors. An interface box has to be used:

The interface box is used because:

- the electrical signals from the sensors may not match the inputs of the computer
- connecting sensors directly to a computer may cause damage to the inputs of the computer if there is an electrical fault with the sensors or cabling so it protects the computer

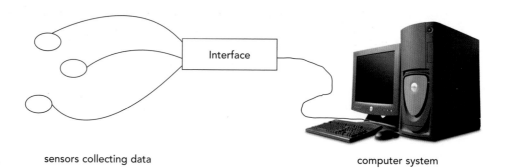

sensors collecting data   computer system

Interface box

- connecting sensors directly to a computer may cause damage to the sensors if there is an electrical fault with the computer or cabling so it protects the sensors
- users holding the sensors are isolated from the computer in case of an electrical fault
- it can be used as an analogue to digital converter.

The data collected by sensors is transferred to a computer system and analysed. For analysis it can be transferred to a spreadsheet or database where calculations or other manipulations can be carried out on the data.

If data on weather is collected, average temperatures or rainfall can be calculated or charts can be made to display the data so it can be easily understood or used in a slideshow presentation or report.

This data was recorded by the UK Meteorological Office in 2007 at Oxford in the UK:

	Month	tmax °C	tmin °C	rain (mm)	sun (hrs)
2007	Jan	10.4	4.8	73.3	79.8
2007	Feb	9.7	3.7	81.0	67.6
2007	Mar	12.0	3.7	36.9	165.4
2007	Apr	17.8	5.6	1.8	210.7
2007	May	17.5	7.1	135.2	165.5

WEBLINK

http://www.
metoffice.gov.
uk/climate/uk/
stationdata/index.
html

This has weather
data for the weather
recording station in
the UK.

	Month	tmax °C	tmin °C	rain (mm)	sun (hrs)
2007	June	20.5	11.3	78.8	149.0
2007	July	20.6	12.2	105.5	195.1
2007	Aug	21.7	12.0	38.2	209.2
2007	Sept	19.2	10.3	17.7	142.6
2007	Oct	15.1	7.9	68.9	102.5
2007	Nov	11.3	4.3	56.0	86.9
2007	Dec	8.3	2.4	606.0	57.2

and later used to create this chart:

ACTIVITY 2

Collect some data
about the weather
in your area over the
past week or so and
create a chart.
  Look up the
rainfall for your
area in 1999 and
compare it with the
rainfall for 2009 by
making a chart. Has
it been wetter or
drier overall?

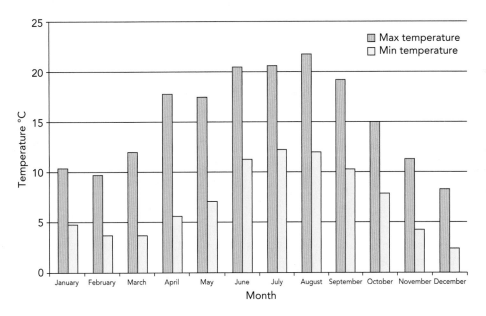

Temperature chart

Monitoring

In security systems the sensors can be used to detect intruders; in science experiments or geography lessons the sensors can be used to record changes during the experiment or in the environment or weather, as they happen and stored ready for later analysis.

Engine management systems

The data collected from sensors can be used to monitor events as they

ACTIVITY 3

Find out the main pollutants that are produced from petrol car engines and what their effects on the human body are.

ACTIVITY 4

Find out what a EODB connector is, where it can be found and what it is used for.

WEBLINKS

http://www.gendan.co.uk/article_3.html

http://en.wikipedia.org/wiki/Controller_area_network

http://www.gendan.co.uk/article_9.html

These explain about connecting cars to ICT systems.

http://en.wikipedia.org/wiki/Automobile_emissions_control

This describes emission controls for cars.

http://en.wikipedia.org/wiki/Automobile_emissions_control#Specific_pollutants

This details specific pollutants.

happen. Car engines are fitted with sensors that connect to an onboard computer system. This is the engine management system and all modern cars have these. An engine management system will adjust the settings of a car engine automatically as driving conditions, speeds and other factors change to ensure that the engine is running efficiently and producing as few pollutants as possible.

Garages, car mechanics and individual owners can connect their own computers to sockets in the car to check the settings and watch the output from the sensors. These are typical screens of data from a running car engine.

This shows the speed of engine, some temperatures and the battery voltage of a family car:

Data screen showing speed of engine

This shows the output from sensors measuring the contents of the exhaust system:

Data screen showing output from sensors measuring the contents of the exhaust system

Using sensors with people

Sensors can be connected to the human body to measure changes in the heart or breathing rates, or other body functions during exercise, sporting events or illness.

Hospitals use sensors connected to computers to monitor patients automatically, e.g. patient's heart rate, blood pressure, oxygen levels in the blood. The data is sent to a computer system which records it for later study or displays it on a screen.

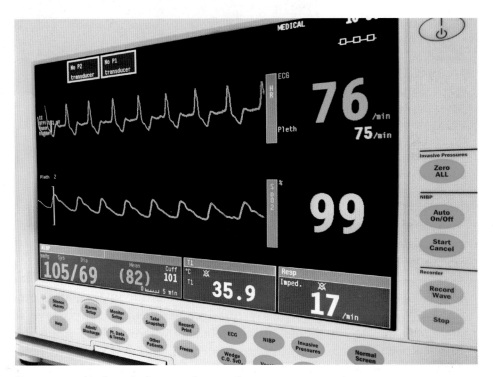

Sensor used in hospital to monitor patients

WEBLINK

http://www.
teach-ict.com/
ecdl/module_1/
workbook12/
miniweb/pg9.htm

This describes how ICT is used in health care.

Often the display is accompanied by an audible beep so that everyone knows that all is as it should be. If the readings go too far from what is expected, the computer system will sound an alarm to attract the attention of a nurse or doctor.

Nurses need to take breaks, often have many things to do at once and may not take readings as accurately as computers so the use of ICT to monitor patients can free nurses to do other things, allow them to look after more patients than they would normally, monitor the patients all day and night without a break and to be alerted at once if the condition of the patient changes.

Sports events use sensors to stream live data to spectators watching at the event or at home over the internet. In Formula One motor racing, fans can use their computers at home to watch the lap times be updated during a race. A typical screen of lap times is shown here:

WEBLINKS

http://www.
formula1.com/
services/live_timing/

This shows Formula
One live data during
races.

http://www.stats.
com/playertracking_
technology.asp

This explains about
tracking events and
players.

http://www.
teach-ict.com/
gcse/software/
datalogging/
miniweb/index.htm

This provides
information on data
logging.

http://en.wikipedia.
org/wiki/Monitoring

This explains about
monitoring.

http://www.bbc.
co.uk/autumnwatch/

This has more
information about
observing wildlife.

P	No	Name	Lap time	Gap	Sec 1	Sec 2	Sec 3	Pits	Lap
1	22	BUT	1:28.318	0.0	32.9			0	10
2	15	VET	1:28.798	4.2	33.0			0	10
3	14	WEB	1:28.784	9.2	33.0			0	10
4	9	TRU	1:28.918	12.5	33.3			0	10
5	16	ROS	1:28.960	15.1	33.0			0	10
6	3	MAS	1:29.247	16.9	33.5			0	10
7	7	ALO	1:29.336	19.6	33.1			0	10
8	5	KUB	1:29.620	22.7	33.5	31.4	24.5	0	10
9	4	RAI	1:29.675	23.3	33.8	31.2	24.5	0	10
10	17	NAK	1:30.020	26.5	33.8	31.6	24.5	0	10
11	2	KOV	1:30.087	30.3	33.7	31.9	24.3	0	10
12	10	GLO	1:30.158	31.9	33.9	31.6	24.5	0	10
13	6	HEI	1:30.476	33.8	33.9	31.8	24.6	0	10
14	20	SUT	1:30.512	35.2	33.9	31.8	24.6	0	10

Typical Formula One screen of lap times

Sporting events such as the Olympic Games have so many events that watchers and commentators need help in just keeping up with what is happening.

Security

Web cameras (webcams) can be used to watch over people or businesses just like CCTV except that the images, and sometimes sounds as well, are viewed over the internet. People can observe what is happening in their homes using webcams wherever they might be when away from home. Scientists can watch animals and plants or natural events using webcams and they can make the images available to everyone on the internet if they wish. The webcams can be placed in situations which are not suitable or safe for humans to stay for long – or even go at all.

Placing a webcam in areas where wildlife are to be found is preferable to intruding on the lives of the animals living there and is often used for remote monitoring of nesting birds.

Monitoring of people

Specialised electronic tags can be placed on people or animals to track their movements.

Tagging animals

Birds can be tracked using marker rings placed around the legs but to check these rings the birds must be recaptured and the data manually recorded each time and it doesn't tell the scientist where the bird has been on its travels. Using electronic tags with built-in GPS devices can be used on larger birds and marine animals to record their progress around the world.

WEBLINKS

http://www.scor-int.
org/Tech_Panel/
SCOR-tagging.pdf

This provides an
explanation of the
use of tagging of
marine animals.

http://en.wikipedia.
org/wiki/Electronic_
tagging

http://news.
bbc.co.uk/1/hi/
uk/4365175.stm

This explains about
electronic tagging.

Tagging people

Sometimes the electronic tag can transmit the position of the wearer so that observers know where it is. This has been used to track people who suffer from various conditions that make them forget things but this use can be seen as an intrusion into their privacy. More often, electronic tags are used on people convicted of a criminal offence instead of sending them to prison.

The tag seen here is fixed around the leg and must not be removed. If it is removed it will inform the central controller and the offender will be arrested. The tag uses a GPS system to keep track of its location and the mobile telephone network to keep in contact with a central control station. If the tagged person moves from where they should be, or goes out at times when they should be at home the control station is informed and the wearer arrested.

Elecronic tag

Monitoring alcohol use

A monitor fitted into an anklet can be used to monitor the alcohol that a person has drunk. This device is now common in the United States and is used to tag people who drink too much alcohol and need to be monitored. Many people use it voluntarily but the courts can order an offender such as a drunk driver to wear one.

Sensor fitted into anklet
to monitor alcohol use

ACTIVITY 5

Find out how
sensors and ICT can
be used in some of
the experiments that
you have done in
science where you
had to record data
as the experiment
progressed.

How it works

Once an hour, the device fires a jet of air into the skin and vaporises any alcohol found there. The amount is measured and recorded. Every night the data is sent using a modem in the wearer's house to a monitoring company for analysis.

The data is used to keep track of the amount of alcohol being drunk, to inform the court if the person violates any restrictions or help the person know how much they have taken in.

Security systems

Simple security systems do not use ICT. A simple switch on a window frame can be used to set off an alarm if the window is opened and older burglar alarms were no more than switches or sensors connected to an alarm.

Using ICT has made alarm systems more effective because they can be programmed to meet the individual needs of the user. Systems can be set to cover parts of a building or even individual objects, not to go off if the owner's cat comes into a room or to make a silent call to the owners mobile phone or to a security company if the alarm is triggered. Most security systems do not call the police directly as there are too many false alarms which waste police time!

ICT can be used to monitor who goes in or out of a building and to record when they did so. This allows companies to keep track of their employees in case of emergencies or to check up on when they are working!

ICT can also be used to allow only certain persons into some areas of the building. Locks on doors to some areas can be set with access codes known only to those allowed to go in. The security or access code can be entered manually using a keypad or stored electronically on an identity card. The card is swiped though a reader or passed over a scanner and the code read into the lock system. Using a card system is more secure than manually entering a code because the user does not have to remember it so will not write it down; the card has to be present for the system to work so only the person with the card can use it and the card may hold more information than just the access code. A photograph on the card or some biometric data can be added to the card to make sure that the proper person is using the card.

KEY WORD

Biometric

Biometric information uniquely identifies people using fingerprints, face recognition, DNA, iris and retinal scans.

Control

Data from sensors can be used to control devices or machinery. ICT can make this control very sophisticated indeed.

Central heating systems

A simple house central heating system uses a thermostat to detect when the temperature is too cold or too hot and turn the heating on or off. There is no control other than switching the system off when the temperature is too high or on again when the temperature drops.

Using ICT to control a central heating systems involves using sensors to measure the temperatures of rooms and the outside air. The data from the sensors is sent to a central control unit that contains a microprocessor. This unit can be programmed by the user to turn the heating on or off depending on the outside temperature, the temperature of the rooms and the time of the day or night.

Data received by the microprocessor is compared to preset values that the user has put into the unit. These values include the temperature that the user wants, the time of the day that the heating can come on, and possibly which of the rooms are to be heated. The microprocessor will send instructions to the heating boiler to turn it on or off and to valves in the system to send heat (in the form of hot water) to where it is needed.

By monitoring the data from sensors at regular intervals, the microprocessor can keep the temperature very close to that required by the user.

KEY WORD

Feedback

Feedback is when the output from a system is used to affect the input to that system. For instance, a heater warms up a room which becomes too hot so the heater is turned off. The room gets colder so the heater is turned on again and the room warms up. When the room is warm again the heater is turned off and so on.

ICT and control

ICT can be used to control machinery or other objects such as medicine dispensers in hospitals because it allows for users to program their requirements into a system. Just like the temperature and times can be programmed into a heating system so the microprocessor can make decisions; machinery can also be controlled by programming instructions.

Warehouses that are very large may have trucks and trolleys that can be programmed to find and fetch items to be shipped out. This is one type of fork lift truck that can be programmed to fetch or deliver items in a warehouse:

Programmable fork lift truck

These vehicles use sensors and programmed instructions to get them to and from their destination.

Airport shuttles and some light railway train systems use automatic control systems, sometimes with no drivers, to carry passengers. Automatic systems stop, start the train, open and close doors and may control when passengers can approach the train or platform.

WEBLINKS

http://www.teach-ict.com/gcse/software/control/miniweb/index.htm

This provides information about control technology.

http://en.wikipedia.org/wiki/Automated_guided_vehicle

This explains about computer controlled vehicles.

http://en.wikipedia.org/wiki/Rapid_transit_technology

Explains about controlling transport systems.

KEY WORDS

Turtle
In the ICT world, a turtle is a mechanical vehicle that is controlled with a computer system by issuing it with commands typed into software application. On-screen turtles are representations of a real turtle but on screen and are controlled in the same way.

Turtle graphics
A turtle can be used to draw objects on screen or on paper by using commands to define its position, orientation and movement. The turtle moves along a grid of squares according to the commands given to it by the programmer.

Controlling on-screen or mechanical turtles

There are a number of software applications that can be used to program and control a turtle or on-screen turtle.

Logo language

LOGO (Logic Oriented Graphic Oriented) is a computer programming language used for turtle graphics. The language can be used to draw all sorts of shapes by programming the turtle with simple commands.

These commands:

FD 3   which means go FORWARD 3 squares or steps
RT 90   which means turn RIGHT 90 degrees
FD 1   which means go FORWARD 1 square or step
LT 90   which means turn LEFT 90 degrees
FD 1   which means go FORWARD 1 square or step

move the turtle from A to B along the line on the grid.

There are more commands and you can make long lists of program instructions to draw complex shapes on the grid.

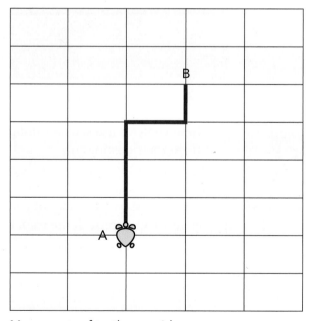

Movements of turtle on grid

WEBLINKS

http://www.extremenxt.com/walter.htm
This describes early mechanical turtles.
http://en.wikipedia.org/wiki/Logo_(programming_language)
This explains the Logo language.
http://en.wikipedia.org/wiki/Turtle_graphics
This describes the origins and use of turtle graphics
http://www.bbc.co.uk/schools/gcsebitesize/ict/
measurecontrol/1logocontrolrev1.shtml
This describes the use of ICT to control devices.
http://mckoss.com/logo/
This shows how to program in Logo.
http://learninglogo.com/
This allows Logo programs to be tried out.

WEBLINK

http://en.wikipedia.org/wiki/Industrial_robot

This explains about robots in manufacturing.

Control in manufacturing

ICT can be used in manufacturing to control machinery. Sensors can be placed on assembly lines to check that an item is present before it is sprayed with paint and ICT can be used to program the painting system to use different paints on different objects.

Machinery that can be programmed to carry out manufacturing or other actions are often called industrial robots. They look and act nothing like the robots of science fiction and may carry out some actions over and over again or be flexible enough to carry out complex tasks.

CAD/CAM

Computers running design software are now commonly in use by architects, engineers and other designers. The software contains a variety of specialist tools and libraries of shapes and measurements for designing items.

Once a design has been finished, it can be analysed by a computer system and the details sent directly to a computer-controlled machine to make it. This is computer aided manufacturing.

KEY WORDS

CAD
This is computer aided design. Designs for new buildings, clothes, vehicles and almost any other product can be done using design software on a computer.

CAM
Computer aided manufacturing has transformed the production of consumer goods ranging from small items like watches, televisions, DVD players to large industrial vehicles.

WEBLINKS

http://en.wikipedia.org/wiki/Computer-aided_design
This provides an explanation of CAD.
http://en.wikipedia.org/wiki/Computer_aided_manufacturing
This provides an explanation of CAM.

The advantages and disadvantages of using robots in manufacturing

There are a number of advantages to a company of using robots in the manufacture of their goods:

- They don't need to have humans in dangerous areas on assembly lines.
- They don't need to employ so many workers skilled in manufacturing so can save the cost of their wages.
- Robots don't need to stop or take breaks or holidays, and can work all day, every day.
- The end product is more consistent in its accuracy so that all the products are of very similar quality.

The only disadvantages that companies using robots may have are:

- the initial setup and purchase costs of the robots and machinery may be high
- they will have to employ IT experts to maintain and service the systems and these may have to be paid high wages
- power cuts and breakdowns of robots may cause damage to products or cause the factory to stop altogether while repairs are carried out.

Workers may find that they become redundant or have to be retrained when robots are first introduced to a factory but eventually the workers who remain and who learn new skills will earn more. There will be job opportunities for those workers who can maintain, program and service the robots.

EXAM TYPE QUESTIONS

1 Describe the advantages of using ICT to monitor a patient in hospital.

2 What are the advantages of using ICT to monitor and control the performance of a car engine?

3 Discuss the issues arising from the electronic tagging of people.

9 ICT and Modern Living

What you will learn in this chapter

- How ICT systems have changed the way people go about their daily lives at home and at work
- How ICT systems have changed the way people communicate
- How ICT systems have changed the way people shop and buy and sell goods and services

Changes in the way people work

Working at home

Advances in communications have changed the way people work and where they work. There is no longer any need for some people to actually 'go to work' in the sense of travelling each day back and forth to a place of work – they can stay at home and use ICT to do their work and send to their employer. They can co-operate with others on projects and each contribute their work without ever meeting their work colleagues.

Using ICT at home

This has become possible because the internet allows fast communications and the exchange of documents to happen easily. Employees can communicate with their fellow employees and with their employers wherever they happen to be.

When working at home, employees can have the same software as if they were at work and use email, fax machines and other methods, e.g. file uploads via FTP and document sharing software to exchange or send their work to others. Most general office software is compatible and specialised software such as Computer Aided Design software would be supplied by the employer if needed. Those who don't work for any particular company, i.e. work for themselves or contract themselves to several companies while working at home, can easily be working on several projects at once.

There are many advantages, and some disadvantages, of people working from home, for both employees and for employers, and these include:

Advantages to employees

A person who works at home saves the costs of travelling as there is no need to buy fuel or pay for parking, spend money on tickets or to spend time on travelling to and from work. This is important in the world today as the cost and time spent on travelling are increasing all the time. Also, any small reduction in the amount of travelling will help to save the environment and combat global warming but the extra use of electrical power and its generation will make any savings much less than they seem.

Working at home allows people to decide when they want to work and adjust their working times to suit themselves and their families. They are not restricted to set working hours.

Disadvantages to employees

Working at home requires the employee or worker to have a reliable and good internet connection and this is not always possible. Some areas of the country do not yet have broadband or it may be too expensive to install and use.

The worker must have a computer system that is sufficient to carry out the tasks needed, and there must be provision for keeping the files and data safe and secure. Proper backup and security procedures must be used and these may be expensive and may be difficult for non-computer experts to set up and use.

When working from home, workers may be interrupted by friends, family or others who do not realise that they are actually working.

There is reduced contact with other workers and the worker may feel isolated from the management and not kept informed of changes, progress of work or any possible promotions.

Advantages and disadvantages to employers

Employers do not have to provide so many offices or so much office equipment at work but may have to provide computer equipment and software for their employees to use at home. This may be cheaper but they have less control over the use of the equipment.

Employers will not have to pay any travelling expenses or provide parking spaces for their employees.

Employers cannot supervise their workers so closely and may not know how the work is progressing.

Weather forecasting

The use of computer technology in weather forecasting allows the collection and manipulation of the data in complex computer models to produce more accurate predictions of weather patterns. Advances in science and computer technology have allowed weather forecasters to show the data and use it to try and make predictions about weather patterns.

Online banking

Many people have a bank account or a credit card or both.

Today, a bank account allows people to manage all their financial affairs such as paying bills, receiving money and saving money. Many banks now offer online banking where account holders can access their account over the internet.

Online banking offers customers facilities for checking the account balance, for electronic bill payment for paying bills such as telephone, gas, electricity and water bills, electronic funds transfer for moving money between different accounts such as into savings accounts, applying for loans, making financial investments, sending money abroad, electronic statements and the ability to download details for bank transactions for use in personal financial software or spreadsheets.

Online banking requires customers to have a user number, a password and a secure way of checking that these are being used by the correct account holder. Banks often use Personal Identification Numbers (PINs) or a private phrase that only the account holder knows. Banks insist that the PIN numbers or phrases are not written down and when accessing the account will only ask for a few, usually three, numbers or letters from the PIN or phrase. This is to ensure that the PIN or phrase is not seen by others, or intercepted and used by others. If only three numbers or letters are asked for, and in any order, then it is unlikely that the whole PIN or phrase will be discovered by any unauthorised person who may try to intercept it or memorise it.

Online bank statement

Using a bank PIN number

If your PIN is 3465, then when your try to access your account online, the bank's computer will, for instance, ask you only for the 4th, 2nd and 3rd numbers. The next time you access your account, the numbers asked for may be the 2nd, 4th and 1st. This means that the same numbers are not sent over the internet every time.

Online banking has a number of advantages and disadvantages, both for the customer and for the bank.

For the customer, there is the ability to use the internet to access their bank account at any time, even when bank branches are closed, from wherever they are. This means that the customer can monitor their bank accounts much more closely than if they had to go to a branch of the bank each time. Payments from the account can be arranged in advance and money can be moved into other accounts easily.

There is no need to travel to a branch of the bank and the customer will save time and money. In some areas where there is no local branch of the bank, savings in time and money can be considerable.

There is no need for the bank to send paper copies of bank statements so this will cut down on waste paper and the need for the customer to store, and dispose of, the statements safely.

However, customers who use online banking must ensure that their passwords, PINs or private phrases are kept very secure. Banks will not pay back any money that may be fraudulently taken from the account if the customer has not kept the details secure.

Not all customers have a computer or internet access so not everyone can use online banking.

Security token

WEBLINK

http://www.teach-ict.com/gcse/theory/banking/miniweb/index.htm

This provides information about banking and ICT.

KEY WORD

Disaster recovery
Companies and organisations have to ensure that in the event of a total computer failure or data loss, they can recover their systems as soon as possible and with as little loss of data as possible.

Disaster recovery procedures will include all the documents, policies and instructions for recovering the software and data to put the system back as it was before the problem occurred.

Banks can save money by having fewer branches with less staff if their customers use online banking. Branch staff such as bank clerks, security staff and cleaners are not needed if there are fewer branches.

The bank must employ technicians to service and maintain their computer systems and the software need for online banking. There must also be people who answer customer queries by telephone and the bank will have to have call centres with many operatives. The overall savings in staff wages may not be very much but the cost of branches in high streets will be saved as call centres can be anywhere in the world.

Bank staff may be able to work part-time, to job share, and work from home as there is no need for set working hours or places of work if the customers do not have to come to branches. Technicians, in particular, can work from anywhere and may choose to work from home using the internet to access the bank computer systems.

The disadvantages to the bank include the need to invest in complex and sophisticated computer systems, to employ many IT technicians.

Banks must ensure that their computer systems are secure both to prevent unauthorised access and use of the computer data.

Passwords and PINs are not considered to be secure enough for some banking transactions so many banks have issued their customers with devices, called a security token, into which the customer places their bank card. When the customer PIN is entered a new number is generated and this number is used to access the bank account. This number is called a Transaction Authentication Number and is different for each time the customer uses the device.

Any exchange of data for online banking, as for online shopping, must be secure so it is encrypted before it is sent. The web browsers do this automatically.

Banks must also make sure that the data is kept safely with proper backups and have procedures for disaster recovery.

Credit card companies also provide online services that allow the card holders to view their statement and to pay their bills over the internet.

Online buying and selling of goods and services

Many people use the internet to buy and sell goods. Internet shopping has many advantages over conventional shopping although people still like to visit the shops!

For the customer, internet shopping means that they can shop whenever they like even when shops are closed, and can buy goods from all over the world. Buying goods when normal shops are closed is more convenient for people who have to work all day and there is no need to travel to the shops. Not having to travel to the shops saves money on fuel, tickets and the

Credit card

A credit card is provided by a company who, when a purchase is made using the card, will pay the company for the goods and then send a statement to the customer asking for payment. This is credit.

Debit card

A debit card is provided by a bank who, when a purchase is made, will check the customer's account balance and only allow the purchase if the account has sufficient funds to cover the cost.

costs of parking. There is also a saving of the time taken to travel although many people will spend more time shopping online than they would if they visited the actual shops!

Customers can also use the internet to find the cheapest place to buy the goods although they may have to pay more in delivery charges or shipping than if they had collected it themselves. Using the internet to search for and choose the cheapest price is an advantage of online shopping.

Buying goods from other countries will give the customer more choice but these goods may eventually cost more when delivery, import taxes and customs duties are all added to the cost of the items.

Companies who sell goods online can sell the goods more cheaply as they do not have to have shops in expensive areas, do not need so many staff so can save money on wages although they do need technicians and packing staff to ship the goods, and they must have facilities for customers to pay for the goods online.

Customers will have to use a credit card or a third party payment method to pay for the goods.

KEY WORD

Third party payment methods

There are companies such as PayPal© who take the payment from the customer and pass it to the supplier. These methods are used by people who do not have credit cards or do not want to use them for online shopping, or by suppliers who do not accept credit or bank cards.

There are bank cards that can have 'money' added to them and this can be used to pay for goods over the internet as well as in real shops.

Advantages and disadvantages of online shopping

To the customer:

Advantages	Disadvantages
Can buy goods at any time	May be difficult to contact the seller
Can compare goods easier and more quickly than visiting may shops	May be too many choices to look at
Have more choice of goods	Goods may not be the same as those viewed online, or the goods may be damaged or different size

Advantages	Disadvantages
Can buy from all over the world	Goods from abroad may cost more to deliver and may have to pay taxes and customs duties
Goods may be cheaper	May have to pay delivery costs
	Must have a credit card or use a third party payment method
May be able to obtain the goods more quickly if the customer has no opportunity to visit a shop	May have to wait for delivery or goods may not arrive at all
	May have difficulty in returning goods or having faulty goods replaced
	Shopping site may not be secure so personal details may be seen by unauthorised persons and used for fraud

Online shopping

To the company selling the goods:

Advantages	Disadvantages
Do not need a proper shop so save money on rent, heating, security	Need a warehouse or somewhere to keep stock
Do not need shop assistants so save money on wages	Need technicians and warehouse staff so have to pay their wages

Advantages	Disadvantages
Goods may be sold cheaper so will have more customers and business will expand	More business may mean that there is difficulty meeting demand so customers go elsewhere
No need to handle cash	Must have facilities for secure payments
	Must have facilities for contacting customers and for customers to contact the company
	Must have provision for customers to return goods
Can have customers from all over the world and not just in the local area	Must have a system for delivery to anywhere in the world
Do not need to stock large quantities of goods as some can be ordered from manufacturers or wholesalers as and when they are needed	Goods ordered 'just in time' may not be delivered so customers may be dissatisfied

Many people are worried that online shopping is unsafe and that their personal details will be used by unauthorised people for fraud and that they will have to pay for goods that they haven't ordered, that their bank accounts will have money stolen from them or that their credit cards will be used without their permission.

While using other people's details for fraud is not very common, it is becoming more of a global problem. Credit card and bank details can be intercepted if the customer and bank do not take care and the details used anywhere in the world. Fraudsters will use the stolen details of credit cards to buy a few items costing very little to see if the fraudulent purchases work. If so, they then buy expensive items quickly. If the customer or bank do not notice, they buy more but if they are noticed it will be too late anyway! For this reason, people are advised to keep their personal details secure and follow safe practices when purchasing goods online. They are also advised to check their bank and credit card statements regularly – they can do this easily online.

CCTV cameras

WEBLINK

http://en.wikipedia.
org/wiki/Biometrics

This provides
information about
biometrics.

Monitoring and security issues

Modern computer technology allows close monitoring of people as they go about their daily activities.

Sensors and CCTV cameras that are placed so that they can be linked over a network or the internet can be used to track people and this raises a number of issues. The images can be stored on a computer system and checked by people or by the system against images already stored or against images of known criminals to try and identify anyone who is likely to be a threat.

Some authorities maintain that monitoring and watching people makes the public safer and more secure because it allows them to track individuals and check what they are doing.

It is also argued that using identity cards with biometric data will help combat crime and terrorism because it is possible to check who the person actually is.

However, many people believe that this does not actually reduce crime and is an invasion of the privacy of the individual who is innocently carrying on with their lives.

This is a complex debate but the use of ICT has made the surveillance of public places, transport systems businesses much easier as ICT can quickly search and compare data such as images so that the movements of people can be recorded by the authorities.

KEY WORDS

CCTV
Close-circuit television cameras linked to central control rooms and computer systems allow observers to watch and record the movements and locations of individuals or groups of people.

Identity card
A card that holds the details of an individual. The details can be printed on the card, stored on a chip in the card or both. Details include names, addresses and biometric data.

Biometric data
Data created from DNA, fingerprints, retinal or iris scans that uniquely identify the individual.

Artificial Intelligence

Artificial intelligence (AI) is a system that can perceive its environment and act accordingly. In computer science, it is a computer system or machine that mimics how a human being would perceive and act in its environment. Only today, after more than half a century of research and development, is it becoming a reality.

ICT systems can learn from their 'experience' (such as 'teaching' a computer system to recognise your voice for commands), learn your frequent commands, learn from your repeated tasks and suggest alternate software for you to use to complete the task more effectively. These are not from the science fiction world of artificial intelligence, with talking, thinking androids or robots but they are examples of ICT systems learning from 'experience'.

Artificial intelligence is used in the banking industry to detect credit card fraud, in telephone systems to interpret speech, and in some expert systems to assist a human worker, for example, in medical diagnosis.

WEBLINKS

Information about Artificial Intelligence can be found here:
http://en.wikipedia.org/wiki/Artificial_intelligence
http://library.thinkquest.org/2705/
The history of AI:
http://library.thinkquest.org/2705/history.html
Examples of AI in use:
http://library.thinkquest.org/2705/programs.html
http://www.cs.washington.edu/homes/lazowska/cra/ai.html

Robotics

Robotics is the part of engineering science which deals with the design, creation, and use of automated machines. Robots for use in factories are not designed to look and move like humans because this would not be suitable. A machine used for the manufacturing and assembly of cars or washing machines needs only to be able to move the parts around and does not need to be able to walk or run. Robots used in transporting goods, or in space exploration do not need to be copies of human beings and perform far better with wheels than with two legs. However, there are some tasks that robots or artificial limbs might be needed for and this is why research into robots or machine parts that mimic human limbs is carried out.

This is an artificial hand called the Shadow hand. It is designed to mimic a human hand.

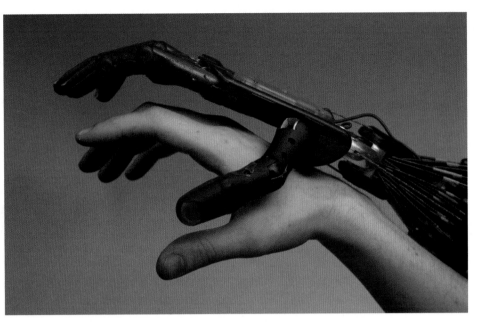

The Shadow hand

WEBLINKS

The Shadow Robot Company:
http://www. shadowrobot.com/

Robots in Industry:
http://www. robotics.utexas.edu/ rrg/learn_more/low_ ed/types/industrial. html

Most robots, however, are designed to carry out a specific task such as welding, spraying paint, moving objects around in a factory or warehouse or assembling parts of, for example, cars or kitchen appliances.

ID cards and Passports

Biometrics are used in identity cards and passports to store data about an individual so the person can prove that they are who they say they are, or the person with the card can be checked against stored data.

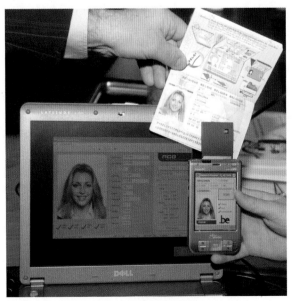

Passport being read electronically

National identity cards will contain data about the fingerprints and facial features of the holder so the person can prove their identity. Biometric data stored on chips in the cards can be read by machines and checked against sorted data very quickly.

A biometric passport issued by the United Kingdom contains a chip that stores, along with personal details, information about the person's face such as the distances between the eyes, nose, mouth and ears. These details are extracted from the photograph that is sent to the Passport Agency when the person applies for a passport.

The data can be read electronically and should make it quicker for the holder to pass through border controls. The passport can be read by a chip reader from a distance of a few centimetres so the holder just has to 'wave' the passport at the chip reader as they walk past. The data can be checked and recorded quickly.

The Identity and Passport Service (IPS) can use the stored data to check the photograph supplied on any renewal applications to prevent the issue of a false passport.

WEBLINKS

http://en.wikipedia.org/wiki/Biometrics#Current.2C_Emerging_and_Future_Applications_of_Biometrics

http://newsinitiative.org/story/2006/09/01/walt_disney_world_the_governments

http://www.youtube.com/watch?v=pj1Wj59lCeU

http://www.engadget.com/2006/09/01/walt-disney-world-to-start-fingerprinting-everyone/

WEBLINK

Using ICT to enhance vision:

http://www.tc.gc.ca/innovation/tdc/projects/access/a/9540.htm

Vision Enhancement

ICT can help people to see better!

As well as making objects on screen easier to see or to read with the use of zoom facilities or enlarged text, ICT can be used, for example, to help people see at night or when driving cars.

Night vision goggles can send images to ICT systems which can process them and enhance them so that the user can make out objects that would otherwise not be seen.

Car drivers with poor vision can be helped by displays that point out important objects when driving.

Computer Assisted Translation

ICT systems can be used to help human translators.

Common tools for translation include:

- spell checkers and grammar checkers found in word processing and other software
- terminology checkers found in specialist software – these can usually be customised with new terms
- dictionaries that can be used to find specific words
- thesaurus' for finding alternative words

Software exists that will translate whole sections of text into different languages and free versions can found on the internet.

There are main two types of computer assisted translation:

- Translation Memory which remembers how previous translations were carried out and does the same, or similar, again.
- Machine Translation which follows a set of rules to translate the text.

Authors and readers of technical articles or scientific publications often use computer aided translation.

WEBLINK

http://www. traduzioni-inglese. it/computer-aided- translation.html

Quantum Cryptography

Most people do not like their messages or letters to others to be read by anyone except their intended recipients. Usually, it does not matter if someone else reads the message or letter but some things have to be kept secret for all sorts of reasons. Over the centuries, cryptography has been developed to scramble messages so that only those who should be able to read the message can do so, and others cannot.

Encrypting whole messages can take a great deal of time and effort so usually a 'key' or code is encrypted and the key is used to scramble and unscramble the actual message. This takes less time and works well, provided the key is kept secret.

It is very important to keep the key secret as anyone with the key can quickly unscramble the message. The problem is how to get the key to the person who will receive the message without it being intercepted and copied. Before computers, it was common practice to send couriers around the world carrying the keys in secure bags from one place to another to make sure they were received by the correct people.

Using computers to encrypt and decrypt keys and messages has made communication more secure and there are now very safe encryption methods available. Encryption keys can be made, scrambled and sent around the world electronically. The keys made by computers can be far more secure than those made by people.

However, the cracking of secret keys and codes has also been made easier and quicker by computers. Before computers, working out secret keys or codes would take far too long and take a lot of effort, but modern computers can be used to work out (crack) codes very quickly.

Quantum cryptography is an extremely secure way of encrypting data because the quantum property of light or photons is used.

Quantum cryptography is usually involved in the encryption and sending of the secret key used to encrypt the actual data. This involves less computation and computer power than encrypting all of the data. Most scientists say it is not possible to measure the quantum state of photons so quantum cryptography is believed to be unbreakable.

An important feature of quantum cryptography is that if anyone attempts to read the encrypted data, the sender and receiver will know that this has happened. This is because one of the basics of quantum mechanics is that anyone attempting to observe (or eavesdrop on) the secret key must measure it and this will make it different in some way. The differences will alert the sender and recipient.

So, not only does quantum cryptography secure the data, it allows the sender or receiver to know when someone else has tried to examine or read it.

Quantum Cryptography has been used in the transmission of voting results in elections and by banks when making electronic transfers of money between different countries.

WEBLINKS

http://en.wikipedia.org/wiki/Quantum_cryptography

http://www.perimeterinstitute.ca/personal/dgottesman/crypto.html

3D and holographic imaging

Holograms use recorded light patterns scattered from objects to recreate images of those objects that appear to be 3-dimensional. The technology for creating holograms is still in its infancy but ICT is being used to enhance video conferencing with 3D or holographic images so that the participants see an image of each other that resembles a real person.

Images for computer games can be created by computers with rendering techniques to achieve lighting and other effects that give the images an appearance of being 3D. Movies have been created by computer systems to appear 3D, but when displayed, most require the use of special screens or televisions and the use of special glasses.

WEBLINKS

http://en.wikipedia.org/wiki/3D_computer_graphics
http://en.wikipedia.org/wiki/Holography#Holographic_recording_media
http://www.youtube.com/watch?v=8hg-m_wT9qQ

WEBLINKS

http://en.wikipedia.
org/wiki/3D_
printing#Equipment

3D printing

Just as printing on flat paper is often carried out by adding ink to the surface of the paper, 3D printing works by adding layers of material onto a surface. By adding layer on layer, a 3D object can be built up (printed) by a computer controlled machine.

Copies of objects can be made by using 3D scanners, and printing them with 3D printers.

Virtual reality

Virtual reality is an environment generated by a computer system to simulate the real world.

Users of virtual reality require input and output devices that allow them to interact with the environment, so that they can manipulate objects or items in the virtual world and see or feel the results. A mouse, keyboard, monitor and speakers are often not enough to experience the full effects so wired gloves, headsets or helmets are used which allow the user to properly experience the virtual reality.

Use of virtual reality

WEBLINK

http://en.wikipedia.
org/wiki/Virtual_
reality

Virtual reality is used in video games, for training pilots or drivers, and for the training of search and rescue personnel, such as firefighters and oil rig workers. It can also be used in safety proceedure training, such as aircraft evacuations, in marketing to show potential buyers new properties and their layouts.

Virtual reality is also used in health care, to train surgeons in anatomy and to treat phobias and post traumatic stress disorder.

EXAM TYPE QUESTIONS

1 An artist wants to sell her paintings but does not have a shop or a gallery. Describe how she could use the internet to sell her paintings.

2 A shop selling DVDs is to start selling them online. The manager of the shop is worried that this may cause him some problems. What might the manager be worried about?

3 A school uses sensors and security cameras to watch the school entrances and exits as well as the playgrounds.
   (a) Describe how the sensors could be used to control the security cameras.
   (b) How could a computer system be used to identify unwanted visitors?

Practical Applications in ICT

UNIT 2

Chapter 10   Investigating a Need

Chapter 11   Practical Use of Software Tools to Produce a Working Solution

Chapter 12   Practical Use of File and Data Structure to Produce a Working Solution

Chapter 13   Present a Solution

Chapter 14   Evaluation

Introduction

Before undertaking this task you will have looked at a wide range of software applications and be able to manipulate and process data and other information effectively and efficiently. You will also need to present information in a format suitable for audience and purpose.

Audience and purpose

When we talk to someone face-to-face, we usually know who we are talking to and why we are talking to them. We have a purpose for the conversation. We automatically adjust the language we use to be sure we are communicating our message.

When you are presenting data, information or your ideas to different audiences, you must first think about who will be reading what you write and why you are communicating with them. To be sure that you communicate clearly, you need to adjust your message and how you present your data and what information you will include.

There are three main categories of audience the 'lay' audience, the 'managerial' audience and the 'experts'.

The 'lay' audience has no special or expert knowledge. They usually need background information; they expect more definition and description; and they usually want attractive graphics and visuals.

The 'managerial' audience will have more knowledge than the lay audience and they need knowledge so they can make a decisions. Any background information, facts, statistics needed to make a decision should be highlighted.

The 'experts' may be the most demanding audience in terms of knowledge, presentation and graphics or visuals. Experts are often 'theorists' or 'practitioners'. For the 'expert' audience, document formats are often elaborate and technical, style and vocabulary will be specialised or technical. Source citations should be reliable and up-to-date, and documentation is accurate. The examiners who will look at your work are an expert audience.

When presenting to your audience you will need to consider:

- What kinds of data or information does the audience need? (purpose and audience).
- What are they going to do with it? (purpose).
- Are they going to use it for further actions? (purpose).
- Are they going to use it to make a decision? (purpose).

Different audiences require different ways of focusing. Let's look at a presentation given about the same topic, a new football stadium to two different audiences:

Audience 1: City council

This audience will want to know why another football stadium is necessary. They will need to know about the football team. They should also be informed of how much money is made from spectators coming to view the games, as well as of any funding raised by existing football teams to help support a new stadium. Every detail they read should support why city council should consider supporting the new stadium.

Audience 2: Football players

This audience will already know why the stadium is needed. Ultimately, they will want to know what is required of them to get a new stadium. How much time will they need to donate to fundraising activities and city council meetings? How will practice hours be increased? Every detail they read should inform them of the benefits a new stadium would provide.

10 Investigating a Need

What you will learn in this chapter
- Assessing user needs
- Researching information from a variety of sources
- How to analyse and present information
- Developing a solution to an ICT problem

ACTIVITY 1

How do you think businesses functioned before the arrival of ICT?

Introduction

The world of business never runs entirely smoothly: it is fast changing and demanding and finding solutions to ICT problems can help a company to maintain a competitive edge. You will almost certainly at some point have to assess user needs – what staff in the business need to carry out tasks

CASE STUDY

eSpares

eSpares is the UK's number one leading spare parts retailer, selling spares, accessories and consumables for all the electrical appliances for home and garden. It offers a catalogue of 500,000 different spare parts, and has over six million unique users every year. If the online shop goes down, business stops, so it's vital to maintain business continuity.

Initially, the website ran on an off-the-shelf e-commerce solution but as the business developed, the system outgrew the structure. In 2005, the company decided that the technical challenge of maintaining business continuity would be best met by signing up a specialist company, and after much research, they chose TelecityGroup.

Jason Duffet, systems administrator for eSpares, explains why: 'We made the decision to move to a hosted environment for extra resilience. It also offloads concerns about power supplies and network connectivity, and the cost benefit of moving to TelecityGroup has been huge.'

TelecityGroup now hosts all critical systems including its website, content management system, stock control system and warehouse system.

'I am now free to work on new projects to enhance the IT infrastructure and improve the web site and customer experience,' says Duffett. 'As our business grows and we make improvements to the site, we need to grow systems, and TelecityGroup gives us scalability.'

Without TelecityGroup's ICT solution, eSpares would never have been able to meet the increasing demands of its customers and maintain its position as leading spare parts retailer.

(http://www.computing.co.uk/computing/features/2231727/hosted-environment-ensures-4370973)

or produce goods – by investigating exactly what is required to solve a particular ICT based problem, and then provide a detailed, viable solution. If you make a careful list of the requirements at this stage it will be easy to plan and evaluate your ICT solution at the end.

Assessing user needs

When planning an ICT solution for an organisation, it is important to collect as much information as possible so that you can build up a detailed picture of the current issues facing the people who will eventually use the solution. Accurately assessing the needs of the organisation and the people within it is the **first stage** in developing a solution so it must be carried out thoroughly. You will need to identify exactly what you and they want to achieve and also think carefully about the constraints you are working under.

Things you may also need to consider:

Who to talk to 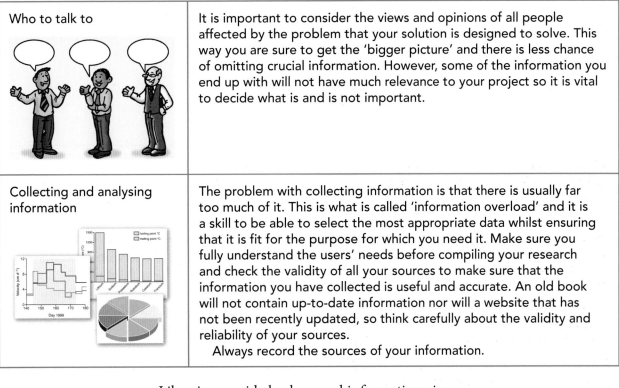	It is important to consider the views and opinions of all people affected by the problem that your solution is designed to solve. This way you are sure to get the 'bigger picture' and there is less chance of omitting crucial information. However, some of the information you end up with will not have much relevance to your project so it is vital to decide what is and is not important.
Collecting and analysing information	The problem with collecting information is that there is usually far too much of it. This is what is called 'information overload' and it is a skill to be able to select the most appropriate data whilst ensuring that it is fit for the purpose for which you need it. Make sure you fully understand the users' needs before compiling your research and check the validity of all your sources to make sure that the information you have collected is useful and accurate. An old book will not contain up-to-date information nor will a website that has not been recently updated, so think carefully about the validity and reliability of your sources. Always record the sources of your information.

Libraries provide background information via:

- textbooks
- encyclopaedias
- bibliographical sources listed at the end of an article
- magazines
- newspapers.

The internet provides background information via:

- keyword specific internet research
- databases
- online versions of magazines and newspapers
- published documents and articles.

Information can be collected in a number of ways using both **primary** and **secondary** sources.

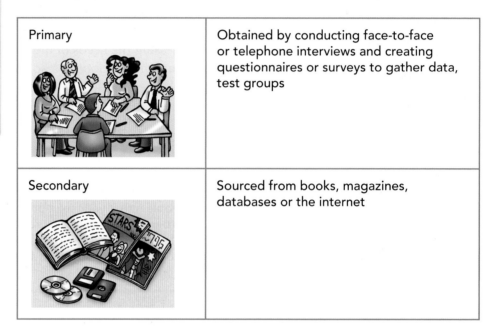

Primary	Obtained by conducting face-to-face or telephone interviews and creating questionnaires or surveys to gather data, test groups
Secondary	Sourced from books, magazines, databases or the internet

Always remember when using information from other sources to consider copyright issues. Always seek permission to use images or work that is protected.

Once collected, you need to consider the best method for analysing the information and presenting it in a manner that is easily understood.

At this stage you need to be sure that you have fully understood your user's needs. You will begin this process by agreeing a **design brief**. Once you have agreed the design brief you will be ready to **analyse** your user's needs in detail and produce the **design specification** for your ICT system.

Large chunks of text-based information can be broken down. Try using mindmapping software or spider diagrams to note down all the issues. This will help you to consider all of the factors and allow you to see things logically as an overview.

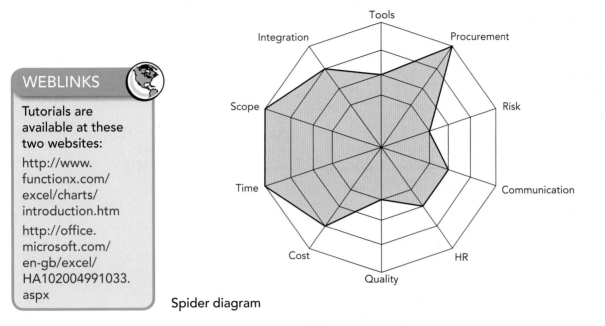

Spider diagram

Which model in which application?

Word-processor software, e.g. Word	Tables Diagrams Pictures Imported graph Spreadsheets
Spreadsheet software, e.g. Excel	Graphs Pie charts Spreadsheets Pictures

Presentation software, e.g. PowerPoint 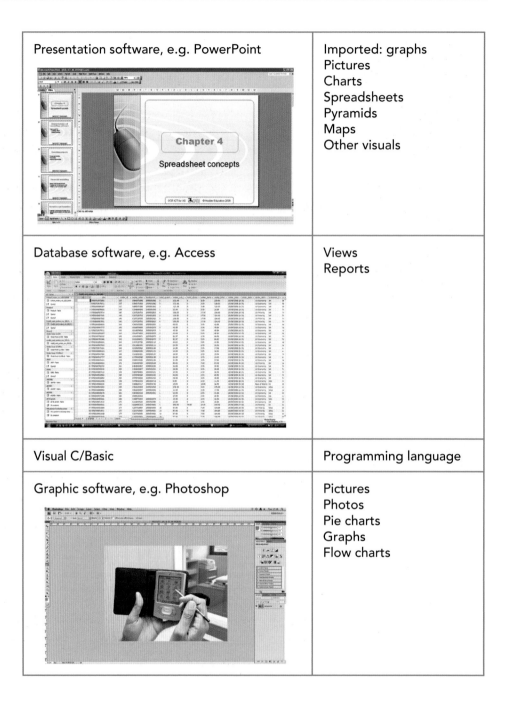	Imported: graphs Pictures Charts Spreadsheets Pyramids Maps Other visuals
Database software, e.g. Access	Views Reports
Visual C/Basic	Programming language
Graphic software, e.g. Photoshop	Pictures Photos Pie charts Graphs Flow charts

Documenting sources of information

You need to record all of your sources in a chronological order by keeping a bibliography or webliography. Using a table format helps to structure information, but you need to be as accurate as possible so that it is clear where you obtained your information from.

When sourcing information from websites you should record the URLs and date accessed. A book should have details of the title, author and publisher, along with the page numbers containing the information sourced.

Keeping information safe

Any information that you collect needs to be organised and stored safely so that you can easily revisit it when needed. Therefore, good file management is essential and you need to make sure that regular backups are undertaken. Always keep secure information safe by preventing unauthorised access. Using techniques such as password protection and encryption for files/folders on your computer and/or your storage media (e.g. memory stick) will prevent the average IT user from accessing important files.

KEY WORDS

Bibliography, e.g. **Drucker, P. (1992).** *Managing for the future: The 1990s and beyond.* New York: Penguin.

Webliography, e.g. Bradley, Ben. 'Time for a portal', Darwin Magazine, March 20004, available at: http://www.darwinmag.com/read/030104/portal.html

ACTIVITY 2

Go to the internet and do a search on file management. Find a website with some simple advice and write a short paragraph outlining the ways the article suggests you can keep files safe. At the end, don't forget to credit the article with the name of the author, etc., under the title 'References'.

WEBLINKS

Microsoft Word http://en.wikipedia.org/wiki/MS_word
Spreadsheets http://en.wikipedia.org/wiki/Spreadsheets
Picture software http://picasa.google.com/

Developing a solution

Once you have gathered all of your research about the needs of an organisation and the people working for it, the next step is to develop a solution. How you do this will determine how successful the outcome is in meeting their needs. If you rush in without considering all of the factors your solution may have gaps and will not work.

Try not to think of the most obvious solution, use your imagination and creativity to consider other approaches. Again, mindmapping software can help here or simply making a list of all your ideas. Make sure you are logical in your thinking by adapting a structured step-by-step approach. This will help you to see things much more clearly. Above all, think critically about your proposed solutions.

Are there any obvious drawbacks, potential barriers or difficult issues to resolve?

Drawbacks	Cost, budget, time, training, expertise, hardware available, software available, technical problems, sufficient manpower, copyright/licensing issues
Difficult issues	Potential causes of disagreements, personality clashes, lack of structure, poor communication, negative attitudes, lack of defined goal/agenda
Potential barriers	What existing systems contribute to the problem? Do existing systems provide an obstacle to effectiveness? What current systems need help?

Working with others

Sometimes it is much easier to work as part of a group to explore an issue. This way you will be able to share different ideas and opinions with people. First of all agree on what must be done, decide who will do what and set a time frame against the task. Make sure that all group members have a role that they are comfortable with, and that larger tasks are broken up into manageable chunks and shared out equally.

Matching people to the skills they have is important so make sure you allocate roles according to strengths. For instance, some people will be more adept at thinking about design whereas others might be better at project management – making sure everything is being done properly and on time.

Drawing up a plan will help you to work towards finding a practicable solution. This way everybody will know roles and responsibilities and this can be checked by holding regular team meetings to monitor progress.

Don't forget to set some ground rules for collaborative working. Always consider the opinions of others, even if you do not agree. Be constructive in your feedback to others and in return respond positively to feedback given. This will help you to improve and develop your solution much more effectively.

Spence's basic rules

Spence identifies seven rules for all collaboration[1]:

---

1 Spence, Muneera U. *'Graphic Design: Collaborative Processes = Understanding Self and Others.'* (lecture) Art 325: Collaborative Processes. Fairbanks Hall, Oregon State University, Corvallis, Oregon. 13 Apr. 2006

Look for common ground	Find shared values, consider shared personal experiences, pay attention to and give feedback, be yourself and expect the same of others, be willing to accept differences in perception and opinions
Learn about others	Consider their perspectives and needs, appeal to the highest motives, let others express themselves freely
Critique results, not people	Do not waste time on personal hostility, make other people feel good, avoid criticism and put downs
Give and get respect	Show respect for others' opinions, be considerate and friendly, put yourself in the other person's shoes, be responsive to emotions, speak with confidence but remain tactful
Proceed slowly	Present one idea at a time, check for understanding and acceptance of each idea before moving on to the next. Speak in an organised and logical sequence
Be explicit and clear	Share your ideas and feelings, pay attention to nonverbal communication, speak clearly and make eye contact, select words that have meaning for your listeners
Remember the five 'Cs' of communication	Clarity, completeness, conciseness, concreteness and correctness

Producing a design brief and specification

The next stage is to actually produce the design brief and specification itself:

- A design brief is a summary of your intentions. It is written by the client and designer. It outlines the aims and objectives of the project.
- A specification is a list of what has to be done to ensure the design brief meets the needs of the user. It lists exactly what you intend to achieve.

Good organisational skills are required here so that the information you have is logically presented. Start by identifying the current problem, outlining how you carried out your research and what you found and – finally – drafting your proposed solution.

You will have gathered plenty of information during the research stages so how you present this back is important. It has to be clear, structured and easy to follow. What method will you use? Perhaps you will decide upon a traditional format such as a formal report or a presentation? These are perfectly fine but have some constraints as well as benefits and you may want to think of other methods instead to make it more engaging.

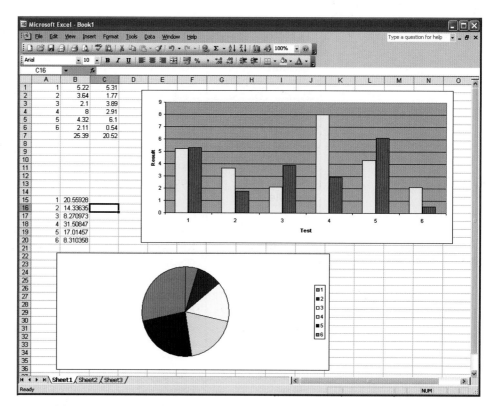

Spreadsheet in Excel with charts

Once you have presented your case and produced a suitable **system specification** there is still some work to be done. Once the specification is implemented – produced as an IT solution – it will be necessary to monitor the impact of changes to the specification that are made as the project progresses. Note what the positive and negative factors were and record all details of the changes. The following pages will help you to effectively use a range of software tools to produce a working solution.

ACTIVITY 3

Find out exactly what writing a design brief involves. Go to the internet and do a search on something like 'ICT design brief'. Pick a website that looks interesting and write down what are the basic elements that make up a design brief.

KEY WORDS

Design brief
Document outlining the problem, aims and desired results of a project written by the designer and business representative.

Specification
The process that will solve the problem outlined in the design brief.

System specification
A structured collection of information that embodies the requirements of the system.

11 Practical Use of Software Tools to Produce a Working Solution

What you will learn in this chapter
● Choosing the right software
● Good working practices

Introduction

Once the investigation process outlined in Chapter 10 has been completed, the next stage is to produce a fully working solution for a given task. For this you would need to use different tools within different software applications.

Choosing the right software package

Deciding upon the correct application for the given task is important. Information such as customer details is best stored and demonstrated using a **database**, whereas if you wanted to calculate projected profit or loss for a business, **spreadsheet software** would provide the best option. Using spreadsheets would allow you to use more complex formulas and advanced features, as well as showing numerical data in a pictorial format using charts and graphs generated from the data in the spreadsheet.

Most people will choose to use **presentation software** to convey a message or they might choose to create a **web page** as an alternative way to present information. Knowing exactly what applications are capable of and selecting the best application for a particular task will help you to provide a working solution to a given problem.

Spreadsheet software 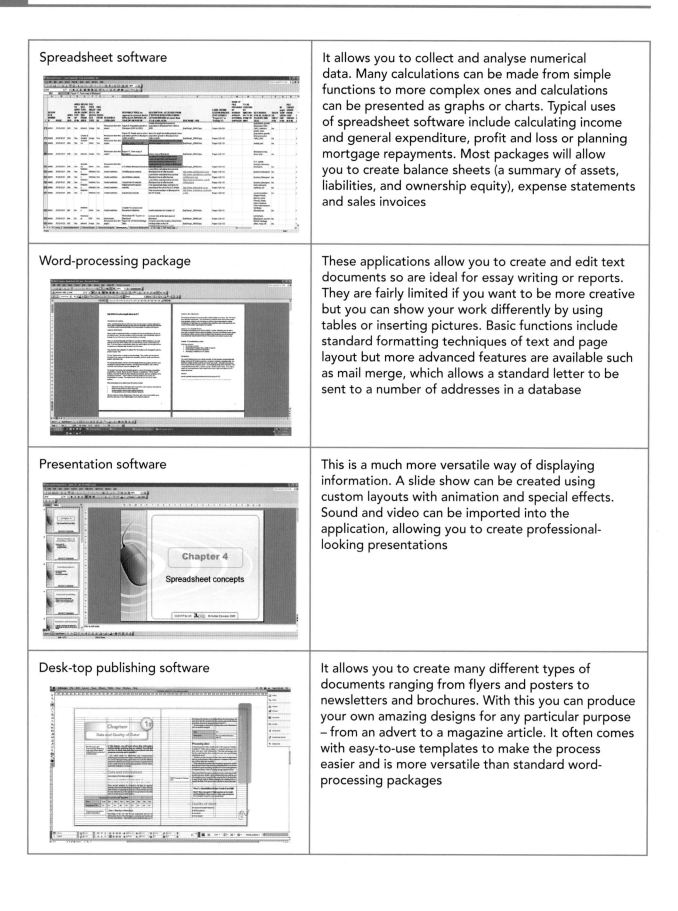	It allows you to collect and analyse numerical data. Many calculations can be made from simple functions to more complex ones and calculations can be presented as graphs or charts. Typical uses of spreadsheet software include calculating income and general expenditure, profit and loss or planning mortgage repayments. Most packages will allow you to create balance sheets (a summary of assets, liabilities, and ownership equity), expense statements and sales invoices
Word-processing package	These applications allow you to create and edit text documents so are ideal for essay writing or reports. They are fairly limited if you want to be more creative but you can show your work differently by using tables or inserting pictures. Basic functions include standard formatting techniques of text and page layout but more advanced features are available such as mail merge, which allows a standard letter to be sent to a number of addresses in a database
Presentation software	This is a much more versatile way of displaying information. A slide show can be created using custom layouts with animation and special effects. Sound and video can be imported into the application, allowing you to create professional-looking presentations
Desk-top publishing software	It allows you to create many different types of documents ranging from flyers and posters to newsletters and brochures. With this you can produce your own amazing designs for any particular purpose – from an advert to a magazine article. It often comes with easy-to-use templates to make the process easier and is more versatile than standard word-processing packages

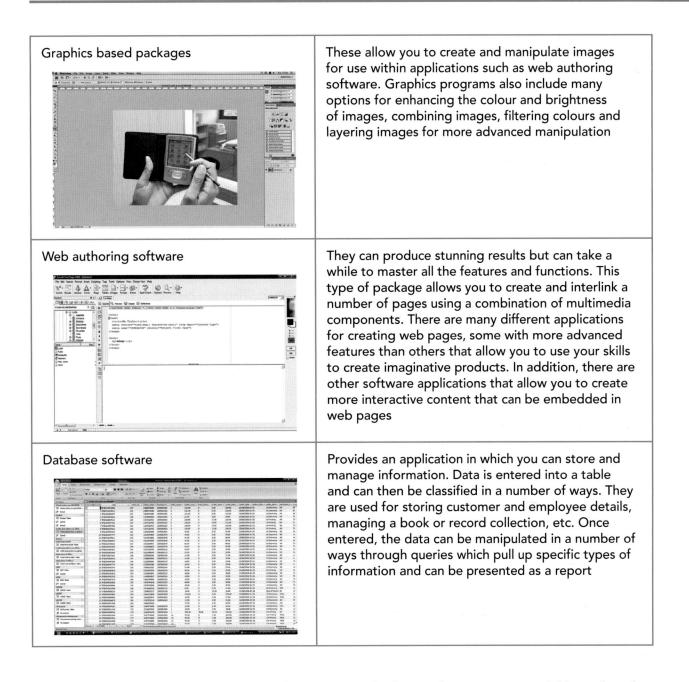

Graphics based packages	These allow you to create and manipulate images for use within applications such as web authoring software. Graphics programs also include many options for enhancing the colour and brightness of images, combining images, filtering colours and layering images for more advanced manipulation
Web authoring software	They can produce stunning results but can take a while to master all the features and functions. This type of package allows you to create and interlink a number of pages using a combination of multimedia components. There are many different applications for creating web pages, some with more advanced features than others that allow you to use your skills to create imaginative products. In addition, there are other software applications that allow you to create more interactive content that can be embedded in web pages
Database software	Provides an application in which you can store and manage information. Data is entered into a table and can then be classified in a number of ways. They are used for storing customer and employee details, managing a book or record collection, etc. Once entered, the data can be manipulated in a number of ways through queries which pull up specific types of information and can be presented as a report

Having a good awareness of what applications are available and understanding what they are best used for will allow you to plan which ones to use to provide your solution to an ICT-based problem effectively. Look at the different software packages on your school computer or use the internet to research for different applications making a note of their purpose and potential.

WEBLINKS

A list of free word-processing applications can be found here:

http://wordprocessing.about.com/od/choosingsoftware/tp/topwordalternatives.htm

Free spreadsheet software:

http://www.openoffice.org/

http://docs.google.com

http://projects.gnome.org/gnumeric/

Free presentation software:

http://prezi.com

http://www.openoffice.org/product/impress.html

http://docs.google.com

A list of free desktop publishing applications can be found here:

http://desktoppub.about.com/od/findsoftware1/tp/freedtpsoftware.htm

A list of free graphics software can be found here:

http://graphicssoft.about.com/od/freesoftware/Free_Graphics_Software.htm

A list of free HTML web page authoring tools can be found here:

http://webdesign.about.com/od/htmleditors/HTML_Editors_Web_Page_Authoring_Tools.htm

A list of free databases can be found here:

http://www.freedatabasesoftware.net/

http://www.openoffice.org/

http://docs.google.com

Within each application there are many features and functions that will allow you to carry out a variety of tasks using different tools and techniques. It can be quite daunting knowing exactly what each toolbar function does, but one of the best ways is to simply try it! All applications have a help facility which will allow you to search for the answer to a particular problem and the internet is full of useful tutorials. Of course, there is also your tutor who can demonstrate how to use a particular function, and as long as you save your work as you go along you can always undo what you've done.

Combining different software packages

There can be compatibility issues between different office suites. Suites are software bundles that include applications such as word-processing, presentation software, spreadsheets, etc. Compatibility issues are one of the main reasons why Microsoft Office has remained the most popular office suites despite stiff competition. However, now there are some office suites that can work perfectly well together such as Open Office and Google Documents, both of which are free to use.

ACTIVITY 2

There are many different types of applications. If you are interested in drawing, for example, Google 'free animation software' to obtain a list of what is available.

Applications within software packages can integrate quite well, allowing for more freedom and creativity. A chart or graph created in a spreadsheet package can be imported into a presentation package; data stored in a spreadsheet can be imported into a database, and animation can be used within web pages. With the right tools and software the options are endless. Using your initiative and being more adventurous will allow you to exploit the potential of new and more advanced ICT tools within applications. Don't be afraid to try more complex tools and techniques – as always, practice makes perfect.

Adopting safe, secure and responsible working practices

KEY WORDS

Office suite applications
Compatibility

RSI – Repetitive Strain Injury
Health & Safety

Data protection
Data backup

When using ICT, there is a common sense approach to making sure that you adopt safe, secure and responsible working practices. So where is the danger in using applications you may ask? First of all, think of your health and well being. Sitting at a computer for long periods can cause tiredness, headaches and lead to **RSI (Repetitive Strain Injury)**. Taking regular breaks is therefore essential, and always follow **Health and Safety** policies.

Your work is important too so protect it! Keep your computer secure by using passwords and up-to-date security software. Files created can also be password protected to stop unauthorised alteration of your work and don't forget to back up your work regularly. The loss of data can sometimes be catastrophic and more costly than replacing an entire computer system!

CASE STUDY

1 A young doctor, Dr M., was awarded a one-year fellowship to an American hospital to study and work. He was invited to go to a children's hospital in Dallas, Texas, famous for the quality of its treatment. There, he saw many more patients than in his hospital at home. He took hundreds of photos of rare conditions and built up a valuable library on his personal computer.

  When he got back home, his computer crashed and he lost his entire library of photos because he hadn't backed up his files. His entire year's worth of photographic work, and source material for future publications was lost and there was no way for him to either restore the files or go back and start again.

2 Another example is a prominent Chicago-based advertising firm that nearly lost everything due to one mistake. Shortly after settling into their new office space, administrators and staff left for the night while maintenance stayed behind. After cleaning, a member of the maintenance crew turned off a hallway switch, unaware that it also turned off every computer in the control room. While the company was able to save a bit of data, most of the machines were only configured to back up only once per week. This caused them to lose a week's worth of creative planning. (http://www.spamlaws.com/data-disaster.html)

ALWAYS BACK UP YOUR DATA!

CASE STUDY CONT'D

3 Thousands of businesses lose millions of dollars worth of data to disasters like fires, power outages, theft, equipment failure, and even a simple operator mistake. Studies show that nearly half the companies that lose their data in a disaster never reopen. 90 per cent of these data losses occur because of power failures, leaks, loose cables, user mistakes and other hardware, software, and human errors. (http://www.protect-data.com/information/index.html)

ACTIVITY 3

Find out how to back up your data here:
http://www.spamlaws.com/how-to-backup-data.html

Practical Use of File and Data Structure to Produce a Working Solution

What you will learn in this chapter
- Assessing data solutions
- How to manipulate data

Introduction

When using different applications it is important that you are aware of their features and functions. The best way to do this is to try things out. It's only by using software that you can really understand how to use it. It's even better if you develop a need, because then you'll have to find a solution.

Software can be rich in features. Word, for example, is incredibly powerful with many functions – you can even program automatic functions called macros – but do not use features just because you know how. Features are only effective if they are relevant and help to improve or illustrate better what you are doing. Try experimenting with the different features within toolbars in several applications to help build up your skills.

The more confident and competent you are at doing this, the easier you will find it to model data to help explore and develop ideas. Knowing the best application for manipulating and presenting your data is the first important stage to developing an ICT-based solution so think about this carefully.

ACTIVITY 1

If you are a collector, or have a library of books or films, or football programmes, create a database to manage your collection. Design a table so that you can enter the author and title of the book and whether you've read it; or design a table for movies with title, actors and a star rating.

Problems and solutions

ACTIVITY 2

Databases are used every day by businesses, the medical world, the government, industry the police, etc. How important is it to have accurate data in the databases? Important decisions are made based on information collected. What sort of important decisions are made:

- in the medical/pharmacological world
- by the police
- by the government
- in industry?

Problem	Solution
What would be the best way to manipulate a collection of data such as names, addresses, phone numbers and email addresses?	A database
Which application would be best for calculating profit and loss and producing charts and graphs?	A spreadsheet
How would you present a report?	With presentation software
What would you use to write up a report?	A word-processing software
You have to create a budget for a company	A spreadsheet
What software would you use to prepare a business plan?	Word-processor
What software would you use to write up a design specification?	Word-processor
What would you use to manage a library of books?	A database

Manipulating data

Before you can manipulate data, you have to check for accuracy. Looking at the information obtained from questionnaires, focus groups, mail surveys and so on, check that it is legible and that all the questions have been answered.

Once you have the data, you need to enter it into the relevant software. One method that can be used for checking the accuracy of data is called the **double entry procedure** where a special program is used to check the second set of data you enter against the first set. Alternatively, random checks can be made on specific entries, or the data can be validated by the software program which would allow you to identify typing errors or incorrectly answered questions. For example, you might have typed 572 instead of 57 for someone's age, or in a question giving options 1–5, the person responded with 8.

You should always keep a record of the original data so that if you ever needed to trace a result from your data, you could consult the original forms.

Once the data is entered accurately, you can then consider **formatting** techniques to ensure that it is processed appropriately and that it is fit for the target audience. Most applications provide automatic formatting so that with the click of a button, your work is transformed into a professional-looking piece of work.

When we talk to someone face-to-face, we usually know who we are talking to and why we are talking to them. We have a purpose for the conversation. We automatically adjust the language we use to be sure we are communicating our message.

When you are presenting data, information or your ideas to different audiences, you must first think about who will be reading what you write and why you are communicating with them. To be sure that you communicate clearly, you need to adjust your message and how you present your data and what information you will include.

Formatting toolbar in Word

You should be able to demonstrate to your tutor that you have a good knowledge and understanding of ICT tools such as methods to import and export data effectively. Use different programs to create and manipulate data and then try to export it into other applications. For example,

- data in a spreadsheet can be imported into a database
- charts created using spreadsheet software can be exported into word-processing programmes or presentation software.

To make sure that the data is accurately entered or imported, use validation rules to help to reduce errors.

Mail merge is a powerful function. It allows a document that has to be sent to many people to be created using a word-processing package. The text is usually fixed but there are fields for the addressees which are inserted automatically by the software. Each letter printed off will have a different name and address. Publicity letters can be personalised in this way, with the name of the recipient inserted into a 'Dear [recipient]' field.

Multiple documents can be created by using data from a spreadsheet or database. As it runs, a document is created for each record leaving the text the same but replacing the data variables, i.e. the address details in the template with the new data in the matching columns of the spreadsheet or database. Try creating a letterhead template and use a suitable data source to carry out a mail merge using fixed text but different addresses. You will be amazed how quick and simple this is.

Numerical data can be imported into a spreadsheet to produce charts or graphs that give a pictorial representation.

Try to choose the best chart for the information.

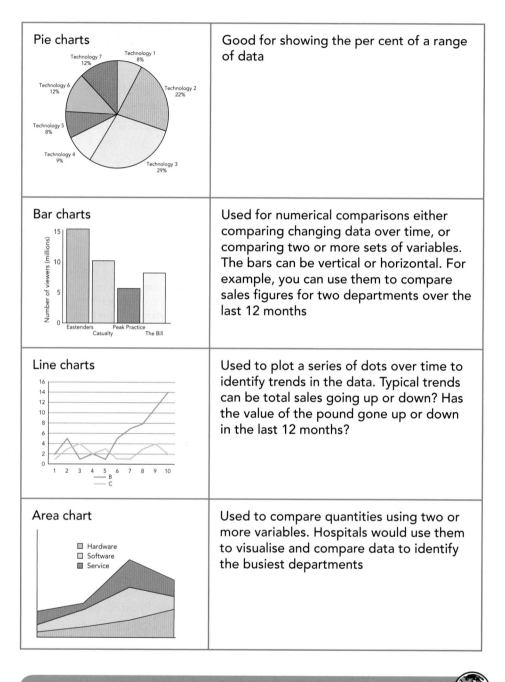

Pie charts	Good for showing the per cent of a range of data
Bar charts	Used for numerical comparisons either comparing changing data over time, or comparing two or more sets of variables. The bars can be vertical or horizontal. For example, you can use them to compare sales figures for two departments over the last 12 months
Line charts	Used to plot a series of dots over time to identify trends in the data. Typical trends can be total sales going up or down? Has the value of the pound gone up or down in the last 12 months?
Area chart	Used to compare quantities using two or more variables. Hospitals would use them to visualise and compare data to identify the busiest departments

WEBLINKS

Information on data preparation can be found here:
http://www.socialresearchmethods.net/kb/statprep.php

A good tutorial on how to do a mail merge can be found here:
http://office.microsoft.com/en-us/word/ch060832701033.aspx

To use data from a database as part of a mail merge, see here:
http://office.microsoft.com/en-us/word/HP051901661033.aspx?pid=CH063560211033

Examples of bad science and data manipulation here:
http://www.badscience.net/

KEY WORDS

Formatting
Changing the visual appearance of the elements on a page in a document.

Double entry procedure
Data entered twice is checked automatically for accuracy.

Mail merge
A form letter is linked to a database of varying information for mass distribution.

Importing data
Information is brought from one software into another, e.g. names and addresses from a database into a word processor.

Exporting data
Information is sent from one software to another, e.g. information from a spreadsheet is exported into a database.

Template
A form letter used as a base for a mail merge.

ACTIVITY 3

Create a table to hold the names and addresses of your friends and family. Imagine you're going to have a party and you want to invite everyone to the celebration. Create an invitation in a word-processor then insert the data from the table you have created to produce a set of personalised invitations.

13 Present a Solution

What you will learn in this chapter
- Communicating data and information
- How to prepare an argument
- How to make a presentation
- How to write a report

ACTIVITY 1
Find out from people around you what they think makes a good presentation. You can ask adults you know, or ask a question on your Facebook or other social-networking site, or send it out as a Twitter tweet. Collate the information into a mini report and create a short presentation.

Introduction

Once a solution has been realised the next stage is to present it back to the client in a format that shows an awareness of the purpose for which it was created and the audience that is going to use it. In most cases you will probably be required to produce a report as well as a presentation. A report can be much more detailed whereas a presentation will focus on the main or major points of your solution.

Communicating data and information

The most important thing to remember when communicating data and information is who you are presenting it to – know your target audience. Make sure that your presentation is suitable for the people it is meant to inform.

Make sure that your presentation is suitable for the people it is meant to inform.

Language	Is the language used set at the correct level?
Structure	Is it formally structured?
Technical terms	Does it have appropriate use of technical terms?
Font	It should be consistent throughout. You can use a different font for headings, but be consistent
Photographs, charts	Use photographs and charts rather than animated GIFs or cartoon type images which would be too flippant if you're trying to make a serious impression

The whole point of your presentation is to persuade the client to implement your solution so you need to show that you know exactly what you are talking about, that your ideas are workable and achievable. The presentation needs to show that you are professional, have prepared well and are persuasive in your argument.

Prepare the argument

1 Identify the problem
2 Strengths of the situation – what is right
3 Needs – what's necessary
4 Explaining the solution
    (a) how it solves the problem
    (b) how it meets the needs
5 Added benefits or advantages to the solution
6 Conclusion

The best presentations are often the simpler ones. Plain background colours should be consistently used throughout. Chopping and changing themes will irritate your target audience and they may lose interest. Make sure that the font colour can be seen against the background colour. Slides should have just enough information and it needs to be relevant to what needs to be said.

How to make a presentation

Do's	Don'ts
Use a presentation software	Don't overload the audience with lots of slides
Stick to your allotted time	Don't overload the slides with too much written information
Present the right information to the right audience	Don't give a presentation unprepared or unrehearsed
Use three sections: Start with the big picture, continue with appropriate detail, conclude with a summary of the key themes	Don't confuse your audience with irrelevant information
Use lists of three – people remember easily in groups of three	Don't go on for so long you leave no time for questions
Use the software essentially for relevant visual aids (graphics)	
Keep the number of slides to a minimum – the audience has come to listen to the speaker, not admire the presentation software	
Less is more	

How to write a report

Alternatively, you may choose to present your information in the form of a report. Again, simplicity is the key although you need to consider how it is structured and decide upon the best way to present your information.

Use a 'sans serif' font such as Arial as it is generally easier to read and consider using tables, charts and images to enhance the report. Provide a structure so it makes it clear for the audience. An introduction outlining the issues and what you hope to achieve helps set the scene. Follow by discussing your research methods and sources of information as your recommendations will be based upon this. You should then offer your recommendations but you must be able to justify them as this is the crucial part of presenting your solution.

The important thing to consider is that the audience needs to be engaged in order for them to consider the proposal seriously. Be professional, be convincing and there is more chance that your proposal will be considered!

Writing good reports[2]

1 Know your audience reader – what they know, what they don't know.

2 A report should have a beginning, middle and end – introduction, development, conclusion:

   (a) **Introduction** – a summary outlining the report's scope, purpose, and a recommendation on how the results of the report should be applied.

   (b) **Development** – present the key issues and use them as subheadings to help maintain a logical structure to the report. In each subheading, identify causes and consequences of the problem, explore solutions and cover implications such as cost. You can help your readers reach the same decision as you in solving a problem if you present the options logically.

   (c) **Conclusion** – summarise the points made, ensure you have left no loose threads without comment, state your solution to the problem and what needs to be done once the decision has been taken.

Include an executive summary that is no more than a few paragraphs long, and identifies the report's content and outcome. It goes at the beginning, but write it after you've written the report when everything is clear and presented logically.

What to avoid

- Writing long reports full of too much detail. Include only information essential to understanding the logic and purpose of the report, plus relevant background.

- Writing a subjective report full of unsubstantiated statements and emotional outbursts.

> **ACTIVITY 2**
>
> Now you know how a good report should look, rewrite the mini report that you prepared at the beginning of this chapter using the techniques you learned above. Compare what you found out with the suggestions in this chapter.

---

2 from http://www.bnet.com/2410-13074_23-59954.html

Evaluation

What you will learn in this chapter

- How to think critically
- How to evaluate your contribution to a solution
- How to evaluate the contribution of others
- How to improve
- How to test

Introduction

When evaluating the outcome of an ICT-based solution there is a tendency to describe what was done rather than commenting on overall effectiveness. You should consider:

- what worked well
- what did not work well
- what the problems were and what was done to overcome them.

It is also important to think about how your ideas developed and what has been learned. Look at strengths and weaknesses, how you responded to feedback from others and what areas for improvement have been identified.

Developing critical thinking skills

Developing good critical thinking skills is important because it will help you make better decisions. Why do you think this? Why do you believe that? If you don't know why you think in a certain way, it's because you have not developed a critical capacity. Thinking critically means challenging and analysing our own motivations, thought processes and conclusions.

A basic definition of critical thinking skills is:

'Reasonable and reflective thinking focused on deciding what to believe and/or how to act.'[3]

You can cultivate critical thinking skills by acquiring knowledge so you know if people are talking accurately or not, and by asking yourself some questions as a way of practising critical thinking skills.

---

3 http://ezinearticles.com/?How-To-Develop-Your-Critical-Thinking-Skills&id=1004309

Ask for evidence	Where did you read that? Did they do a test on that? Is there some basis for the claim or belief?
What are the sources?	Consider the sources of information and evidence. Does that person remember facts correctly? Is the source they are referring to reliable?
What's the motivation?	Why have these facts been reported? What bias is likely? What facts are being ignored or passed over?

Evaluating your and others' contribution

Once the solution has been realised and completed it is good to look back and consider how well you contributed, particularly if it was a team effort. You should also comment on the team performance overall, the effectiveness of the team, was there a good mix of personalities and how well did individuals contribute?

The evaluation should:

- be well organised
- be clearly structured, making it easy for the user to read
- present information logically and avoid repetition
- have specialist terms that are correctly and appropriately explained
- give arguments that are backed up with good, clear evidence or sound reasoning.

Start off by saying whether you worked as part of a group or on your own. Justify your choice of working alone or with others. What were the advantages/disadvantages to this? Explain what the problem was and what you set out to achieve. What were the research methods used? They should be a mix of primary and secondary and from a variety of different sources, i.e. paper-based, electronic. How effective was your research? Did it give you the answers you were looking for? How reliable was the data collected? How well did you complete the task? How did you present your solution?

- Other considerations checklist:

Did you meet all of the objectives and on time?	
What went well? Why was this?	
What did not go well? Why was this? What were the reasons?	
How did you manage your time?	

Did you keep to deadlines and targets?	
How well did you work during the task?	
If in a group, how well did the group work together?	
How have you benefited from working on the task?	
What have you learned? What skills have you developed?	
Don't forget you should have gathered feedback from test users to help you evaluate your finished solution and identify ways in which it could be improved.	
What did others think?	
Did you make good use of feedback?	
How did this affect your ICT based solution?	
Were changes made based on feedback?	
Did you choose the right people as your test users and reviewers?	
Did you provide feedback to others and how was this given?	

Evaluating how well the development went

In the planning stage, once you had researched your user's needs you came up with a plan of how you would organise your work. It's a good idea to include this in your evaluation with notes about what went well in each session and any problems you encountered. The notes should briefly explain how you overcame the problems.

Evaluating your system

You spent a lot of time developing a detailed **design specification** when you were planning your project. Now is the time to review how well your system matches the specification. One way to do this is to use the different requirements in your design specification as headings in a brief report. Under each heading explain what you included in your system to meet this need and whether or not it was successful.

How does your system measure up to the identified success criteria?

Another useful item to include in a detailed evaluation is a table showing how well the system meets the success criteria – you will need to suggest improvements in any areas where they might be needed. It can be a little worrying to notice the need for improvements at this stage but in reality there is always something that can be done to make a system even better, however expert the developer!

Identifying strengths and weaknesses

Whilst developing a solution for an ICT-based problem it is important to identify areas to improve. This may be something you have recognised yourself or has been pointed out by a reviewer. It would be a good idea to create a table listing the areas for development whilst recommending suitable changes. A column justifying why the changes are needed and how they benefit the project would enable you to tackle future problems with more confidence.

Testing your solution

It makes good sense to try out your solutions on test users. This will allow you to review what you have done and make suitable modifications. Creating a test log to check that your solution works as intended would be a good idea. This provides the opportunity to review your work and make suitable amendments. Handing over a solution without proper testing would not only be unprofessional but also potentially embarrassing.

Conclusion

Finish by giving an outline of how well the solution met its objectives overall and examine what the factors were that contributed to this? What suggestions for improvement can you make? What could you have done differently? Was the client happy with the solution that you produced?

> ### ACTIVITY 2
> Draw up a document that provides you with a checklist of everything you consider important when making an evaluation. Make a table with a column you can tick when you've finished the item. It'll help you remember everything you need to check.

ICT in Context

Chapter 15   ICT Innovation in Five Businesses: Introduction

Chapter 16   Art Gallery: IndepArt

Chapter 17   A Fashion Retailer: Ote KoKotur

Chapter 18   A Theatre: Pea Hints on Halfsbery Avenue

Chapter 19   A Dentist: Dr Jay Maloden

Chapter 20   A Manufacturing Company: Hedsup

UNIT 3

15 ICT Innovation in Five Businesses: Introduction

What you will learn in this chapter

- How different businesses use the internet
- How different businesses use software
- Some of the specialist software available for specific businesses
- IT innovation in action

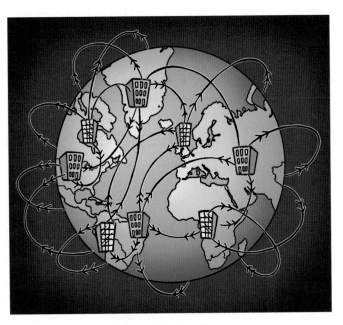

How the internet links and helps businesses

Just as you may find it difficult to imagine your world without information and communication technology, today's businesses simply couldn't function without it. The business world has become both complex and streamlined, and it's only by using computers that companies can maximise their profits. In this section you'll be learning how different companies use specific technologies. There is no one-fix solution for all because the business world is so diverse. However, tools such as the internet are used by all companies enabling them to communicate and collaborate despite their differences.

For the examined component you will need to know about these new technologies. Although the technologies are explained in relation to a specific company, any of the companies listed could be using the innovation described. You will need to read all of the sections to understand the range of emerging technologies required for the examination.

ACTIVITY 1

Name three companies as different from each other as possible. How would you imagine they use ICT? Write two uses for each company.

ACTIVITY 2

Name three pieces of specialist equipment used by businesses. What does the specialist equipment do?

Art Gallery: IndepArt

Introduction

Art gallery

IndepArt is a gallery devoted to finding new artists and promoting their work in special themed exhibitions. Exhibitions take place in the gallery and in selected locations offering maximum visual impact. The gallery owner is called Inis Deppard who is a dynamic and creative force for the cause of promoting new artists. She uses every means at her disposal to bring as wide an audience as possible to her gallery and the work it does. She gives talks at local schools and encourages the artists who exhibit with her to give workshops within the community. Every year they hold a charity event, the proceeds of which go to community projects helping disadvantaged children.

Inis and her team make as much use of information technology as possible to manage the gallery and promote the artists.

IT innovation

Websites

Nearly all companies these days have a website. Websites are the easily accessible face of companies. With a website, people anywhere in the world with access to the internet can find a company. This represents enormous business potential, but to be really effective, the website needs to be attractive, dynamic, easily navigable and well-designed.

Websites have:

- a domain name
- an IP address which, when associated with a geographical location, identifies their 'geolocation'
- and pages that are written in text with HTML (Hypertext Mark-Up Language) formatting.

Web 2.0

IndepArt uses a range of Web 2.0 technologies. Like many important concepts, Web 2.0 doesn't have a hard boundary. It was designed to improve the interactive aspect of the web.

Web 1.0		Web 2.0
Netscape	→	Google Chrome
DoubleClick	→	Google AdSense
Machine based software	→	Online software
Kodak Gallery (Ofoto)	→	Flickr
distributed computing	→	BitTorrent
mp3.com	→	Napster
Britannica Online	→	Wikipedia
personal websites	→	Blogging
domain name speculation	→	Search engine optimisation
page views	→	Cost per click
publishing	→	Participation
content management systems	→	Wikis
directories	→	Tagging

The World Wide Web was originally invented in Europe by a British researcher, Tim Berners-Lee at the CERN laboratory in Switzerland. He invented the HTML protocol which converted documents created on a word-processor into a file viewable on the internet, plus the notion of the hyperlink which linked a word on the document to another document on the web. He said that 'the original idea of the web was that it should be a collaborative space where you can communicate through sharing information'.[4]

To understand the differences between the Web and Web 2.0 you only have to look at the internet. Originally the internet was seen as a platform with a desktop application. You accessed it, just like the other software you had on your computer. The user was able to view the data or pages they wanted but there was no interaction. All that a user could do was to contact the author by using the contact form or write his opinion on the guest book maintained in that website. If the user found the page useful then they could bookmark it in their web browser to return to later. The bookmarks stayed within the users' software.

---

4 http://www.catalogs.com/info/gadgets/who-invented-HTML.html

WEBLINKS

Discover some websites considered among the world's best[5]:

http://www.keo.org/

to send a message 'back to the future'.

http://www.questacon.edu.au/

a superb educational resource.

http://www.penguinclassics.com/

the world's largest online resource dedicated to classic literature, 1600 titles, essays and education resources.

Web 2.0 is different as it allows the users to interact with the webpage in the following ways:

1 Wikis which allow users to edit the content on a page.

2 Weblogs popularly known as Blogs. The user is able to write a comment in a form associated with a blog post and the comments get displayed in the same page.

3 RSS which when expanded is Really Simple Syndication. The users can view this in a RSS reader and can choose to visit only the page or topic in which they are interested.

4 Podcasts which allow media files like audio, video, etc. to be displayed across the internet using the above mentioned RSS.

5 Web services which allow computer systems to collaborate by calling services with web protocols (http, xml, etc.) which are platform independent (before then, it was possible to call services on a remote computer but the caller had to have the same processor and operating system as the callee; this is because these exchange protocols were binary whereas web exchange protocols are text-based and thus platform independent).

6 Social bookmarking which is an advanced form of bookmarking and allows users to bookmark sites that will be available online and which a user can retrieve irrespective of the computer they use.

7 Social software are websites that allow users who are logged into their website to interact with one another by using instant messages that were previously sent using instant messaging software outside the web browser.

KEY WORDS

Website

A collection of related web pages.

Domain name

Identifies the name of the website.

IP address

Identifies the network and geolocation of the computer. 'A name indicates what we seek. An address indicates where it is. A route indicates how to get there.'

HTML

The language of formatting web pages.

Web 2.0

A recent development in the use of the internet, where users exchange and share information, for example, Wikis.

WEBLINKS

You can read more about websites at:

http://en.wikipedia.org/wiki/Website

Find out more about Web 2.0

http://en.wikipedia.org/wiki/Web_2.0

---

5 According to http://www.worldbest.com/gold.htm

KEY WORDS

Social networking
On the internet, a website where members interact with friends, post photos, communicate via email or instant messaging.

Profile
Summary of the social networking member – personality, likes, location, friends.

Network
A member's list of friends makes up his/her network.

Company pages
Pages used by professional companies to expand their client base through networking and develop customer loyalty.

ACTIVITY 1

Look up the following questions on Google:

- what is HTML?
- what is Web 2.0?
- what is a website?

Link your answers to produce a short history of Web 2.0.

Social networking

Facebook

Facebook is a social networking website. Individuals can post a profile then add friends and communicate with them via messages. Networks are created by organisations (schools, companies, charities, groups) on company pages which recruit members from individual profiles.

Twitter

Twitter is a social networking and micro-blogging service. People who have an account post 140 character max 'tweets' which their friends and followers can respond to by the internet, instant message or SMS.

ACTIVITY 2

Do you have a favourite website? Describe why you think it's a good website – is it well-designed? Is it easy to navigate? Does it fulfil its purpose? Is it creative?

Blogs

A blog is a contraction of weblog and is a kind of online diary. Often used to give updated information such as commentaries, descriptions and accounts, they are written with the most recent entry at the top. Blog software is widely available and easy to use.

You can make blogs more varied and entertaining by inserting photos, videos and podcasts into them. You can make them easier to find by RSS and indexing. The following table lists some of the different ways to vary the content of blogs and increase blog traffic (readers to a blog).

Flickr http://www.flickr.com/	Flickr is an online photo storage and photo management site. Members can upload their photos into their account and then share them with family and friends, or keep them private. If they want to be creative, they can print off photos into cards, posters, photo books, calendars and onto canvas
YouTube http://www.youtube.com/	YouTube is an online video sharing website where members can upload their home movies and share them with the world
Podcasts	Podcasts are digital audio or video files. Certain radio programmes are converted into podcast format of MP3 so that they can be listened to either on the computer or downloaded on to an MP3 player at any time
RSS	RSS (Really Simple Syndication) is used to subscribe to the feed of a blog, website or other media content (such as music or video) and saves the trouble of having to visit favourite websites to see whether they have been updated. That information comes straight to a feed reader such as Google Reader which the user sets up with sources of interest
Technorati http://technorati.com/	Technorati is an internet search engine for indexing and searching blogs. Technorati sends out electronic automated 'spiders' to identify and categorise the material plus any incoming and outgoing links, and return that information to the Technorati database. It is then added to the information coming from millions of other blogs, cross-referenced, and made available to users searching for specific topics

ACTIVITY 3

Make a list of three things which interest you. Do a search on each one in Google. For example, if your interest is whitewater rafting, search 'whitewater rafting blog' and see how many hits you get. Then click on the ones which appeal to you. Write up this process in a short paragraph:

1 subjects of interest
2 number of hits
3 what are the interesting blogs for each subject?

The gallery and the internet

The internet is an important showcase for the gallery. Inis contracted out the design and development of the online gallery to a third party specialising in the needs of the art world. The **website** offers a comprehensive service to the artists who are exhibited at the gallery and other locations.

Each artist has a page with a display of paintings. The artist can add a biography and contact details, email address, links to other websites and a visitor's book for those who wish to leave a comment. Images of the paintings can be uploaded and protected with a highly sophisticated encryption. This stops them being copied from the screen and used elsewhere without permission. Each image is accompanied by its details – size, title, medium and a possible comment on its inspiration, plus its price and shipping weight. Paintings can be bought online via the e-commerce system and paid for by credit card or an online electronic payment intermediary service (PayPal).

The website also has a monthly newsletter on what's been happening at IndepArt, a section on tips and legal advice for artists, and information on administrative issues such as insurance, copyright, taxation and valuing.

IndepArt has a **Facebook** page where exhibitions are announced. It's used essentially to promote previews. Members are invited via email in a special 'events' announcement, and can indicate whether they intend to participate or not by clicking on a special button.

IndepArt's Facebook page has lots of members because all the artists join and they get their friends to join too. Other members include buyers and those who appreciate the work the gallery does for new talent both locally and elsewhere.

IndepArt's **blog** is regularly updated with information such as ideas on new artists, calls for new artists, stories on the day-to-day running of the gallery and preparations for exhibitions, news on outreach programmes within the community (e.g. schools), other art information and news on exhibitions by artists.

Inis does not have time to write the blog on a regular basis so one of her team – Tony – volunteered to do it, and is committed to updating it two to three times a week. He makes it as interesting as possible by embedding other sources within the blog, e.g. a slideshow of paintings through **Flickr**. This changes the image every couple of seconds from IndepArt's Flickr online photo album.

Another embedded source he uses is **YouTube** to display, for example, interviews with the artists. Material is also provided by the artists themselves who film themselves creating a work of art then speed it up to show how the work emerges. They also use it to give short lessons in drawing aimed especially at children – how to draw cartoon characters, how to draw monsters, how to draw facial expressions.

Tony also subscribes to **podcasts** on art-related subjects, and posts the

WEBLINKS

Tate Gallery podcasts
http://channel.tate.org.uk/podcasts

BBC podcasts
http://www.bbc.co.uk/podcasts/

Tate Modern Blog
http://modblog.tate.org.uk/

ArtActif
http://www.artactif.com/uk.php

Apple iPhone applications
http://www.apple.com/uk/iphone/apps-for-iphone/

most interesting ones on the blog. These are digital audio or video files, often of an interview, or analysis by an art critic of a new exhibition, art book, historical overview, etc. He subscribes to the podcasts via an RSS feed. Tony subscribes to the Tate Gallery podcasts and the Tate Modern blog. Whenever these sites post a new item, Tony knows about it by consulting his RSS reader which collects all his feeds into one place.

The IndepArt blog is claimed on **Technorati**. Whenever Tony writes a post, the blog software sends a 'ping' to Technorati to inform it of the new material.

Inis uses **Twitter** to develop a network of professionals who are not necessarily on Facebook. She finds it an excellent communication tool to find out about new ideas, get instant feedback on issues and for information gathering. IndepArt has a strong physical presence in the local community, but Inis extends its visibility much wider by using the internet and Twitter. Her Twitter profile is claimed as a blog on Technorati and as such, her tweets are available for consultation by any of its users.

Inis' website has its own domain name (www.indepart.co.uk) which also enables all the staff to have their own work-based **email**. Inis' email address, for example, is inis@indepart.co.uk. Having the gallery domain name email address instead of an email service-based one such as Gmail or Hotmail is an important element in promoting the gallery as a credible business. Spammers and scammers usually use free email service addresses so by using the gallery's domain name, Inis helps reassure recipients that her communications are authentic. Email is used essentially for everyday communication and sending out electronic invitations to previews thus saving on postage.

iPhone

The Apple iPhone is not just a simple telephone. There are 90,000 applications which can be downloaded ranging from games to music, keeping track of your money, the Great Outdoors, recipes, restaurants and many more.

One art-centred application is Artnear, and IndepArt is a member of this iPhone application which tells subscribers about art galleries, venues and artists around the world. Wherever they are, subscribers can discover not just the most nationally and internationally famous galleries but local venues which they might never have known about otherwise. Inis has already had several visitors who, by using the application, found IndepArt and bought paintings.

EXAM TYPE QUESTIONS

1 (a) Which of the following statements about websites are true and which are false?

	True	False
All websites have a domain name		
Not all websites have an IP address		
Hyperlinks identify a website's geolocation		
Web pages are written in text with HTML formatting		

(b) What is the main difference between Web1.0 and Web 2.0?

(c) Identify 3 features of Web2.0 and explain what they are used for.

2 Frantic Art is a gallery that has its own blog. The gallery owner wants to liven it up with embedded sources.

(a Identify 2 possible embedded sources, and explain how each one could liven up the blog.

(b) Describe how Frantic Art could make use of Facebook.

A Fashion Retailer: Ote KoKotur

Introduction

Ote KoKotur is a sizable, successful fashion retail outlet based in a large town near London. It is owned by Ote Kosamui, a second-generation immigrant from Thailand. His target customers are young professionals who have disposable income, live in the area and often work in London but who don't want to have to shop in London at the weekend. He attends the major fashion shows, has a network of contacts who inform him on upcoming trends and ideas. The clothes are made in factories all over the world including Thailand, China, Brazil and Bulgaria. He has plans to open more stores in other towns and if these are successful, maybe ultimately franchise the business. To this end he is currently developing the store's image with the help of his sister who is a marketing consultant. He relies on ICT[6] to operate efficiently and increase profitability.

ACTIVITY 1

Think of your three favourite clothes shops. What technology does each one use?

IT innovation

The retail trade is a demanding business and the most innovation in information communication technology can be seen in the software that's been developed to meet these demands.

Software

Line of Business (LOB)

LOB applications automate core business processes. LOB applications are essentially data driven and tie into databases and database management systems. The information stored there is then accessed and exploited to improve business systems. In the retail business, there are several key processes. These include:

Point of Sale (POS)	The POS is the cash register/till. The software manages all of the possible details of this process such as sales, returns, voids, quotes, work orders, layaways, shipping, tax collection, credit checking and receipt printing. Layaways are a payment plan in which a buyer reserves an article of merchandise by placing a deposit with the retailer until the balance is paid in full. The POS system uses optical scanners with the cash register connected to the online central computer and LOB application
Natural User Interface (NUI)	NUI technology is used on the screens attached to cash registers. The screens are touch-sensitive, activated by pressing and tapping the screen
Inventory management	Includes purchasing, receiving, billing, stocking and pricing. The application checks on stock levels and can order new items automatically via the internet
Customer engagement	Delivers purchase histories – what customers have bought and when; customer preferences, and contact information
Barcodes	Scanners read barcodes. When you scan the barcode its data is sent to the computer as if it had been typed on the keyboard. Barcodes come in many different forms these days, from lines to dots, colours to 2D matrix codes

ACTIVITY 2

Look at the keywords and write out what each abbreviation stands for.

How do you feel about the manipulation of your behaviour as a customer from the analysis by businesses of what you do and what you buy?

Retail demand forecasting 	Barcodes are also used in conjunction with **retail demand forecasting** software to improve retail performance (higher sales), and predict trends in customer behaviour and demand
Radio frequency identification (Digiprice) 	This is smart chip technology for handling real time inventory checking, dynamic labelling, antitheft processes and customer loyalty all on one platform. It streamlines these processes by concentrating them into one system. Time-consuming actions such as repricing before or after sales, for special offers or implementing price increases will be instant as the electronic tags can be programmed from the central computer and the changes made for the range of garments automatically over radio waves. RFID enables tracking the geolocation of items
Near Field Communication (NFC) 	It enables payment for goods by mobile phone using near field communication technology. Customers use their NFC-equipped phones to collect loyalty points, check their balance and receive rewards via text message. The data-processing centre, connected via broadband to the cash registers, automatically registers new purchases and then sends out text messages to customers with their points totals and any discount vouchers to which they are entitled. In the future, customers will also receive text messages whenever new collections arrive in the store and at the start of sales[7]

Ote Kokotur

Ote uses a sophisticated, integrated **Line of Business** application which is specifically designed for the retail trade. At the **Point of Sale** he has cash registers which use **Natural User Interface** technology and scanners.

Integrated into the software is **inventory management** as presented at the Point of Sale. The application checks on stock levels and can order new

7 http://www.nearfieldcommunicationsworld.com

Natural User Interface barcode scanner

RFID tag

items automatically via the internet. The internet enables key suppliers and clients to communicate via their browser with the company server's extranet site which is connected to the company database.

Through the **customer engagement** application Ote can analyse purchase histories and customer preferences, and collect contact information. The automation of these functions improves his bottom line by reducing costs such as labour, contracted services and inventory. Instead of contracting out specialist consulting tasks, the software does it all for him.

Scanners read the **barcodes** on labels which are attached to the clothes at the factory. Fixing labels on clothes is normally a time-consuming process so having it done at source is an important saving in labour. Ote uses the standard worldwide retail UPC system of vertical lines.

Barcodes are also used in conjunction with **retail demand forecasting software** to improve retail performance and predict trends in customer behaviour and demand. They enable Ote to monitor the effects of repositioning a given item within the store. This allows more profitable, fast-moving items to occupy the best space, and ensures that the right products are in the right place at the right time.

The position of goods is so important that Ote recently added more sophisticated software – an in-store system which analyses customer movements around the store in order to maximise exposure of high-value goods in key areas. It uses a camera which feeds data back to the software. The data is analysed and a picture of customer 'hotspots' is generated. Ote can then place clothes with the highest value in these hotspots knowing they will generate more sales than if they languished in an area with little footfall.

Ote keeps a small warehouse for stock and uses **electronic tags** to track items. This is done by radio frequency identification (**RFID**) which is also useful in inventory keeping and theft prevention. In case of theft, the tag sets off an alarm as it passes through the electronic panels by the front doors. This technology has been around for some time, but Ote is just about to invest in the latest Digiprice technology of a **Magic Mirror**. Whenever a customer displays an RFID-tagged piece of clothing in front of the Magic Mirror, they will instantly be greeted by displays featuring brand messaging, garment description, availability of colours and sizes, as well as other helpful fashion tips. If they are trying the garment on and it's the wrong size, they can call up a sales assistant over the WiFi device to bring one in the right size.

Ote is preparing for the near future when customers will be able to pay for goods by mobile phone using near field communication technology (**NFC**) in conjunction with Digiprice when real time inventory checking, dynamic labelling, anti-theft processes and customer loyalty will be handled all on one platform.

The LOB application integrates seamlessly with the spreadsheet accounting system which is used to analyse its data.

Outside the shop is a **store window 'touch' movement** identification system which projects an image of the catalogue onto the store window and allows customers to navigate around the catalogue from outside the shop. It works by analysing the movements of customers from outside enabling an interactive, highly original experience. Ote KoKotur is an innovator in hand gesture technology.

Gesture-based controls

Gesture recognition is one of the most exciting new **input** technologies. So what are gesture-based controls? Gesture-based controls is the name given to the way you can control a technology device by hand, arm or finger gestures, like waving your arms around in circles to make something happen on the screen. Thanks to the iPhone and the Wii they are now being used in everything from phones to televisions and game consoles. A variety of companies are developing new ways to interact with ICT systems.

Even in TV remote controls the range of keys and buttons are getting so complex that consumers need a less-intimidating way to navigate through all of the data, movies, stored TV shows, music and pictures.

To understand gesture-based controls you need to understand some of the technology that is being used. The main input devices to a gesture based control system are:

- touch screens and touch pads
- accelerometers
- cameras and location sensors.

Touch screens and pads

Touch screens have been around for many years but the Ote KoKotur system is very advanced because it is gesture-based. The growth in touch screen mobile phones and finger gesture pointing devices has been rapid. Multi-touch, a system where you can use more than one finger to indicate gesture control has opened up a whole new world. The iPhone multi-touch panel was designed to let you control everything using only your fingers. This multi-touch technology, being integrated into Windows 7, makes it very likely that we'll see more and more gesture-based appliances and computers in the future.

How does it work? A panel underneath the display's glass cover senses your touch using electrical fields. It then transmits that information to operating system software that interprets gestures and transforms them into commands.

iPhone multi-touch panel

Accelerometers

Wii remote

An accelerometer is an electromechanical device that will measure acceleration forces. These forces may be static, like the constant force of gravity pulling at your feet, or they could be dynamic – caused by moving or vibrating the accelerometer. The Wii remote revolutionised the use of accelerometers in ICT systems.

So how can accelerometers be used? By measuring the amount of static acceleration due to gravity, you can find out the angle the device is tilted at with respect to the earth. By sensing the amount of dynamic acceleration, you can analyse the way the device is moving. An accelerometer can help a system understand its surroundings better. Is it going uphill? Is it going to fall over? Is it travelling horizontally? Apple and other manufacturers are even using accelerometers in their laptops to protect hard drives from damage. If you accidentally drop the laptop, the accelerometer detects the sudden freefall, and orders the hard drive head into a safe parking spot.

Even advanced mobile phones such as the iPhone respond to motion using a built-in accelerometer. When you rotate them from portrait to landscape, the accelerometer detects the movement and changes the display accordingly.

iPhones have accelerometers

Cameras and location sensors

The Wii remote has two main sensors: the Pixart camera+point tracker (tracks the Sensor Bar), and an accelerometer.

An accelerometer cannot sense in which direction the remote is pointing. The Sensor Bar and the camera tell the system the orientation of the remote in relation to the screen.

But whilst cameras are one type of location sensor there are many others used in modern ICT systems. When you lift an iPhone to your ear, a proximity sensor immediately turns off the display to save power and prevent accidental dialling. The ambient light sensor in an iPhone automatically brightens the display when you're in sunlight or a bright room and dims it in darker places. This technology is also available in car dashboard computers.

Internet

The store has a **website**, but with just one shop, there is no immediate need for an e-commerce capability. Once the business expands and the brand is better known, Ote intends to add e-commerce to the website so that customers who can't physically get to a shop can still buy its clothes. As a small but growing company Ote KoKotur uses a wide range of cloud technology and hopes to expand by using off-site technology support.

Ote KoKotur also has a **Facebook** page to announce the arrival of new season's stock and invite fans to special discount evenings in convivial surroundings. These are private evenings, by invitation only through the Facebook invitations page, where customers are greeted with a drink and nibbles so they can relax and browse through the clothes comfortably. There is always a Christmas special with mince pies and mulled wine or spiced fruit juice that regular customers come to appreciate after a day's work.

Ote has his own **Twitter** account which is vital in such a quick-changing business. He has to be able to hear the latest news coming from his contacts in the fashion industry in real time. Rumours are rife in the fashion world, and being able to react quickly to sudden trends is important.

The factories are located in areas where wages are lower than in the UK, but Ote visits them all to be sure they maintain good business practices and adhere to health and safety regulations. He refuses to do business with factory owners who employ children or exploit their staff. However, he cannot be flying over to China or Thailand for all his meetings with manufacturers so uses **smart camera video-conferencing**. The camera automatically identifies who is speaking and turns to focus on that person.

Cloud computing

Cloud computing is a style of Web 2.0 computing which is **scalable** and uses virtual resources that are provided as a **service over the internet**.

To work, the cloud uses a number of key elements:

- Infrastructure as a service (IaaS).
- Platform as a service (PaaS).
- Software as a service (SaaS).

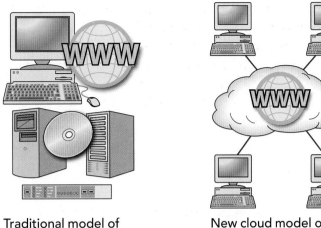

Traditional model of
computer system

New cloud model of
computer system

Traditionally an organisation would own its own computers, software, servers, etc.

In the cloud model, software, servers, databases and even computers are external to the company; the organisation simply has a connection to the cloud (internet).

PaaS (platform as a service) provides the infrastructure needed to run applications over the internet. It is delivered in the same way as a utility like electricity or water. Users simply 'tap in' and take what they need without worrying about the complexity behind the scenes. And like a utility, PaaS is based on a metering or subscription model so users only pay for what they use. If a company needs a lot of access, for example, on Mondays only, the cloud's scalability would enable them to access sufficient resources on that day, and reduce it for the other days. The company would only pay for the resources actually used at any time.

IaaS (infrastructure as a service) is where a user uses online technology including storage, hardware, servers and networking components rather than buy them for themselves. The service provider owns the equipment and is responsible for housing, running and maintaining it. The client typically pays on a per-use basis.

One example of **SaaS (software as a service)** is Google's App Engine, a place where web application developers can upload code and let Google's infrastructure take care of deploying the application and allocating computer resources.

KEY WORDS

Cloud computing
Computing using virtual resources over the internet.

Scalable
Can be increased or decreased according to demand.

PaaS
Platform as a Service

SaaS
Software as a Service

Security
The susceptibility of a system to attack.

Drawbacks

The main drawback of cloud technology is the speed of the connection. To use the resources the connection to the internet must be both fast and reliable. Another drawback is security. Any online activity is susceptible to security issues from hackers.

WEBLINKS

Magic Mirror news
http://www.rfidjournal.com/article/articleview/2854/
Near Field Communication
http://en.wikipedia.org/wiki/Near_Field_Communication
Barcodes
http://en.wikipedia.org/wiki/Bar_codes
Find out more about cloud computing here
http://en.wikipedia.org/wiki/Cloud_computing
http://www.computerworld.com/s/article/321699/Cloud_Computing

ACTIVITY 4

In ten years' time, do you think we'll still be using cash, cheques and credit cards? What about 20 years' time?

ACTIVITY 5

What is the difference between working with cloud computing and working off a LAN?

Legal use of ICT

With a large number of workers working from home Ote KoKotur are keen to ensure that they act within the law.

Legal use of data in the UK is governed by the Data Protection Act of 1998. It defines how personal information such as name, address, contact information, medical and criminal records is protected by law within companies. The Act defines 8 data protection principles.
Read more about the Data Protection Act here:

http://en.wikipedia.org/wiki/Data_Protection_Act_1998#Data_protection_principles
You can find the whole Data Protection Act here:
http://www.opsi.gov.uk/Acts/Acts1998/ukpga_19980029_en_3

Ethics

Ote KoKotur also want to be an ethical company. Ethical issues include:

- stealing software – making/using illegal copies
- plagiarising
- making illegal or unethical use of ICT facilities such as accessing inappropriate or offensive websites

- damaging, destroying, stealing and illegally using ICT facilities and files that belong to others
- cyberbullying
- hacking
- piracy.

Waste disposal

Disposal of ICT equipment comes under the WEEE directive (Waste Electrical and Electronic Equipment)

```
http://weeeman.org/html/directive/glance.html
http://www.berr.gov.uk/whatwedo/sectors/
sustainability/weee/WEEE%20in%20the%20UK/
page35967.html
```

and the related Restriction of Certain Hazardous Substances (RoHS) Directive. The aim of both directives is to control the disposal of equipment and ensure that it is carried out sustainably.

The main objectives of the WEEE directive are:

- to **increase re-use, recycling and other forms of recovery**, leading to a reduction in the amount of waste going to landfill or incineration
- to **improve the environmental performance of all operators** involved in the life cycle of electrical and electronic equipment
- to set criteria for the **collection, treatment, recycling and recovery of WEEE**
- making producers responsible for financing most of these activities – private householders are to be able to return WEEE without charge.

Teleworking

The environmental impact of ICT can be affected by modified working practices such as teleworking. Cloud computing is part of the teleworking trend which allows employees to work from anywhere that has an internet connection. Ote is not always at the shop because he does much of his thinking and creating at home, connected to the business computer by the internet. This saves him a lot of time travelling to the shop, reduces his carbon footprint, and means he/she can work whenever he/she wants.

ICT enables people to work flexibly in a results-driven environment. If managers prefer to physically monitor employees, it will not be compatible with teleworking which requires a lot of trust.

Working from home

Advantages of the system are:

- environmental – less strain on traffic infrastructures, fewer traffic jams, saves fuel and energy which reduces the carbon emissions
- social – widens the employee base including work at home parents, the disabled, retirees, people working in isolated areas
- financial – reduces costs for businesses, increases productivity, reduces the spread of illness.

There are disadvantages, however:

- Such employees often feel isolated and disconnected from the workplace.
- Employers find the loss of control a problem and distrust teleworkers.
- Security – potential theft of mobile devices loaded with sensitive information.

WEBLINK

Read more about teleworking here
http://en.wikipedia.org/wiki/Telecommuting

EXAM TYPE QUESTIONS

1 (a) Identify 3 key processes of Line of Business applications.
  (b) Discuss how a retail store could use software and its associated hardware to maximize the effects of repositioning.

2 (a) What are gesture-based controls?
  (b) How can an accelerometer save a falling laptop computer?
  (c) Analyse the appeal of the MagicMirror and store window 'touch' movement identification system to attracting customers into a retail store.

3 What are the advantages and disadvantages of cloud computing?

18 A Theatre: Pea Hints on Halfsbery Avenue

Introduction

Pea Hints Theatre Company is a popular independent theatre located in a small town. It has a regular troupe of actors but also puts on productions by visiting or other independent companies. Music groups can also rent the stage and there is a Sunday lunchtime jazz band that plays in the sizeable foyer. This is a very popular occasion for local residents who come to buy food and drink in the independently managed cafeteria and can then sit listening to the music as they eat. In the summer, the foyer sliding windows are opened up and they all move outside and sit on the grass. Other lunchtime concerts are also put on during the week, often by classical musicians who can choose either to play in a casual event in the foyer, or a more formal concert in the auditorium. Wherever possible, the theatre puts on plays that are being studied at local schools so that children can enjoy a physical performance of the texts and deepen their understanding of the characters and the action. The theatre also offers drama workshops as an evening class which take place in the practice rooms. The theatre manager is called Lucien Fried and he relies on information technology to promote the theatre and manage its different functions.

ACTIVITY 1

Have you ever been to see a show or a concert? How did you buy your ticket? What was the technology involved?

IT innovation

Information communication technology is everywhere, even within the theatre, a place dedicated to live performance.

Software

It's important for a theatre to have a box-office system which is as flexible and all-inclusive as possible. Audiences have to be able to buy tickets in the way that suits them whether by telephone, on the internet or at the box-office point-of-sale itself.

Pea Hints uses a specialist **integrated box-office software**. It combines an online sales system with point-of-sales solutions. At any time, the theatre management knows how many tickets have been sold for an event or a show whether those tickets have been sold over the internet or the phone or via the box office. The software manages in real time all the ticketing from the

KEY WORDS

Desktop publishing (DTP)
Publishing software to produce professional-looking documents.

Integrated box-office software
Combines online ticket purchasing and issuing with ticket sales management.

WEBLINKS

The most comprehensive website for stage design and theatre technology resources can be found at www.artslynx.org/theatre

Seat advisor box-office software
http://www.seatadvisor.com/

box office and website. It also handles season tickets, subscriptions and promotional offers.

It provides reports on ticket sales and prints tickets with a facilitated mailing address system. A special printer is used which prints the address to coincide with envelope windows. This speeds up the process as there is no need for either labels or reprinting an address on the envelope.

The publicity department of the theatre uses **DTP software** (desktop publishing) to design and print programs. It is used to design posters, but these are printed by a professional printer as the size of poster is too big for a conventional office printer.

Software is used to control many of the technical systems in the theatre such as lighting and sound.

Internet

The internet is an integral part of the box-office software. From the theatre's **website**, people can click on a link that sends them to the reservation page where they see a representation of the theatre's auditorium seating. This means they know exactly where their seats will be and how the price structure works according to how far away they are from the stage or whether there is a slight obstruction to their view. The reservations page enables them to order tickets, pay for them by credit card and even print them off as a PDF file or pick them up at the box office before the show.

The internet is also useful for research on theatre design resources like costumes, lighting, props, sets, make-up, special effects, scenery and technical manuals. Also for finding specialist suppliers of costume-hire, obtaining materials for unusual set designs and scriptwriters.

Facebook

The theatre has an active Facebook page which has many local fans. Lucien uses it to inform them of upcoming events, special offers and a review of the production showing at that time.

Blog

This is maintained by Lucien's PA, Jeff, who is also a writer. He uses it to inform readers about each production and invites audience reviews in the comments. The blog is updated nearly every day as there is always something going on at the theatre whether it's the workshops, the concerts, the productions or the Sunday lunchtime jazz sessions. Because it's such a lively blog, it has a great following and gets many comments. Excerpts from shows are filmed for **YouTube** and inserted into blog posts. He also has a slideshow of images from theatre productions that he embeds into the blog via **Flickr**, the online image manager.

iPhone

There's an application for helping actors learn their lines!

The digital divide

As an international group of artists with musicians and actors from all around the world the members of Pea Hints are concerned at the digital divide.

The term **digital divide** refers to the gap between people with effective access to digital and information communication technology and those with very limited or no access at all. New forms of enterprise, new types of skills, new sources of wealth and new forms of social interaction – these are among the benefits of the 'Information Society'.

But, if these developments are seen as being beneficial, then the lack of them is seen as a cause for concern. Many people, mostly those already poor or socially disadvantaged in some other way, cannot or do not have access to the new technologies and the opportunities they bring. These people – 'socially excluded' in the current jargon – stand on the wrong side of the 'digital divide'.

The digital divide can exist because of a number of reasons:

- **Geographic location**: some countries lack the infrastructure needed to support ICT.
- **Income**: some people lack the financial resources to purchase the technology.
- **Gender**: some technologies are more attractive to one gender than another.
- **Knowledge and skills**: some people lack the knowledge and skills to make use of the technology.

So the digital divide includes the imbalances in physical access to technology as well as the imbalances in resources and skills needed to effectively participate as a digital citizen.

Some facts

- The G8 countries are home to just 15 per cent of the world's population – but almost 50 per cent of the world's total internet users.
- There are roughly around the same total number of internet users in the G8 countries as in the rest of the world combined.
- It is estimated that the top 20 countries in terms of internet bandwidth are home to roughly 80 per cent of all internet users worldwide.
- There are more internet users in London than in the whole of Pakistan.

KEY WORDS

Digital divide
Gap between those who have access to computers and those who do not.

Information Society
A society in which the creation, distribution, diffusion, use, integration and manipulation of information is a significant economic, political, and cultural activity.

WEBLINK

http://en.wikipedia.org/wiki/Digital_divide

- Denmark has more than twice the international internet bandwidth than the whole of Latin America and the Caribbean combined.
- There are 30 countries with an internet penetration of less than 1 per cent.
- The 14 per cent of the world's population that lives in the G8 countries accounts for 34 per cent of the world's total mobile users.

ACTIVITY 2

Find out more about the digital divide from people themselves. Go to YouTube.com and enter 'digital divide' into the search engine. Click on some of the videos to find out how the digital divide is being bridged in different countries. Write up your findings.

EXAM TYPE QUESTIONS

1 (a) Why is it more efficient for a box office to use integrated software?
  (b) What is the advantage to the client?

2 How does the digital divide affect the information society?

19 A Dentist: Dr Jay Maloden

Introduction

Dr Maloden's surgery is a state-of-the-art theatre dedicated to the treatment of teeth. Gone are the mouthwash basins – waste material is flushed out and vacuumed up directly from patients' mouths. Dr Maloden's time is valuable and he relies heavily on specialist IT to maximise his paid time and reduce administrative chores.

IT innovation

Many dentists belong to the National Health Service which enables patients to get treatment at a reasonable price. It's a huge and complex organisation but aims to simplify procedures with the help of information communication technology.

Augmented reality

Augmented reality blurs the line between what's real and what's computer-generated by enhancing what we see, hear, feel and smell. After the military, video games and cellphones are driving the development of augmented reality. Imagine a game where the monsters are superimposed in your own home. Dentists too can now benefit from the ability to place computer-generated graphics in their field of vision.

Augmented reality is changing how its users see the world. Augmented-reality displays, which will eventually look much like a normal pair of glasses, allow the dentist to see informative graphics in their field of view, and audio that will coincide with whatever you hear. These enhancements will be refreshed continually to reflect the movements of the dentist's head. Similar devices and applications exist, such as smartphones like the iPhone.

Internet

The National Health Service (NHS) has been working on centralising patient data so that dentists throughout the country are linked up to its

> ### ACTIVITY 1
> What do you see when you look at your teeth? Do you have baby teeth or permanent teeth? Maybe you have a combination. How many teeth do you have all together?

Connecting for Health system which is the NHS's national programme for IT. Within **Connecting for Health** are a number of systems:

Picture Archiving and Communications System, (PACS)	The PACS enables images such as X-rays and scans to be stored electronically and viewed on screens, so that dentists and other health professionals can access the information and compare it with previous images at the touch of a button
NHS Care Record Service (NHS CRS) http://www. connectingforhealth.nhs.uk/	PACS will be tightly integrated with the NHS CRS thus removing the traditional barrier between images and other patient records and providing a single source for clinical information
Summary Card Record (SCR) http://www.nhscarerecords. nhs.uk	The NHS CRS will keep an individual's SCR on a national database while detailed records are held locally. Over time, NHS organisations will keep health care records on computers that link up patients' notes, allowing them to get access to information in a safe and secure way
Choose and Book http:// www.chooseandbook.nhs.uk/	The Department of Health also aims to include dentists in systems such as 'Choose and Book' which allows patients to book an appointment with a health specialist over the internet, and the Electronic Prescription Service, which allows a patient's prescription to be sent electronically from their dentist to a pharmacy
Dental Services NHS Business Services Authority (BSA) http://www.nhsbsa.nhs.uk/ DentalServices.aspx	Dentists can access the Dental Services NHS Business Services Authority online site for information on payments, general regulations, financial management services such as pensions, and patients' claims for refunds
Electronic Data Interchange (EDI)	Transmits data electronically to the BSA through a broadband connection

Dental surgery

Despite being very busy with many patients, Dr Maloden is interested in progressive dentistry and collaboration with colleagues on projects. One of the collaborative interfaces he uses is the 'Medline Publications'

KEY WORDS

Facebook API (Application Programming Interface)
A software interface that enables interaction with other software.

Medline publications
Database of biomedical articles published in journals.

(MP) Facebook application which is an API (Application Programming Interface) to help researchers find colleagues who may be working on similar or complementary projects. It is based on the US National Library of Medicine's PubMed database which catalogues all articles published in journal and comprises more than 19 million citations for biomedical articles from MEDLINE and life science journals.

The internet is also a useful resource for ordering specialist materials, getting information on training courses, seminars and conferences; receiving online professional training, online management training, joining professional associations. There are services such as cosmetic imaging to show patients the potential effects of treatment, provide education for patients and find out where to buy specialised dental software.

Software

WEBLINKS

Dental software
http://www.fusionsoftwareuk.co.uk/

PubMed
http://www.ncbi.nlm.nih.gov/pubmed/

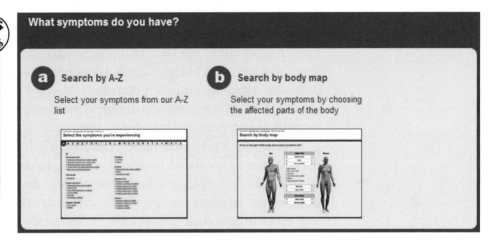

Patient Treatment Plan software

ACTIVITY 2

Go to the PubMed website and enter in a search such as 'adolescent dental health'. How many articles come up? Scroll down until you find one that sounds interesting, click on the title and read the abstract.

Specialised software enables Dr Maloden to have a panoramic view of each patient's teeth for each record. He just has to click on a tooth for all the details of treatment and X-rays taken to come up on the screen. Digital X-rays are taken and loaded into patient records. The digital X-ray camera is a major breakthrough in health safety as it exposes patients to only 10 per cent of the X-ray dose that older, traditional cameras gave.

The software also schedules appointments, sends out recalls, manages billing, provides patient education, clinical charting, treatment planning, electronic patient records, management reports, insurance management and a document centre.

Networking

WiFi

Bluetooth

Due to the nature of his work Dr Maloden uses a range of network devices.

WiFi (also written Wi-Fi) stands for Wireless Fidelity. It is a wireless network technology that allows computers and other devices to be connected to each other into a LAN (local area network) and to the internet without wires and cables. WiFi is also referred to as WLAN, which stands for wireless LAN. A WiFi hotspot is the area around a WiFi source (a wireless router, WiFi antenna, etc., generating WiFi signals) in which computers and devices can connect through WiFi. WiFi typically has a range of about 25 metres although walls and other obstacles can reduce this distance. Dr Maloden uses a laptop which connects to his network via WiFi. He also has a mobile phone than can connect to his network this way.

Although WiFi gives greater flexibility in terms of movement it is unlikely that it will ever be as fast as cables, particularly given the speeds of fibre optics.

Bluetooth is a system that uses low-power radio communications to wirelessly link phones, computers and other network devices over short distances. Wireless signals transmitted with Bluetooth cover short distances, typically up to ten metres.

Bluetooth technology was designed primarily to support simple wireless networking of personal consumer devices and peripherals, including cell phones, PDAs, keyboards, mice, printers and wireless headsets. Dr Maloden uses a range of specialist Bluetooth devices in the surgery.

Infrared technology allows computing devices to communicate via short-range wireless signals. With infrared, computers can transfer files and other digital data bidirectionally. Infrared communications span very short distances. The two infrared devices need to be less than five metres of each other to communicate with each other. Unlike WiFi and Bluetooth technologies, infrared network signals cannot penetrate walls or other obstructions and work only in the direct 'line of sight'.

The Mobile Web

The **Mobile Web** refers to browser-based access to the internet or web applications using a mobile device connected to a wireless network. As mobile browsers gain direct access to the hardware of mobile devices (including accelerometers, cameras and GPS chips), and the performance of browser based applications improves a whole new world of computing has opened up. Sophisticated user interface graphics functions may further reduce the need for the development of platform-specific native applications. Mobile developments have led to **technological convergence**.

Technological convergence

Technological convergence refers to previously separate technologies such as voice (and telephony features), data (and productivity applications) and video that now share resources and interact with each other. Modern mobile phones have built in music players, cameras, palm top computers and a wide range of technologies that used to be separate.

Today, we are surrounded by a multilevel technology convergence in a media-driven world where all modes of communication and information are continually changing to adapt to the demands of developing technology and user demands. This is changing the way we create, consume, learn and interact with each other.

Technological convergence can also refer to how technologies developed for one use are then used in many different contexts. Military and space research developed technology is used in our homes as well as most types of machine tools and silicon chips.

Data security

Dr Jay Maloden deals with a large amount of confidential patient information. Data needs to be secure and safe.

Data security is an important feature of ICT. Data can be lost by system crashes, stolen via hackers or corrupted by viruses. Backing up data and making it secure protects it and the business.

To protect against system crashes, data should always be backed up onto another source, either an external hard disk or USB key, or burned on to a CD-ROM. Hackers can be prevented from entering a system simply by logging off or turning the computer off when not in use. Use antivirus software to scan incoming emails, and never open an attachment unless you personally know the sender.

Information can be made more secure by encrypting it. Not everyone who has access to data necessarily needs to know everything. Total or partial encryption of sensitive information makes the encrypted data illegible to unauthorised users. Authorised users have passwords to access the encrypted data. Layers of encryption can be protected by a hierarchy of passwords. The system administrator would have access to all passwords, and depending on their need to know, employees and management would have access to a hierarchical structure of passwords to protect data from unauthorised access.

Monitoring a system can by done by transaction logs on databases. These track modifications performed on a database so if a problem arises such as loss of power, users can 'rollback' or undo the results of a transaction.

More information here:

http://databases.about.com/od/sqlserver/a/disaster_3.htm

More robust physical security measures include biometric scanning and electronic passes. Biometric scanning includes:

- fingerprinting, but any fan of action movies knows that fingerprints can be lifted
- eye retina scan
- finger vein scan using a CMOS sensor, designed by Sony, which is an image sensor using an array of pixel sensors which contain a photo-detector. It is much faster and more accurate than fingerprinting, and is used to provide access to mobile phones and laptops.

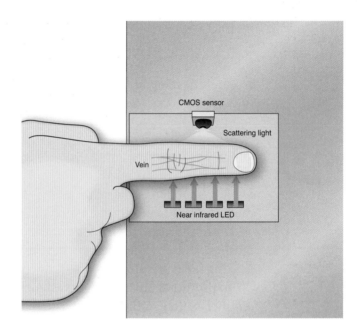

Finger vein scan using a CMOS sensor

Electronic passes are worn by employees and visitors to businesses. The passes contain a chip that identifies the wearer as s/he passes through a scanner. The scanner is connected to a terminal which uses software to control and analyse the information received. At any moment, the system controller knows who is in the building, and where they are, and who has left, and the time when they entered or left.

Security breaches are a major threat to businesses and come from cyber attacks such as malware and spyware which result in losses such as downtime, loss of customer or employee personal data and theft of corporate data. Other causes of loss are from hardware failure, natural disasters, human error, lost or stolen mobile devices, deliberate sabotage by employees, outdated security measures and improper security solutions.

Breaches can be avoided by implementing robust automatically updated antivirus and endpoint protection software, password protecting mobile devices, educating staff as to safe ICT procedures to guard against malware attacks and backing up data in case of loss.

EXAM TYPE QUESTION ?

1 State 2 ways that businesses use WiFi.

A Manufacturing Company: Hedsup

Introduction

Hedsup is a company based just outside London which manufactures pinheads within three divisions: industrial, hobbies & crafts, household & lacing. It's part of a global group whose head office is in New York. The CEO of Hedsup is called Lynne Sepingle. The pins are made of polished steel and there is a range of finishes including nickel-plating, brass, coppered and gold, and they are exported throughout Europe both to personal customers and other businesses. It's essential for Ms Sepingle to be able to contact both suppliers and customers as well as head office.

IT innovation

ACTIVITY 1

How many items do you own that have been manufactured?

There are many different types of manufacturing but they all have similar basic aims – produce as much as possible as efficiently as possible as well as possible. There is specialist software aimed at maximising the manufacturing process, keeping costs down and increasing profits.

3D computing

In normal life our two eyes sense two different images. This gives us the ability to see in 3D. But for many years computer monitors have been 2D output devices. Initially, 3D computing was thought suitable only for video game enthusiasts and Hollywood animation studios. But now it is recognised that everyone from manufacturing companies like Hedsup to doctors can benefit: doctors who will be able to examine detailed, three-dimensional X-rays over the internet; oil exploration companies and stock market investors who can dramatically improve their forecast models, and everyday consumers who can watch high-definition movies streamed over the internet or create 3D presentations for work and school. 3D video images suspended in mid-air above the operating table could even help surgeons target tumours more precisely; they could also help air-traffic controllers prevent air accidents and drug designers better understand the structures of promising molecules.

On a 2D screen, a protein molecule looks like tangled spaghetti. But when it appears in 3D, you begin to fully grasp its 3D structure.

The biggest problem with 3D computing was the need to wear special glasses. These glasses used colour or polarised lenses to separate the two images on the screen. All 3D systems must send separate images to the viewer's left and right eyes and the glasses helped to do this. But now computer monitor developers are tackling the problem in a new way. One company, Sharp gets around the need to use glasses, which filter one eye's image from the other, through what is called a parallax barrier: The monitor uses two LCD panels, one in front of the other. The front panel displays the image. The back one angles the light coming from the backlight, sending alternate columns to the left and right eyes. In 2D mode, the rear panel simply shuts off so that all pixels are seen by both eyes.

A parallax barrier is a device to allow a liquid crystal display to show a 3D image without the need for the viewer to wear glasses. Placed in front of the normal LCD, it consists of a layer of material with a series of slits, allowing each eye to see a different set of pixels, so creating a sense of depth. This system has even been used in a car navigation system, allowing the driver to view GPS directions, while a passenger watches a 2D movie on the same screen.

Software

3D CAD software

Database management systems, enterprise resource planning systems and simulation and computer-aided design tools have become indispensable to most manufacturing enterprises. In the pursuit of the five Rs – produce the right product, with the right quality, in the right quantity, at the right price and at the right time – IT plays an essential role in providing correct and timely information.

Lynne's most indispensable IT item is **3D CAD software** (Computer Aided Design) for the pins to ensure the engineering is practicable, aesthetic and financially viable. The software is a major investment purchase bought because the company is seeking large contracts with international space programmes. IT has often been assigned a supporting role in manufacturing, but it's now considered a catalyst for product and process change.[8]

For example, integrated into the 3D CAD software is an **Overall Equipment Effectiveness** (OEE) software which serves as a key measurement of efficiency in manufacturing processes at machine, manufacturing cell or assembly line levels. OEE is a standard indicator that combines performance (are your lines making at their target speed?), machine availability (are they running all the available time?) and quality (is product coming off 100 per

8 http://www.computer.org/portal/web/csdl/doi/10.1109/2.751328
Krishnamurthy Srinivasan, Sundaresan Jayaraman, 'The Changing Role of Information Technology in Manufacturing,' Computer, vol. 32, no. 3, pp. 42–9, Mar. 1999, doi:10.1109/2.751328

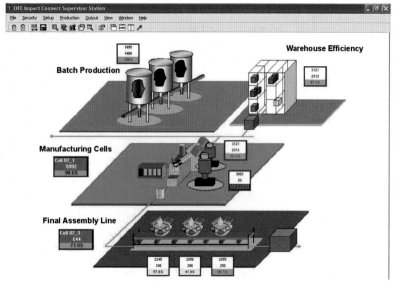

3D Overall Equipment Effectiveness (OEE) software

Factory planning software

cent right first time?) as a baseline for improvement. OEE has a direct link to profitability since it enables increased output with the same overheads.

Also integrated into the 3D CAD software is a factory planning software. This is used to maximise scheduling, reduce lead times, lower inventory and reduce overtime and premium shipments.

IKBS and expert systems

Part of artificial intelligence is IKBS (intelligent knowledge-based system) which uses data stored in a database to make deductions. It could be used in a doctor's surgery to ask patients about their symptoms and then present the doctor with a range of diagnoses. It is also used in businesses where a range of data on a problem would provide management with a range of solutions. IKBS transforms information into knowledge, in effect, replacing the human 'expert' with an artificial one.

Internet

The internet is used to maximise the commercial potential of the business. Business to Customer (B2C) orders are taken over the internet via the website which provides the company with a global presence. Premium orders such as the gold-plated pins are sent out via a preferential courier service while standard orders use the standard service overland.

Business to Business (B2B) orders, for key customers, are made directly through electronic links to Hedsup's computer system via extranet. Such

GPU chip

instant access speeds up the ordering process, and customers appreciate the privilege of being in such close contact with their supplier.

While Google referencing helps customers find Hedsup on the internet, the factory also has a sales team which services current customers and tries to find new ones. The sales reps are helped in organising their tasks by a **sales cloud** interface (salesforce.com) which is a customer service and support application suite to ensure that customers have consistent, high-quality interactions on an ongoing basis. Part of the package enables the company to monitor what is being said about them in online communities – on Facebook and other networking sites – and engage directly with customers to resolve issues.

With the head office being located in America, meetings either involve a lot of travelling or, more recently, **holo-conferencing**. This is a conferencing system that produces holograms of the people talking giving the impression that they are in the same room.

CPU vs GPU

Computers have used a CPU (Central Processing Unit) as their heart for many years. A CPU is excellent at doing one task after another very quickly. GPUs (Graphics Processing Unit) are relatively new and were designed to enable complex graphics to be displayed on computer monitors. Hedsup uses very powerful graphics cards in its computer systems. These are necessary to render the 3D designs. Computers started to have GPU driven graphics cards added or GPU chips added to the motherboard when companies such as Hedsup started to require very fast processing. A GPU (also occasionally called Visual Processing Unit or VPU) is a specialised processor that tackles the difficult job of rendering 3D graphics.

GPUs are used in embedded systems, mobile phones, personal computers, workstations and game consoles.

Modern GPUs are very efficient at manipulating computer graphics. They are more effective than general-purpose CPUs for a range of complex tasks involved in graphics rendering.

http://www.youtube.com/watch?v=fKK933KK6Gg

EXAM TYPE QUESTIONS

1 Identify the three ways specialist software helps the manufacturing process.

2 What does IKBS do?

Creative Use of ICT and Coding a Solution

UNIT 4

Chapter 21 Introduction to the Creative Use of ICT and Coding a Solution

Chapter 22 Analysis

Chapter 23 Design

Chapter 24 Development

Chapter 25 Testing your solution

Chapter 26 Evaluating your solution and Working with Others

21 Introduction to the Creative Use of ICT and Coding a Solution

The creative use of ICT unit is an opportunity to demonstrate understanding and skills developed during the GCSE course. You will need to choose from a range of scenarios to produce a multimedia solution, a computer game or a computer program. This choice of scenario opens up a wide range of possibilities and you should choose the approach which best showcases your skills and abilities.

You will have had exposure to various application packages during the course and should identify those which will enable you to produce a solution to one of the problems provided by OCR. There will be at least two task scenarios initially for each option and OCR plan to add more tasks to the bank as the specification progresses, giving an even wider choice of scenarios. They will, of course, retire some tasks after a while as they become less relevant and you should be aware of what tasks are available each year. Your teacher will provide this information and may suggest tasks best suited to your experience and to the facilities available within the institution. It is important to note that these assessments *must* be completed under controlled conditions and you will only be able to use facilities available within the institution to complete tasks; they may not be completed away from the classroom.

The multimedia solution (B064)

One of the choices is to produce a multimedia solution to the problem and this means exactly that: you must use more than one medium in your solution. The choice of media is then fairly open and only limited by the facilities available. You may choose to use sound and video to create a digital movie, or it could be sound, images and animation for some web pages, it could be that a presentation including a variety of media provides a suitable solution, the decision is yours. What is important is your ability to demonstrate the appropriate skills and to provide a functional and effective solution to the problem using the facilities available, within the classroom and within the time available. It may be that you wish to use an application with which you do not currently have sufficient experience to produce an effective solution and this need not be a problem. You are required to plan the development of your solution including relevant timings; remember to include the time to develop the appropriate skills into your plan and practise these skills before starting the assessment task. You will be able to refer to the documentation and help for the application while you are developing your solution so don't think you need memorise every tool and technique for any specific application.

The computer game (B064 alternative option)

If you choose this option then you will need to develop appropriate skills with the chosen application before starting the controlled assessment. You will be able to access documentation and support for your chosen application while working on the task but it is sensible to get some experience of the application and its features beforehand in order to inform your decisions. You will not be allowed to complete your work outside the school or college so remember to make sure the package you choose is available within the institution. Like the multimedia solution you will need to demonstrate good skills with the package to create an effective solution to the problem and this must be demonstrably related to the scenario. Avoid simply creating a computer game without reference to the chosen controlled assessment task.

The coded solution (B065)

This option has the most obvious need for further skills and these are identified within the specification. Basic programming concepts are required and need to be demonstrated within the solution to the problem. These skills should be developed and practised before starting the controlled assessment unit. Access to the support for the programming language can and should be available during the controlled assessment stages; it is the logical process and use of these skills that is being assessed, not the ability to remember accurately every command or instruction you will need. You are required to show how you used the identified techniques effectively and, while you will need to use many of these, it is not a requirement that you include all the techniques listed. This unit requires programming techniques to be used appropriately. You are still required to produce an effective and functional solution to the problem in the chosen scenario but there is an emphasis on producing an efficient and functional solution. You should focus on this aspect rather than spend too much time designing complex graphics, etc. for your solution.

The process

You are required to analyse, design, develop, test and critically evaluate your solution to the chosen controlled assessment task. You will be assessed against each of these criteria. It is not enough to simply put together a multimedia presentation and present this as the solution. While it will gain some credit many of the skills being assessed will not be present and marks will be lost. What is required in evidence is identified in OCR's marking criteria and you should have access to and refer to these throughout the period in which you carry out the controlled assessment. The marking criteria, used by your teacher, are similar for all three units, but as evidence requirements may differ depending upon the choice of scenario, you need to prove that you have followed the process outlined in the OCR specification.

Analysis

You will need to carry out some initial research which should be completed before starting work on the controlled assessment. At this stage you are expected to work with other candidates to research the chosen topic(s) and work together to find solutions to similar problems and evaluate these for their suitability. This can be carried out by using the internet to research similar solutions or situations, or by using more traditional methods of analysis, such as interviews, questionnaires or existing documents. You should identify elements of existing solutions and describe how these are (or are not) fit for purpose. Working with others at this stage is an important aspect of this specification and provides valuable information about what others think makes a good solution. You will later be expected to obtain feedback from other students on your final solution and use this to evaluate critically what you have done in light of their comments and in light of your initial research. At this stage in the process it is appropriate you work with a range of applications you feel might provide the necessary features to develop a solution to the problem. This practical research with potential applications should be used to inform your decision about how you will solve the problem. For those choosing multimedia it may be gaining experience with animation packages, or web page creators, or graphics editing software or sound editing software, or video editing software or presentation software. Those choosing the computer game option will need to gain experience with those packages available within the institution to create computer games and possibly sound and graphics editing software. Those who choose to code a solution will need to ensure they have experience with the identified techniques in a suitable programming language.

After the initial research you will need to work under controlled conditions, this means work must be completed by you within the classroom without reference to other candidates.

- You should take all the research you completed with others and analyse it to identify a suitable solution to the problem.
- You should identify what the steps are in developing your solution, the hardware and software required and a suitable time plan.
- You should refer to the findings from the research, including what you and the others identified as the requirement for the solution.
- You will also need to explain how you will know you have been successful or not in achieving these requirements, the success criteria.

At this stage you will need to complete a plan of action identifying how you will allocate your time to the various stages in completing your assessment work.

Design

The solutions to these problems will not be simplistic linear ones and you need to break down the problem into component parts and show how each of these can be solved. You will also need to show how these component parts form a complete solution to the problem when combined. The design should include all essential design elements including input, navigation paths, output and screen layouts. You will also need to identify how you will test your designed solution. You are required to show how your proposed solution is fit for purpose and solves the initial problem. At this stage you should have a clear idea of how you will proceed through the development and testing of your proposed solution and how you will know if you have been successful.

Development

If you have completed the earlier sections carefully this stage should be relatively straightforward. You need to develop each of the elements for your solution and test them to make sure they function then combine these into an overall solution for testing. It is important you try to stick to your development time plan in order to complete the task and should comment on any issues with this in your report.

Testing

You should use the test plan you created in the design to test your solution against the design criteria. You need to identify how well the developed solution matches the requirements identified in the analysis. It is also time to go back to those you worked with in the research phase and get them to test your solution to see if it matches their expectations. Record their testing and their comments.

Evaluation

You have researched a problem, designed a solution, developed it and tested it. It is time to reflect upon how well your final solution matches the initial requirements. You should use the results from your testing and the testing by others to identify the elements of your solution that worked well, those that did not work so well and how you might have improved upon these aspects. The evaluation should compare the final solution to the designed success criteria and it is also your opportunity to point out to the assessor the best bits of your solution.

Working with others

Elements of this assessment require you to work with others to research the task and to evaluate each other's solutions. You will need to comment on how successful this was, the contribution of you and the others to this work and to comment on how this might have been done more effectively.

Analysis

OCR will provide a range of tasks for you to consider and the first important decision is which one of the tasks you will choose. Whichever one you do decide upon, the initial research is a vital element in the process. The initial research is an important opportunity to demonstrate your ability to work with others to investigate the chosen problem. You will be expected to comment on your and others' contribution to this process in your evaluation; it is a good idea to start to keep an up-to-date diary of your activities to refer to at the end of the process. You should allocate tasks between the members of your group to research your chosen topic effectively; it is important for each member of the group to complete their task and for the group to ensure that all tasks are completed. This initial research forms the basis for all that will follow and good quality research will make a significant difference to the final outcomes. During this phase you should try to use many different sources for information to ensure that you have identified the important factors relating to your chosen solution. You may use the internet, discussion with potential end-users for your system, interviews, questionnaires, magazines, books, television, radio and similar sources. You will also need to research potential applications to identify which will provide the most appropriate features for you to complete your solution. This research will be used to inform and justify your decisions when creating your solution, and while the research has been a group activity, what you do with the research should be your own work.

You must record the sources for all the material you use, commenting on the suitability of these solutions describing how they are (or are not) fit for purpose. Remember this is a collaborative exercise and you should show that you have cooperated with others to collect information explaining how the work was divided among members of the group as well as describing your individual role in this activity.

This stage is similar for all the possible choices of problem but there are some areas of particular significance for each of the possibilities:

- If you have decided to create a multimedia solution you will need to identify suitable images, animation, video clips or sound used in existing solutions and multimedia presentations and comment on their suitability.
- If you have decided to create a computer game then as well as images and sounds you should look at a range of existing games in order to identify elements that are appropriate to your intended solution.
- If you have chosen to create a coded solution to the problem then your research should look at existing programs for similar purposes.

> **Key points:**
> - Start a diary to record the process (try using a weblog).
> - Share the work between the group so you can cover more material.
> - Look at existing solutions such as:
>   - multimedia presentations
>   - computer games with a similar theme
>   - computer programs for a similar purpose.
> - Record all the sources you have looked at in your diary.
> - Keep evidence of these sources and make some comments on each of them.
> - Share your findings with the group and keep a note of your own contribution to the research.

From this point the work must be carried out under controlled conditions and anything you produce must be your own work.

You will need to plan your time effectively because the time allowed to complete the remaining part of the assessment is limited. Excluding time spent developing skills, such as the use of the software or programming techniques and researching the problem, OCR suggest 12 hours be spent on creating your solution. This is not a lot of time and you must plan carefully if you are going to complete the task on schedule. Identify the steps you will have to take to complete your project, allocate a set amount of time for each of these steps and a completion date. In order to do this you will have to analyse the research you have done to identify what form the final solution will take. You will need to think about the elements that make up this solution and in which order these must be completed. You must also take into account testing your solution, completing the report for the moderator and, of course, build in some allocation to cover unforeseen problems and delays.

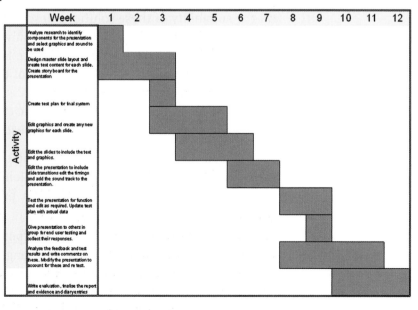

Time plan

A design specification explains what the system must be able to do when it is completed, how it will look and how it will function. This is effectively the agreement between you and the end-user about what they want from the system. You must take into account the system requirements identified in the original task and you must consider what software and hardware will be needed to make your system run. This will include the minimum and recommended specification for the computer, any peripheral devices, the operating system and any specific software requirements such as web browsers and plug-ins.

- If you have decided to create a multimedia solution you will have to decide what form this will take, for example a presentation, a 'movie' or a website.
  - You will need to identify the software which will be needed to produce the solution and the software necessary to create or modify the individual components of the solution.
  - You will also need to specify the hardware required, including the computer and peripherals, for example, devices to import images, any sound requirements and screen resolutions.
- If you have decided to create a computer game then you will have to identify the software in which you will create the game.
  - You will also need to identify the software you will use to create any graphics, the software you will use to edit any sounds you decide to use and any software required on the end-user computer to enable them to run your game.
  - You will also have to identify any hardware requirements for your solution to run, including the computer specification and any peripherals, for example a game controller, sound card and speakers and screen resolutions.
- If you have chosen to create a coded solution to the problem then you will need to identify the programming environment you will use to create the solution.
  - You will also need to identify any software that must be available on the end-user system to run your solution, for example the .net environment or a small basic system.
  - You will also have to consider any computer and peripheral requirements, for example operating system, system specification, plugins, printers, sound requirements and screen resolution.

It is very important for the design to reflect the user requirements and you should show how your design relates to these. You will also need to show how you plan to demonstrate that you have achieved these requirements. In order to do this you must make sure you list the end-user requirements in a form that you can 'measure' and provide evidence of having achieved them. These are your success criteria and you will have to judge the success of the

---

Multimedia Presentation: Design specification

The task is to encourage young people to recycle more.

I plan to use a presentation in PowerPoint 2003

It will include suitable images, text, animations and sound.

The images will appeal to a teenage audience and focus on items they use most, plastic bottles, cans, paper, batteries etc.

The text will comment on issues related to their age, saving the environment and sustainable use of resources.

The animation will be quick and 'edgy' as well as slightly funny.

The presentation will last no more than 30 seconds to avoid being boring.

The music will be mild punk rock style to engage their interest.

I will need to use a PC capable of running the following software:

• Powerpoint 2003
• Audacity to edit the sound file
• Macromedia Fireworks to edit the images
• Windows XP or later

I will need the following hardware:
• Scanner to scan images from drawings and magazines
• Speakers and sound card to play and edit the sound track

I will also need:
• Internet access to download music and images
• CD drive to import music from CD or USB to import music from MPS player

The PC specifications to achieve this will only need to be of a minimum specification for any current computer to run office 2003 and Fireworks

They will both run 128 Mb RAM
Total hard drive space for both is 480Mb
Both run on VGA 600*800 in 256 colours
Both will run on XP and
Both need a CD or DVD drive for installation.

Design spec

development against these in your evaluation of the project. You must decide from the research evidence which are the most important requirements for your solution and judge which of these will be used as success criteria.

- If you have decided to create a multimedia solution you will probably identify navigation paths, timings, clarity and basic functionality as some of the key elements in the success of your solution. Depending upon your choices there will be other factors but remember, you will have to show whether these have been achieved or not, so choose things you can measure or demonstrate to the moderator through your report.

- If you have decided to create a computer game then playability will be a major factor, along with the behaviour of the user interface, timings and basic function, for example do all the elements behave as expected, is the score correct and do the graphics 'work', i.e. are they suited to the end-user requirements?

- If you have chosen to create a coded solution to the problem then you might include functional elements such as the behaviour of the user interface, the responses from the system to correct or incorrect responses, the way data is stored and modified, security of data, etc. as appropriate to the proposed solution and as a result of the research carried out.

Coded Solution: Design specification

Problem: Develop a programme to use as a till in a fast food store

I plan to solve this problem using Microsoft Small Basic.

I will need to design a suitable user interface that will work with a touch screen.

The images/text on the touch screen will need to be easily recognised as products from the menu.

The touch screen buttons will have to be large enough to be 'touched' accurately by the sales assistant.

There will need to be some method of inputting the quantity on the touch screen.

Product details, quantity, unit price and sub totals will have to be displayed.

The overall total will need to be displayed.

The money submitted and the change required will need to be displayed.

I will need to be able to modify the touch screen buttons for product changes.

The prices for the products will need to be stored within the program.

I will need to use a PC capable of running the following software:

Microsoft VB express 2008

I will need the following hardware:
• PC with Microsoft XP or later operating system
• Keyboard, mouse and screen (The touch screen can be simulated with a standard graphical • interface and a mouse)

My solution will be a success if:

• I can select items and quantities from the menu interface
• The display shows:
  – A description of the item,
  – The unit cost and a total cost per menu item
  – The total cost of the selected items
  – The amount tendered and the appropriate change.
• The interface is laid out clearly
• The interface items are all distinct and unambiguous
• The system works sufficiently quickly to avoid delays inputting data
• All calculations are correct

Design spec coded solution

Key points:

● Create a time plan showing the stages you need to complete showing:
  ● each stage in the process
  ● the time you allocate to each stage
  ● the planned finish time and date.
● Analyse the information you and the group have collected to identify useful material and ideas for your solution.
● Write a description for your solution showing
  ● what it must be able to do and
  ● how it might work and
  ● what hardware and software you will need to use.
● Identify how you will know you have been successful and
  ● how you will prove you have been successful.

You will be expected to describe how your proposed solution solves the problem and is fit for purpose. To do this you will have to clarify how your proposals match the success criteria you identified in the previous section and explain how the identified features will provide a completed solution to the problem. The solution you identify will normally contain several component parts and you will need to design each of these and show how they fit together to form a complete solution to the problem.

- If you have chosen to create a multimedia solution then features such as appeal to target audience, aesthetic considerations, functionality, navigation paths or storyboards may be identified and you should show how these produce a solution to the problem.

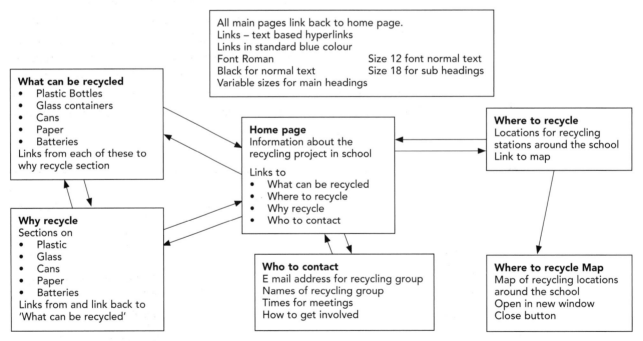

Sample web page structure

- If you have decided to create a computer game then, once again, features such as appeal to target audience, aesthetic considerations, functionality, navigation, storyboards, graphics and sound will all have been identified and you must show how these all work together to solve the initial problem.

  - For the game creation option simple algorithms for game play may be appropriate evidence for this section.

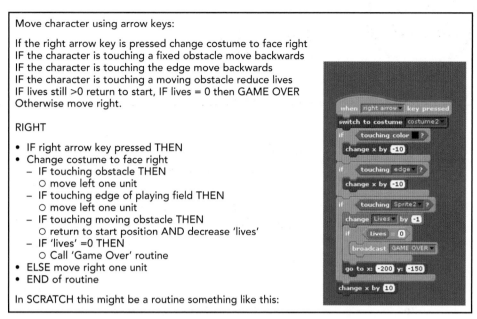

Move character using arrow keys:

If the right arrow key is pressed change costume to face right
IF the character is touching a fixed obstacle move backwards
IF the character is touching the edge move backwards
IF the character is touching a moving obstacle reduce lives
IF lives still >0 return to start, IF lives = 0 then GAME OVER
Otherwise move right.

RIGHT

- IF right arrow key pressed THEN
- Change costume to face right
  - IF touching obstacle THEN
    O move left one unit
  - IF touching edge of playing field THEN
    O move left one unit
  - IF touching moving obstacle THEN
    O return to start position AND decrease 'lives'
  - IF 'lives' =0 THEN
    O Call 'Game Over' routine
- ELSE move right one unit
- END of routine

In SCRATCH this might be a routine something like this:

Sample algorithm to move a character to the right, using SCRATCH

● If you have chosen to create a coded solution to the problem then this is a major part of your solution. You will have to design the individual modules or components for your solution and describe these using suitable algorithms. You will also have to describe how these individual elements fit together to form a complete and functional solution to the problem. You may also have some data handling within your solution and you will have to describe any data structures you will be using and how these are utilised within your solution.

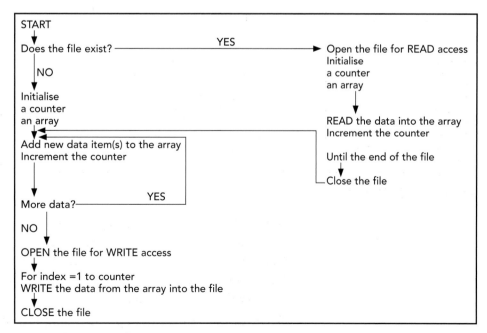

Putting data into a file basic algorithm

- For the functional elements you should produce suitable algorithms describing the processes. These algorithms can be in any suitable format. You can use flowcharts, numbered or bulleted steps, written sequences, diagrams, etc.; the important point is that they demonstrate the logical processes within the proposed solution and how the components combine to form a solution to the problem.

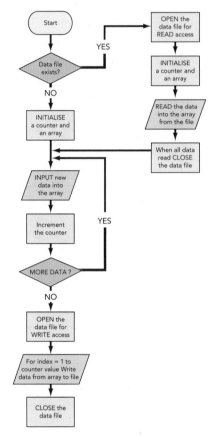

Flowchart data to file

You have shown how your solution will work; now you should show what it will look like. This section should include details of all the component parts of your solution including screen layouts, screen designs and descriptions of any other component parts.

- If you have chosen to create a multimedia solution then you will have to provide screen designs, descriptions (possibly as sketches) of images, animations, backgrounds, video clips and sound clips.
- You will also have to describe the navigation paths, including any alternative routes, through your system and show how these all fit together to form a complete solution. Use diagrams to describe these elements whenever possible with arrows to show navigation and labels to describe individual elements in your designs. Prototyping, using other software to create a sample design, is an acceptable way to design these elements.

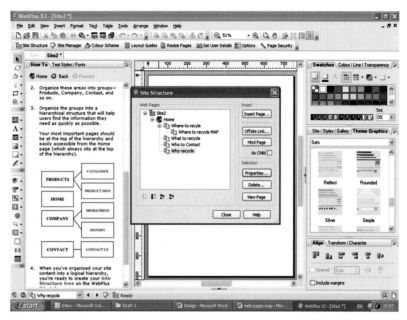

Creating web page structure

MMP web design

- If you have decided to create a computer game then you will have to consider the graphics, sound, animations and control aspects of your game, showing how all these individual elements work together to form a complete solution.

  - You should include details of how the game will progress, showing navigation paths through the game dependent upon the user's input and interaction between the game's components. Use diagrams to describe these elements whenever possible with arrows to show navigation and labels to describe individual elements in your designs. Prototyping, using other software to create a sample design, is an acceptable way to design these elements.

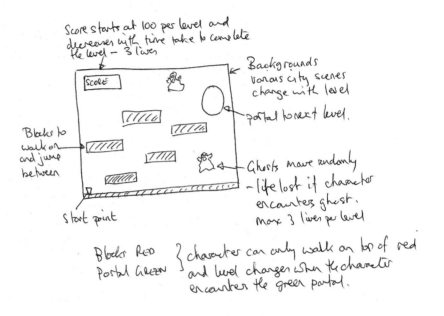

Game design

- If you have chosen to create a coded solution to the problem then you will have to describe the screen layouts which may be simple sketches or more detailed drawings but may also be a list of requirements to be included in a prototype screen layout. For example if you are using Visual Basic you may simply use the list of required features to inform your work whilst designing forms on screen. You should retain sufficient evidence to demonstrate this process. You must show the functional elements are linked and how the other design elements, for example screen layouts and forms, relate to the design criteria.

Coded screen designs

Whichever option you have chosen you will have to produce a test plan including descriptions of the tests which will be employed with the expected results.

- You should produce a table which will indicate the proposed test to be carried out as well as columns for the expected results and the actual results. There should also be a column for comments on the results of the test. This table should be completed during the testing stage. At this stage only complete the description of the test and the expected results columns. Typical tests should include each of the functional elements as well as final testing and perceptions by others at the end of the process. The proposed testing should cover as many paths through the system as required to show that the solution meets all of the success criteria identified earlier.

What I am testing	What data I will use	Reason	Expected result	Actual Result	Comments
Validation routines for data entered	Coke, Small, 2	This is a valid entry	Coke Sm should appear in items column, 2 in the Quantity column and £2.30 in the total column		
	Coke, 2, Small	The data is not entered in the correct order and should be rejected	Error message (Loud Beep) and no data entered into the order summary column		
Validation routines repeated for all items.	Eg Beef Burger, medium, 3 Ice Cream, Vanilla, 5	ALL valid data, should be accepted	Appropriate data entered into order summary columns		
Valid data entered for various products to check correct values returned from data array	The data used above should be used	to see if the correct values are returned	Correct prices shown in the order summary. Compared to manual calculation of these values.		
SEND ORDER works	Key press on SEND ORDER	To check that once the order is complete the addition is carried out	A total should be displayed in the balance 'cell'		
Order value correctly calculated	Data used above	ALL valid data should be accepted and order sent, balance calculated	The total shown in the balance cell should be correct, compared to manual calculation		

Test plan

> ### Key points:
> - Describe how the proposed solution solves the problem and meets the success criteria outlined in your analysis.
> - Produce suitable algorithms describing the processes:
>   - use flowcharts, numbered or bulleted steps, written sequences, diagrams.
> - Show how the individual elements form a complete solution to the problem.
> - Produce a test plan describing the tests you plan to use, the data that will be required and the expected results.
> - The proposed testing should cover as many paths through the system as required to show that the solution meets all of the success criteria.

Development

You will now need to turn your designs into the final product and the moderator will expect to see evidence of this development. It is anticipated that the evidence provided will be sufficient to demonstrate the process without the need for lengthy descriptive explanations, though some annotation may be appropriate. Given the nature of the requirements for multimedia presentations, computer games and coded solutions, the evidence for development may be very different in each case.

Multimedia solution

With the multimedia solution you will have to show how you created each of the multimedia elements you need for your final solution. This may include images, video clips, sound clips or animations. In each case you need to show the development process. For example, if you have modified images downloaded from the internet then provide annotated 'before and after' screenshots as evidence. If you have created images from scratch then two or three screenshots of this process with some annotation will be sufficient.

Once the basic elements are created you will need to develop the screen layouts for presentations or web pages. For video projects with live action this may mean researching and identifying locations or backdrops. In many cases, especially with presentations or web pages, the final product will provide sufficient evidence of this development but you may wish to include some rationale for the choices you have made by annotating screenshots or images.

Your next task will be to create the navigation paths through your solution. For presentations and web pages this may include hotspots, navigation buttons, hyperlinks, links to other slides or websites, for presentations and animations timings and transitions. Importantly you need to show how the end-user will navigate through the system. For video products this will be evidence of timings and transitions between segments of video and evidence of the synchronisation with any soundtrack. You will need to show how these features have been developed. Evidence to show how each navigational element has been completed is not necessary. Include examples for each type of element by means of appropriate screenshots, for example of the linking process or annotated HTML or two or three screenshots of the video editing process.

These elements will now be combined into a single multimedia

Video editing showing segments pasted together

presentation matching the criteria identified in the design process. You should also provide evidence of the time spent on this process and how this compares to your time plan; if you fall behind schedule comment on this and explain why. Once again this process should be recorded in your project diary showing how your actual schedule compares to your planned schedule. Remember the evidence in your diary will be taken into account and comments on the process as you progress may well be valuable evidence of what you have achieved.

Computer game

With a computer game solution you will have to show development of the associated graphical elements, characters, costumes, backgrounds, sounds and basic processes for each component, for example interactions and control. Evidence of the process by way of screenshots will be sufficient in most cases and there is no need to repeat evidence for similar processes. For example, show the steps to create a set of costumes for one character and the existence of similar sets of costumes for others will be sufficient evidence as will evidence for creating one background for a game level and the existence of other backgrounds and game levels.

The control structures, interaction and methods used in the game will form a large part of the evidence for your development. You will need to demonstrate the logic used in developing these items and should provide basic outlines of the logical processes used to control the game. Once again you need only show examples of the key processes. For example, the logic used to control a characters movement to the right on a key press is similar to that for left, up and down movements. These need not be shown, nor do you need to repeat this for other characters moving using the same control structure. You will need to describe the overall navigational and interaction possibilities for the game and show how these work together to create the final product. A series of annotated screenshots to show key interactions and responses will provide sufficient evidence if the game is also submitted for assessment. Given the large number of game development applications on the market evidence will take many forms and it is your responsibility to provide evidence to show how the system was developed and how it functions. Long descriptive commentaries are not required and should be avoided in favour of selective screenshots and key annotation.

Developing the jump routine

These elements will now be combined into a single game matching the criteria identified in the design process. You should also provide evidence of the time spent on this process and how this compares to your time plan. If you fall behind schedule, make a comment saying why this happened. Once again this process should be recorded in your project diary showing how your actual schedule compares to your planned schedule. Remember the evidence in your diary will be taken into account and comments on the process as you progress may well be valuable evidence of what you have achieved.

Coded solution

The coded solution is slightly different in its requirements and you must use standard programming techniques effectively to produce an efficient solution to the problem. While many of the techniques will be required, it is possible that the designed solution does not require one or two of them. Your work will be assessed not on the number of techniques used but on the effective and efficient use of the most appropriate techniques.

You will obviously have to make sure you are able to use the identified techniques and this should be done as part of your preparation for this assessment not as part of the controlled assessment time. The techniques required are listed in the OCR specification and include the following.

The three basic programming constructs to control the flow through a program

- Sequence; instructions are carried out one after another in order.
- Select; the sequence in which instructions are carried depends on a condition being met, for example an IF THEN ELSE statement or a CASE statement.
- Iteration; a set of instructions calls itself repeatedly until a condition is met.

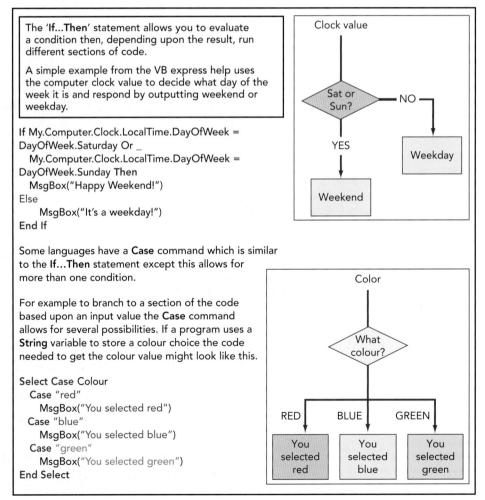

The 'If...Then' statement allows you to evaluate a condition then, depending upon the result, run different sections of code.

A simple example from the VB express help uses the computer clock value to decide what day of the week it is and respond by outputting weekend or weekday.

```
If My.Computer.Clock.LocalTime.DayOfWeek =
DayOfWeek.Saturday Or _
   My.Computer.Clock.LocalTime.DayOfWeek =
DayOfWeek.Sunday Then
   MsgBox("Happy Weekend!")
Else
      MsgBox("It's a weekday!")
End If
```

Some languages have a **Case** command which is similar to the **If...Then** statement except this allows for more than one condition.

For example to branch to a section of the code based upon an input value the **Case** command allows for several possibilities. If a program uses a **String** variable to store a colour choice the code needed to get the colour value might look like this.

```
Select Case Colour
   Case "red"
      MsgBox("You selected red")
   Case "blue"
      MsgBox("You selected blue")
   Case "green"
      MsgBox("You selected green")
End Select
```

IF THEN ELSE and CASE

The use of count and condition controlled loops

- Count controlled loop; a set of instructions is repeated a set number of times, for example a FOR NEXT loop.
- Condition controlled loop; a set of instructions is repeated until a condition is met, for example a REPEAT UNTIL loop or a WHILE ENDWHILE loop.

The '**For – Next**' loop allows a series of commands to be repeated a set number of times with a varying index value

This simple example in VB express uses a For – Next loop with step 5 to show how much an item will cost if discounted by various percentages.

```
Dim FPrice As Double = Val(TextBox1.Text)
Dim discount As Integer

    For discount = 5 To 25 Step 5

        ListBox1.Items.Add("With a discount of " & discount & "the price will be " &
                      FormatCurrency(FPrice * (1 - discount / 100)))

    Next discount
```

There are other ways of setting up loops
Repeat - Until and While – EndWhile

The pseudocode for the same problem is

As a Repeat loop:

```
Input Full Price
Set discount to 5
Repeat
        DiscountPrice is Full price * (1- discount/100)
        Print discount at discount% is DiscountPrice
        discount = discount+5
Until discount =30
```

As a While loop:

```
Input Full Price
Set discount to 5
While discount <=25
        DiscountPrice is Full price * (1- discount/100)
        Print discount at discount% is DiscountPrice
        discount = discount+5
EndWhile
```

Notice how the Repeat loop will always execute at least once, a While loop need not execute at all.

Example flowchart and code: loops

The correct use of a range of data types including Boolean, String, Integer and Real

- Boolean are variables that take just two values, TRUE or FALSE.
- String is a generic name for a variable that can contain any 'string' of alphanumeric characters.
- Integer variables can only contain whole number values.
- Real variables can contain fractional values.

(These variable types may be referred to by various names within specific programming languages but these are the generic type names by which they can be identified.)

The use of arrays to store data when solving problems

● Arrays are simply a set of variable names using the same variable name plus an index value, for example the array defined by value(10) defines a set of variables with names value(1), value(2), etc. up to value(10). (In many languages value(0) is also defined by defining or dimensioning such an array.)

File Edit Utilities Options Run Help

```
DIM Takings(7)
FOR i=1 TO 7
  PRINT "Enter takings for day ";i;
  INPUT Takings(i)
NEXT i

Total=0
FOR i=1 TO 7
  PRINT "Income day ";i;Takings(i)
  Total=Total+Takings(i)
NEXTi

PRINT "Total Income is ";  Total
PRINT "Average Income is ";Total/7
```

(untitled)
```
Enter takings for day 1? 34.50
Enter takings for day 2? 56.79
Enter takings for day 3? 92.34
Enter takings for day 4? 87.56
Enter takings for day 5? 76.59
Enter takings for day 6? 99.84
Enter takings for day 7? 102.45
Income day 134.5
Income day 256.79
Income day 392.34
Income day 487.56
Income day 576.59
Income day 699.84
Income day 7102.45
Total Income is 550.07
Average Income is 78.5814286
>_
```

Example definition of an array in BBC basic

You have designed algorithms as a solution to the problem set by OCR and now you will have to use suitable programming structures to implement these algorithms. The design of your algorithms will, in many ways, dictate the efficiency of your overall solution. However, whilst coding these you may identify more efficient methods of implementing the designs, don't be afraid to do this, but do make sure you comment on this in your diary and in your evaluation.

In your evidence for this section you will have to show how each of the elements has been developed and how these have been combined into a single solution. The most effective way of doing this is to produce your code in modular form with comments or to break up the code into discrete sections with suitable comments describing each section's role in the solution and comments within each section explaining how it works.

Your diary is a very useful document and it can be used to record the process as you develop the code. You will also be testing individual elements as you proceed and evidence of this will also be required to demonstrate your use of the techniques to solve the identified problem. You should also use your diary to keep track of the progress through the project compared to the time plan you developed in the design section. Comment on any changes to the design and schedule during development. Remember the evidence in your diary will be taken into account and comments on the process as you progress may well be valuable evidence of what you have achieved.

Key points:

- Identify all the elements in your solution.
- Show the stages in the development clearly:
  - Avoid long narratives and use screenshots with annotation to show key stages in the development.
  - Annotate all your evidence to explain what is shows.
- Create and explain navigation through your solution.
- Show how these elements go together to form a complete solution.
- For coded solutions include the annotated code explaining what each section does and how it works.
- Illustrate your code with selected screenshots.

25 Testing Your Solution

The solution is completed and now needs to be tested against the success criteria you set using the test plan you designed earlier. The testing should show that the system works and that it is an appropriate solution to the problem for the target audience and defined end-user. You do not have access to the end-user but you will have access to other students who can comment critically on your solution; use these other students as potential end users and use their feedback to inform your evaluation.

To test that the system functions you will have to test as many navigational paths through your system as is feasible. The test data you use will depend upon the chosen solution, but you should try to use typical, valid inputs as well as invalid and extreme inputs, for example values at the limit of the expected range. Using the test data you described, or equivalent test data needed to account for any changes to the design made during development, test the functionality of your system and record the actual results. If these match your expectations then record this, if not suggest why they did not, a reason for this and any suggestions you have to fix the problem. The test output can be in any suitable form but remember the moderator will need to be able to assess this evidence and should not require any special equipment or software to view this evidence.

The solution will probably have been created on one computer system with a specific configuration; you should also test how this works if the conditions are changed.

- Does your system need any specific software or plugins to work?
- Does it work with different screen resolutions?
- Are there any issues with different hardware configurations?
- Will it work on a range of operating systems?
- Will it work (for a set of web pages) on different browsers?

You may not be able to test all or many of these, depending upon the hardware and software available, but you do need to show you have considered these issues and tested your solution in as many different situations and configurations as is feasible.

To test that the solution is suited to the task and is appropriate to the target audience, use other students, and teachers, if they are willing to do this, to try out the system. They will not stick to the data you have anticipated and will not know how the system is supposed to work. Good on-screen information and instructions will be very helpful but you may also provide some written instructions for them if necessary. These 'end-users' should record their comments and any issues they had using your system for you to comment upon in your evaluation.

What I am testing	What data I will use	Reason	Expected result	Actual Result	Comments
Validation routines for data entered	Coke, Small, 2	This is a valid entry	Coke Sm should appear in items column, 2 in the Quantity column and £2.30 in the total column	Coke Sm in items 2 in quantity £2.30 in total. See screen shot 1	Test successful for valid data entry
	Coke, 2, Small	The data is not entered in the correct order and should be rejected	Error message (Loud Beep) and no data entered into the order summary column	Data not accepted	Invalid data not accepted as expected
Validation routines repeated for all items.	Eg Beef Burger, medium, 3 Ice Cream, Vanilla, 5	ALL valid data, should be accepted	Appropriate data entered into order summary columns	Various entries tried all valid data entered resulted in correct output. See screenshots 2–6	Valid data accepted as expected
Valid data entered for various products to check correct values returned from data array	The data used above should be used	to see if the correct values are returned	Correct prices shown in the order summary. Compared to manual calculation of these values.		
SEND ORDER works	Key press on SEND ORDER	To check that once the order is complete the addition is carried out	A total should be displayed in the balance 'cell'		
Order value correctly calculated	Data used above	ALL valid data should be accepted and order sent, balance calculated	The total shown in the balance cell should be correct, compared to manual calculation		

A partially completed test plan

Mains	Beef Burger	Small	Medium	Large		ORDER SUMMARY		
	Chicken Burger	Small	Medium	Large		Item	Quantity	Price
	Vege Burger	Small	Medium	Large		B Burger Sm	2	£1.98
	Extras	Bacon	Cheese			Cheese	1	£0.50
Drinks	Coke	Small	Medium	Large		Coke M	2	£2.30
	7UP	Small	Medium	Large				
	Orange	Small	Medium	Large				
	Milk	Small	Medium					
	Tea	Small	Medium					
	Coffee	Small	Medium					
	Chocolate	Small	Medium					
Sweets	Ice cream	Vanilla	Choc			SEND ORDER		

Quantity	1	2	3	BALANCE	£4.78
	4	5	6	TENDERED	£5.00
	7	8	9	CHANGE	£0.22
	00	0	Clear		

Example screenshot: This is the last of a sequence of images that show data being input to the system and the correct value being output

Key points:

- Use the test plan from your design section to test your solution.
- Complete the actual results column showing that the solution worked:
  - if not comment on why it did not work.
- Get other people to test the various pathways through your solution and record their results and comments.

For a coded solution you should also:
- Include testing carried out during the development phase.
- Test under as many different sets of circumstances as possible to show if it works under different conditions.

26 Evaluating Your Solution and Working with Others

At last you have completed your solution and tested it; you have feedback from your end-users and you now need to evaluate your work. Evaluation is more than saying 'my system works' and that you enjoyed doing it, it is time to reflect on the whole process. It is also your opportunity to tell the moderator about the clever things you did and point out the best bits of your solution and an opportunity to explain how you could solve those issues that have been identified during testing.

Analyse all the evidence produced during the testing phase and identify what worked well, and what didn't work so well. You already have a test plan so use the comments column to provide feedback on the actual results for your planned tests. For those things that did not work well, discuss why and how you might go about fixing the problem. Use feedback from your end-users to comment on other issues not anticipated within this test plan, for example lack of appeal or problems with following navigation paths through lack of information. Once again comment on changes you would make to deal with these issues. You may also have already made modifications to your system during development; comment on these, saying why you made them, how you made them and the effect on your overall solution.

You should also consider how well the solution matches the design criteria and discuss whether it is fit for purpose. For example, is your solution suited to the target audience? If not why not and how would you go about modifying it to make it more appropriate? This is also your opportunity to discuss how your system could be improved and for you to attempt some of these improvements in light of your evaluation. As evidence of this you should simply produce before and after evidence showing the changes made and commenting on how these improve the solution.

The evaluation is your opportunity to demonstrate your technical skills and knowledge and your evaluation report should be well structured using technical language appropriately.

Key points:

- Analyse your test results.
- Use the differences between the expected and actual results to identify those parts of the solution which have not worked as expected.
- Use the results of testing to recommend possible improvements to the solution.
- Comment on how well it matches the original purpose and identify any shortcomings.
- Re-list the success criteria and comment on whether the criterion has been met and, if not, why not.
- Make any necessary improvements to the solution.
- Use this as an opportunity to tell the moderator about any aspects of your solution you consider particularly good or clever or efficient.
- This is your opportunity to demonstrate your technical skills and knowledge and the evaluation report should be well structured using technical language appropriately.

You have been asked to cooperate with others in the group at two stages in this assessment: the research element and the testing element. You should now comment on what part you and others played in this. At the planning stage you were asked to work with others as a team, allocating tasks to each other. Your team should have been aware of each other's role in the process and each member of the team should have understood the objectives. At this stage you should have worked as a team to ensure that not just your own allocated task was completed, but that the tasks allocated to others in the groups were completed. You now need to reflect on this and comment on how the tasks were shared, any shortcomings and how the shared activities could have been improved to provide a more effective process. Don't make personal comments about one person not completing their part of the research; this would be a shortcoming for the whole group and not the individual. During this stage the whole group needs to work together towards all tasks being completed.

Working as a team

Index

3D CAD software 218–19
3D computing 217–18

absolute cell references 75, 76–7
accelerometers 201
access codes 88, 132
accessing a PC 105–7
accidental deletions 84–5
actuators 15, 125
adjusting settings 106–7
adware 93, 95
airlines 119–20
alcohol use monitoring 131
alignment of text 54–5
alphanumeric data 64, 65, 243
analogue computers 3
analogue to digital converter (ADC) 124, 125
analysis 224–25, 227–31
Analytical Engine 2, 3
AND 38, 80
animals, tagging 49, 130
antivirus software 93, 94
application software (applications) 7, 24, 171
  moving data between 62
archives 43, 84, 86
area charts 159
argument, preparing the 177
arrays 244
art gallery 188–95
Artnear 194
ascending order 78, 79
attachments 42, 43
audience 50, 52, 154–5, 176
audio streaming 115
augmented reality 211

Babbage, Charles 2, 3

back button 36
back and neck pains 99–100
backing storage 8, 15, 17–22
backups 84–6, 169–70
banks 92
  see also online banking
bar charts 174
barcode reader 12, 66
barcodes 66, 197, 199
bibliography 161, 162
biometric data 132, 145, 147–8
biometric scanning 216
BIOS (Basic In Out System) 16, 17, 104
blogs 32, 46, 190, 191–2, 193–4, 208
Bluetooth technology 214
Blu-ray technology 19, 20, 20–1, 22
bookmarks 37, 38, 190
Boolean (logical) data 64–5, 243
Boolean (logical) operators 38–9, 80
borders 54
Braille keyboards 14, 102
bullets 53
business to business (B2B) orders 219–20
business to customer (B2C) orders 219

CAD (computer aided design) 135, 218
CAM (computer aided manufacturing) 135
cameras 200, 201–2
Care Record Service (CRS) 212

Carpel Tunnel Syndrome (CTS) 99
cars 121, 127–8
CASE 242
CCTV (close-circuit television) 145
CDs 18, 19, 20, 21, 22
cells 74, 75
central heating systems 132–3
central processing unit (CPU) 10–11, 220
centre justification 55
charts 174
chat rooms 28–9, 44
check digits 73
checking data 70–3, 167
chip and pin systems 12, 87
Choose and Book 212
cloud computing 117, 202–3
coded solution option 223, 227, 229, 230–1, 233–4, 236–7, 241–5
collaboration see group working
colour balance 59
combining software packages 168–9
command line interface 23
communication 28–34, 121
  safety and security 33–4
communication devices 9, 10, 22–3
communications software 60
compatibility 168
compilers 25
computer game option 223, 227, 229, 230, 232–3, 235–6, 240–1
Computer Misuse Act 96–7
computer rooms 101

computer systems 2–7
see also hardware; software
condition controlled loops 243
Connecting for Health 212
contributions,
evaluating 181–2, 250
control 48, 119, 120, 124,
132–6
copy and paste 62
Copyright, Design and Patents
Act(s) 98–9
corporate blogs 46
count controlled loops 243
crawler-based search
engines 39
credit cards 47, 142
fraud 87, 144
criminal offenders 49, 121, 131
criteria (database queries) 80
critical thinking skills 180–1
customer engagement 196, 197
cut and paste 62

data 91
checking 70–3, 172
manipulation 172–3
misuse of 87–8
types 64–5, 243
data acquisition 125
data capture forms 66–9
data entry 66, 70–1
data logging 124, 125
data protection 88–92
see also security
Data Protection Act 97–8, 204
database management software
(DBMS) 60–2, 73, 78–82,
160, 167
database search 78, 80
database sort 78, 79–80
databases 78–82, 167, 172, 215
date/time 65
debit cards 47, 142
debuggers 25
decryption 91
dentistry 211–17

descending order 78, 79–80
design 225, 232–8
brief 163–4
specification 158–9, 229,
230, 231
desktop PCs 3, 4
desktop publishing
(DTP) 50–6, 166, 208
development 225, 239–45
Difference Engine 2
digital to analogue converter
(DAC) 124, 125
digital camcorders 15
digital cameras 14, 15, 66
digital computers 3
digital divide 202–3
digital video cameras 15, 18
digital X-ray camera 213
directory-based search
engines 39
disabilities, people with 13–14,
101–2
disaster recovery 85, 86, 141
document sharing 47
domain names 41, 188, 190
double entry procedure 71,
172
drivers 7
DVDs 18, 19, 20, 21, 22

e-commerce 47–8, 116–17,
120–1, 139, 141–4
editors 25
electronic data interchange
(EDI) 212
electronic passes 216
electronic tagging 49, 121,
130–1, 199
email 30–2, 40–3, 115, 194
features of email
software 42–3
how an email travels 41–2
organising emails 30–1
email addresses 30, 40, 41
email client 40, 41
email inbox 41, 42

email outbox 41, 42
email server 42
embedded computers 6
encryption 88, 91, 92, 109, 215
encryption/decryption key 91
engine management
systems 127–8
eSpares 156
ethics 204–5
evaluation 226, 249–50
of contributions 181–2,
249
'expert' audience 154
exporting data 173
eyestrain 99

Facebook 191, 193, 202, 208
facsimile (fax) 32–3
factory planning software 212
fashion retailer 196–206
favourite button 37, 38
feedback 133
fields 78
file extensions 26–7, 108
file servers 110, 111
file sharing 32, 33, 47, 114
file transfer protocol (FTP) 32,
33, 47, 114
files
designing files for storing
data 69–70
managing 107–8
security of 86–7
troubleshooting when unable
to open 118
types 26–7
finger vein scan 216
firewalls 90, 92
fixed-width text 52
flash memory 9, 17, 18, 20, 21,
34, 105
Flickr 192, 193, 208
floppy disks 17, 18, 20, 21
folders 107–8
fonts 51–2
foot mouse 14, 102

foreign keys 81, 82
fork lift trucks 133
format checks 72–3
formatting 167
formulas 75–7
forward button 37
fraud 87, 144
functions, spreadsheet 74–5

gaming software 60
gesture-based controls 200–2
Google 38, 196
Google wave 47
GPS (global positioning
      systems) 48, 49
graphical user interface
      (GUI) 23
graphic tablets 66, 67
graphics manipulation
      software 58–9, 160, 167
graphics processing units
      (GPUs) 220
group working 162–3, 224,
      226, 227, 249
   evaluating
      contributions 181–2, 249
gutter 68

hacking 87, 91–2, 96
hard disks 9, 17, 21, 22, 105
hardware 7–23
   input devices 7–8, 11–14,
      102, 198–200
   networking 9, 10, 22–3
   output devices 7–8, 14–15
   processing 7–8, 10–11, 213
   storage 7–8, 15–22, 70
head pointers 102
health 99–100, 169
Health and Safety at Work
      Acts 99
Hedsup 217–20
history 37, 38
holo-conferencing 220
home-based working 116,
      137–9, 205–6

home button 36
home page 36
household appliances 6, 48,
      120
HTML (Hypertext Markup
      Language) 35, 113, 188,
      189, 190
hubs 9, 10, 22–3
hybrid search engines 39
hyperlinks 36, 188

icons 23
ICT systems 2–7
   see also hardware; software
identity cards 132, 145
identity theft 87
IF 236
IKBS (intelligent knowledge-
      based system) 219
images 56, 58–9, 65
importing data 173
improvement, areas for 183
IndepArt 188–95
information 91
   collecting 157–8
   finding on the
      internet 38–40
   sources of 157–8, 161,
      162
Information Commissioner's
      Office 97
information overload 157
infrared technology 214
infrastructure as a service
      (IaaS) 203
input devices 7–8, 11–14, 102,
      198–200
instant messaging 28, 29, 44,
      115
integer data 64, 65, 243
integrated box-office
      software 207–8
interface 10
interface box 125–6
internal memory (main
      memory) 8, 16–17

internet 4, 28, 34, 92, 111,
      113–17, 158, 189
   dentistry 211–16
   fashion retailing 202–4
   finding information
      on 38–40
   manufacturing 219–20
   theatre company 208–9
   uses 114–17
   see also World Wide Web
internet service providers
      (ISPs) 41, 42
interpreters 25
intranets 114
inventory management 197,
      198–9
IP address 188, 190
iPhone 194, 201
iteration 242

Java 25
joystick/game controller 12
justification 54–5

key logging software 91–2, 95
keyboards 11
keypads 11

laptops 3, 4, 88–9
'lay' audience 154
left alignment 54
legislation 96–100
length checks 73
line charts 174
line of business (LOB)
      applications 196–8
linkers 25
local area networks
      (LANs) 109
location sensors 200, 201–2
logical (Boolean) data 64–5,
      243
logical (Boolean)
      operators 38–9, 80
login 105–6
Logo language 134

logout 105, 106
loops 243

Magic Mirror 199
magnetic stripe readers 12, 66
mail merge 173
main memory (internal
        memory) 8, 16–17
mainframe computers 4, 5, 6
Maloden, Dr Jay 211–16
malware 92–5
'managerial' audience 154
manufacturing 135–6, 217–20
margins 68
measurement 123–4, 125–7
medicine 121, 129
Medline Publications 212–13
menus 23
mesh networks 111, 112
microphones 13, 66
microprocessors 48, 120,
        132–3
micro-transactions 47–8
misuse of data 87–8
mobile phones 4, 6, 32, 46
        see also iPhone
Mobile Web 214
modems 9, 10
monitoring 49, 120, 121, 124,
        125–32, 145
monitors 15
mouse 11, 14, 102
multilayer disks 20
multimedia software 57
multimedia solution
        option 222–3, 227, 229,
        230, 232, 234–5, 239–40
multiplayer online games 29
multi-touch technology 200

National Health Service
        (NHS) 211–12
National Insurance
        numbers 73
natural user interface
        (NUI) 197, 198

navigational aids 36–8
near field communication
        (NFC) 198, 199
netbook computers 3, 4
network interface card
        (NIC) 9, 10, 22, 109
networking 9, 10, 22–3, 92,
        109–13, 117
    dentistry 211–16
    topologies 110–12
NOT 39, 80
numeric data 64, 65, 243

object code 25
object linking and embedding
        (OLE) 62
office suites, compatibility
        issues with 168
online (defining) 28
online banking 116, 120–1,
        139–41
online chatting 115
online shopping 139, 141–4
        see also e-commerce
operating systems 7, 23–4, 26
    storage of 105
optical character
        recognition 66
optical mark readers 66
optical storage systems 19–21
OR 38, 80
Ote KoKotur 196–206
output devices 7–8, 14–15
overall equipment effectiveness
        (OEE) software 218–19

page not found errors 119
parallax barrier 218
passwords 84, 88, 89–90,
        105–6, 215
patients, monitoring 121,
        129
PDAs 4
Pea Hints Theatre
        Company 207–10
peer-to-peer networks 114

peripheral devices 10, 28, 106,
        111
personal computers 3, 4, 6
personal data 87–8, 97–8
personal identification
        numbers (PINs) 90, 139,
        140
photo-editing software 58–9
physical safety 100–1
physical security 88–9
Picture Archiving and
        Communications System
        (PACS) 212
pie charts 174
pixels 59
platform as a service
        (PaaS) 203, 204
podcasts 32, 190, 192, 193–4
point of sale (POS) 197, 198
point sizes 51–2
pointing devices 23
ports 22
postings 32
presence checks 73
presentation software 160, 165,
        166, 173–4
presentations 56–7, 176–8
primary keys 81, 82
primary sources 158
print server 110
printer 15
    troubleshooting failure to
        print 118
processor/processing 7–8,
        10–11, 220
programming software 25
programming
        techniques 241–4
programs 3
proof reading 71–2
proportional text 52
protocols 32, 113
prototyping 234, 236
public key encryption 91
PubMed database 213
puff-suck switches 13, 102

queries, database 80
questionnaires 67

radio frequency identification
(RFID) 48, 49, 66, 120,
198, 199
random access 69, 70
random access memory
(RAM) 16, 17
range 75
range checks 72
read only memory (ROM) 16,
17
real data 64, 65, 243
records 78
red-eye 59
relational databases 80–1, 82
relationships, in relational
databases 82
relative cell references 75, 76
reload button 37
remote access 115
remote control units 13
removable storage
media 18–22, 88
repeaters 22–3
repetitive strain
injury (RSI) 99
replication 75, 76
reports 176, 178–9
research 224, 227–8
resolution 59
retail demand forecasting 198,
199
right alignment 55
ring networks 110, 111
robots 135, 136
routers 9, 10, 22
RSS (really simple
syndication) 190, 192

safety 33–4, 84–95, 161, 169–70
physical 100–1
social networking 46–7
sales cloud interface 220
scanners 12, 66, 67

scheduled backups 85
search engines 38–9
types of 39
searching a database 78, 80
secondary keys 81, 82
secondary sources 158
security 33–4, 43, 78–9, 84–95,
145, 169–70, 215–16
security systems 131–2
security tokens 141
select 242
sensors 13, 66, 123–4, 200,
201–2
sequence 242
serial access 69, 70
settings, adjusting 106–7
short message services
(SMS) 46
shutdown 106
slide transition 56
slides 56
slideshow software 56–7
smart camera
video-conferencing 202
social bookmarking 190
social networking 45–7, 190,
191–2
dangers of 46–7
see also blogs; Facebook;
Twitter
software 7, 23–7
combining software
packages 168–9
dentistry 212
fashion retailing 196–9
manufacturing 218–19
selecting 165–8
theatre company 207–8
software as a service
(SaaS) 202, 203
solution development 162
sorting, database 78, 79–80
source code 25
sources of information 157–8
documenting 161, 162
spam emails 31–2

spam filters 32, 43
speakers/headphones 15
specification 163–4, 229, 230,
231
spellcheckers 43, 55
spider diagrams 158
sports events 129–30
spreadsheets 60–2, 73, 74–8,
159, 165, 166, 173
uses of 77–8
spyware 93, 94–5
star networks 110–11, 112
startup 104
stop button 37
storage devices 7–8, 15–22, 70
backing storage 8, 15, 17–22
flash memory 9, 17, 18, 20,
21, 105
main/internal memory 8,
16–17
removable 18–22, 88
storage software 69–70
string data 64, 65, 243
success criteria 229–30, 238
Summary Card Record
(SCR) 212
supercomputers 5, 6
surveillance 121, 145
system specification 164

tables 53–4
tabs 53
tagging, electronic 49, 121,
130–1, 199
tape drives 17, 85
team working see group
working
Technorati 192, 194
technological
convergence 214–15
telephone 115
teleworking 116, 137–9,
205–6
template 173
test log 183
test plan 237–8, 246, 247, 249

testing 183, 225, 246–8
text data 64, 65
text messaging (SMS) 46
textspeak 46
theatre company 207–10
third party payment
        methods 142
time/date 65
time plan 228
touch pads 200
touch screens 14, 15, 200
tracking 49, 119, 120, 121
transaction authentication
        number 141
transaction logs 215
transport 119–20
tree networks 110, 111
Trojan horses 93, 94
troubleshooting 118–19
turtle graphics 134–5
turtles 134
Twitter 31, 32, 46, 191, 194
typefaces 51–2

unauthorised users 87, 88
URL (uniform resource
        locator) 36
USB interface 10
USB memory sticks 9, 17, 18,
        34
user interfaces 25–6

user names (user IDs) 88,
        89–90, 105–6
user needs 229
    assessing 157–60
utility software (utilities) 7, 24

validation 70, 72–3
vehicle identity numbers
        (VINs) 72–3
verification 70, 71
video-conferencing 44–5,
        115–16, 202
video-editing software 60
video streaming 115
viruses 92, 93–4
visual checks 71
voice-over-internet-protocol
        (VoIP) 115
voice recognition 66, 101
voice synthesis 101

Waste Electrical and Electronic
        Equipment (WEEE)
        directive 205
weather forecasting 139
Web 2.0 technology 188–90
web authoring software 57–8,
        167
web browsers 34, 35, 38, 42
web browsing 34–8
web exchange protocols 190

web pages 32, 34, 35, 57–8
    page not found error 119
web server 35
webcams 13, 44, 130
webliography 161
weblogs (blogs) 32, 46, 190,
        191–2, 193–4, 208
webmail 42
website home page 36
websites 34, 35, 58, 188, 190,
        193, 208
    e-commerce 48, 195
wheelchairs 102
wide area networks
        (WANs) 109
WiFi 109, 214
wikis 190
windows 23
wireless networking 109,
        112
word-processing 50–6, 159,
        166, 172
working at home 116, 137–9,
        205–6
working practices 169–70
World Wide Web 4, 32, 35,
        113, 114, 189
    browsing 34–8
worms 93, 94

YouTube 192, 193, 208